The Passenger Experience of Air Travel

TOURISM AND CULTURAL CHANGE
Series Editors: Professor Mike Robinson, *Nottingham Trent University, UK* and Professor Alison Phipps, *University of Glasgow, Scotland, UK.*
Associate Editor: Dr Hongliang Yan, *Oxford Brookes University, UK.*

Understanding tourism's relationships with culture(s) and *vice versa*, is of ever-increasing significance in a globalising world. TCC is a series of books that critically examine the complex and ever-changing relationship between tourism and culture(s). The series focuses on the ways that places, peoples, pasts and ways of life are increasingly shaped/transformed/created/packaged for touristic purposes. The series examines the ways tourism utilises/makes and re-makes cultural capital in its various guises (visual and performing arts, crafts, festivals, built heritage, cuisine etc.) and the multifarious political, economic, social and ethical issues that are raised as a consequence. Theoretical explorations, research-informed analyses and detailed historical reviews from a variety of disciplinary perspectives are invited to consider such relationships.

All books in this series are externally peer reviewed.

Full details of all the books in this series and of all our other publications can be found on http://www.channelviewpublications.com, or by writing to Channel View Publications, St Nicholas House, 31-34 High Street, Bristol, BS1 2AW, UK.

TOURISM AND CULTURAL CHANGE: 60

The Passenger Experience of Air Travel: A Critical Approach

Edited by
Jennie Small

CHANNEL VIEW PUBLICATIONS
Bristol • Jackson

DOI https://doi.org/10.21832/SMALL9028
Library of Congress Cataloging in Publication Data
A catalog record for this book is available from the Library of Congress.
Names: Small, Jennie, editor.
Title: The Passenger Experience of Air Travel: A Critical Approach/
   Edited by Jennie Small.
Description: Bristol, UK; Jackson, TN: Channel View Publications, [2022]
   | Series: Tourism and Cultural Change: 60 | Includes bibliographical
   references and index. | Summary: 'Taking a critical approach to the air
   passenger experience, this book considers the representations, embodied
   practices and materialities of air travel. It brings the journey to the
   fore as a complex and meaningful experience, filling a gap in the social
   science research of tourist behaviour, traditionally focused on the
   destination experience' – Provided by publisher.
Identifiers: LCCN 2022025777 (print) | LCCN 2022025778 (ebook) | ISBN
   9781845419028 (hardback) | ISBN 9781845419011 (paperback) | ISBN
   9781845419035 (pdf) | ISBN 9781845419042 (epub)
Subjects: LCSH: Airplane occupants. | Airlines – Customer services. | Air
   travel – Social aspects. | Tourism.
Classification: LCC HE9787 .P375 2022 (print) | LCC HE9787 (ebook) | DDC
   387.7/42 – dc23/eng/20220609
LC record available at https://lccn.loc.gov/2022025777
LC ebook record available at https://lccn.loc.gov/2022025778

British Library Cataloguing in Publication Data
A catalogue entry for this book is available from the British Library.

ISBN-13: 978-1-84541-902-8 (hbk)
ISBN-13: 978-1-84541-901-1 (pbk)

Channel View Publications
UK: St Nicholas House, 31-34 High Street, Bristol, BS1 2AW, UK.
USA: Ingram, Jackson, TN, USA.

Website: www.channelviewpublications.com
Twitter: Channel_View
Facebook: https://www.facebook.com/channelviewpublications
Blog: www.channelviewpublications.wordpress.com

Copyright © 2023 Jennie Small and the authors of individual chapters.

All rights reserved. No part of this work may be reproduced in any form or by any means without permission in writing from the publisher.

The policy of Multilingual Matters/Channel View Publications is to use papers that are natural, renewable and recyclable products, made from wood grown in sustainable forests. In the manufacturing process of our books, and to further support our policy, preference is given to printers that have FSC and PEFC Chain of Custody certification. The FSC and/or PEFC logos will appear on those books where full certification has been granted to the printer concerned.

Typeset by Riverside Publishing Solutions.

Contents

	Contributors	vii
1	Introduction *Jennie Small*	1
2	The Airport Experience *Erwin Losekoot and Jennie Small*	44
3	Passenger–Passenger Interaction *Jennie Small*	73
4	Flying and Appearance *Jennie Small*	97
5	Flying into Uncertainty: Part 1 – Flying with Mobility Disability *Simon Darcy, Jennie Small and Barbara Almond*	118
6	Flying into Uncertainty: Part 2 – Flying with Non-Mobility Disabilities *Jennie Small, Alison McIntosh, Barbara Almond and Simon Darcy*	139
7	Fear of Flying *Jennie Small and Cheryl Cockburn-Wootten*	162
8	The Flyers' Dilemma: Confronting the Negative Psychological Effects of Air Passenger Travel *James Higham and Martin Young*	178
9	Epilogue *Jennie Small*	197
	Index	219

Contributors

Editor

Jennie Small is an Adjunct Fellow of the Management Department, UTS Business School, University of Technology Sydney. Her research interest is tourist behaviour from a Critical Tourism approach, concentrating on equity and social justice issues in tourism. Her specific interests are gender, age, embodiment, body image, disability (vision impairment) and mobility, and how these relate to the tourist experience. The passenger experience of air travel is of particular interest. Employed in much of her work is the feminist research method, Memory-work.

Authors

Barbara Almond is an experienced academic and research project manager at the University of Technology Sydney Business School. She is experienced in sustainability and planning with a Master's degree focused in Sustainable Development and Resource Management. Her research interests and current research areas include sustainable tourism, social inclusion and social capitol, accessible tourism, destination and protected area management, events management, accessible education and innovation.

Cheryl Cockburn-Wootten is a Senior Lecturer and Director of Teaching & Learning at the Waikato Management School, University of Waikato, New Zealand. She aims to facilitate research that informs and makes a difference to our communities. Cheryl enjoys collaborating with others using organisational communication approaches and co-creative methods for social change. Her work examines issues relating to dignity, equity, justice, PR stakeholders, community engagement and social change.

Simon Darcy is a Professor of Social Inclusion at the UTS Business School, University of Technology Sydney. He is an interdisciplinary mixed methods researcher with expertise in developing inclusive organisational approaches for diversity groups. Simon's academic and industry-based work in disability, tourism and accessible tourism has defined the field and led to collaborations with local, regional, national and international destination management organisations including the UN World Tourism Organization. As one of the few researchers with a lived experience of disability as a high-level person with a spinal cord injury who uses a power wheelchair, he brings an insider's perspective that seeks to develop transformative solutions for transport, travel and tourism for the group.

James Higham is a Professor in the Otago Business School (University of Otago). His research addresses tourism and global environmental change, with a particular interest in global aviation emissions and decarbonising tourism. He is the Co-Director of the University of Otago Tourism Policy School (2019–2022) and has served as the Co-Editor of the *Journal of Sustainable Tourism* (2014–2022).

Erwin Losekoot (PhD, FIH, FRGS) is Professor of Hospitality Studies at NHL Stenden University of Applied Sciences. He has previously worked at Strathclyde University in Scotland, AUT University in New Zealand and RMIT University Vietnam. Most of his work has been about the nature of hospitality and how we can make places and people more hospitable. His PhD was a case study of Auckland Airport and the hospitable experience. He is Co-Editor in Chief of the peer-reviewed academic journal *Research in Hospitality Management*.

Alison McIntosh is Professor of Tourism at Auckland University of Technology, New Zealand. Her research focuses on critical understandings of the tourism and hospitality experience, with particular focus on issues of accessibility, social justice and advocacy. A central theme of her research is that experiential, qualitative and social justice analyses reveal subjective, emotional and neglected aspects of tourism experiences, prioritising otherwise unheard voices, personal dimensions and tourism in marginalised contexts. She leads AUT's Tourism For All New Zealand research group to work alongside communities to make tourism accessible for all.

Martin Young is a human geographer interested in the spatial political economy of contemporary leisure consumption with an emphasis on the tourism and gambling industries.

1 Introduction

Jennie Small

Background

It is nearly 50 years since Dean MacCannell (1976) published *The Tourist: A New Theory of the Leisure Class*, putting the subject of tourism, the tourist, centre stage. In the decades since, we have witnessed a growing academic interest in the consumer of travel and tourism. While traditional, industry-oriented research has studied the consumer at all stages of the journey, most tourism social science research has focused on the experience of the traveller or tourist at the destination. Surprisingly, few studies have related to the actual *movement*, the journey to and from the destination. This omission implies that 'getting there' is more a non-event, an *endurance*, with the real event happening at the destination. The poet, Cecil Day-Lewis, in his poem *The Tourists*, warns against treating travel 'as a brief necessary disease, A pause before arrival' (as cited in Crossley-Holland, 1989: 25). One could say that if 'getting there is half the fun', half the fun has been largely ignored by many tourism academics. There are, of course, some exceptions in the tourism literature, with some journeys attracting attention; these generally relate to touring holidays, such as self-drive and grey nomad holidays or cruising, where the transport is seen as part of the attraction. Tourism studies, as a social science field of study, is not alone in its lack of interest in the journey. Sheller and Urry (2006) recognised that a great deal of social science research has been 'a-mobile' with the systematic movement of people, whether for work, family life, leisure and pleasure or politics and protest, largely ignored or trivialised. Travel has been referred to as 'a black box' (Sheller & Urry, 2006: 208), '"dead time" in which nothing happens' (Cresswell, 2010: 18), while the transport terminus has been labelled a 'non-place' (Augé, 1995).

However, since Sheller and Urry (2006) wrote about the a-mobility of much social science, we have seen a cultural change, a strengthening of the 'new mobilities' paradigm brought about by changing patterns of global mobilities. With social life becoming increasingly distanciated (Larsen, 2014), no longer is the focus the sedentary and static aspects of society, but rather the connections, flows, rhythms, networks and movements of people (and ideas, images, objects, information, money etc.)

and at different scales – either at the individual level or global flow. While mobility is about movement, it is also understood in terms of 'forms of place, stopping, stillness and relative immobility' (Cresswell, 2011: 552). Rather than the utilitarian aspect of movement from A to B (the focus of traditional transport geography), mobility is seen as motion that is socially produced (Cresswell, 2006), the focus being social relations in travel, 'the aesthetics, experiences and meanings bound up with movement' (Bissell & Adey, 2011: 1007). Included in this understanding of mobility is the recognition that movements of people are both the producer of power and the product of power (Cresswell, 2006). For social scientists, the new paradigm puts mobility, *the journey*, centre stage. Within tourism studies, it shifts our understanding of travel and tourism from the traditional fixation on *place* to *movement* (Franklin, 2014) and, further, to socially produced motion. It takes us beyond the business concerns of the service sector (the focus of much of the travel and tourism literature) to consider travel and tourism as a social and cultural practice and airports and aeroplanes, not inert physical constructions, but rather cultural spaces that reflect and shape the narratives of the passengers.

No longer is travel time considered as 'dead time' or travel spaces 'non-places'. Seeing individuals' mobility practices as embedded in their spatial, social and cultural context deepens our understanding of the meaning of the journey and the effect of the journey on social relations, for just as the context shapes mobility practices, so, too, such practices shape the context. Mobility now comes to be seen as a political and ethical issue with critical mobilities focused on power relations and disparities in mobilities. It considers who can and who cannot move. While mobility studies has examined different modes of mobility (car, rail, plane, cycling, walking etc.), some forms have been more thoroughly researched than others. It is to air travel and mobility or 'aeromobility', that this book now turns.

Inherent in the mobility research is the belief that air travel, like other means of travel, is 'a meaningfully constituted form of mobility, intricately interwoven with human society' (Lin, 2016). As Adey *et al.* (2007: 776) maintain, aeromobility is not just the outcome of technological advances but 'a complex set of social representations, imaginations and practices'. Much of the focus of mobility scholars has been the role of air transport in the making of global social orders, the ways in which modern, Western, networked and cosmopolitan societies 'are made and constituted by air travel' (Adey, 2010: 6) through movements in the global economy, transnational cultural exchange, surveillance/control systems and civil rights. The airport, in particular, described by Fuller and Harley (2004: 41) as 'a complex techno-cultural machine', has been studied as 'a microcosm of wider society' (Adey *et al.*, 2007: 780), an icon of the global order (Cwerner, 2009), a laboratory for understanding today's global movements (Fuller & Harley, 2004). The aerotropolis is of special interest for its restructuring of urban space. With the airport now at the centre and the city at the periphery, 'the future of cities lies around airports' (Kasarda & Lindsay, 2011: 159). The future of national borders may also lie around airports. When borders move from the edge of territories to the airport, the airport becomes the 'threshold to the kingdom' (Hart, 2015). The picture painted by mobility scholars of air travel's place in the global social order sets the context for the passenger experience of air travel. Mobility scholars can be said to have explored the 'bigger' picture – the global social context in which the modern Western passenger experiences air travel. However, there is still much to be known about the *lived experience* of the air passenger and, especially, the experience *in flight*. While the airport has received much attention from mobilities scholars, with some exceptions (such as Budd, 2009, 2011; Jensen & Vannini, 2016), there has been less interest in the in-flight component of the journey. As Rink (2017: 881) says, in regard to air travel and tourism, 'Although the relationship between flying and tourism is clear, the role of flying as a tourism activity itself is less well understood'. While some mobilities scholars have studied the passenger experience in earlier times, it is surprising that there has not been more interest in the contemporary air passenger, considering air travel is seen as synonymous with the modern world – an everyday part of life. Certainly, when ethnographies of the contemporary air passenger experience are published, the social complexity of the air journey is apparent (Vannini, 2009).

Others interested in (post)modernity and air travel's place in society have studied the discursive context (*representations* of airspace) through which air travel can be comprehended. As Schaberg (2012: 4) argues in in *The Textual Life of Airports: Reading the Culture of Flight*, 'The culture of flight… involves *reading airports* for their symbolic values: airports serve as intermediary yet interpretively charged points amid the accelerating mobilities of twentieth century consumer culture' (Schaberg: 2012: 4). Pascoe (2001: 10) writes in *Airspaces*,

> Versions of airspace are so common that twentieth-century culture resounds with whirling propellers, the whistling roar of jet engines and the shockwaves of accidents smashing into the vacuity of the terminal. Airports lying as they do at the threshold of airspace, should be treated not as the sterile transitory zones with which we are all familiar, but as 'vessels of conception' for the societies passing through them. More than any other building type of the last century, their being seems to depend on cultural identification no less than architectural use, on their aesthetic properties no less than technological function.

However, to understand *airportness*, the *feel* of air travel, Schaberg (2017a) argues we cannot limit ourselves to reading airports, but rather need to read all stages of the air travel process and all cultural forms in society depicting air travel, such as films, poetry, advertisements, children's toys (planes or airport sets) and even our mobile phone (the aeroplane mode icon). Texts are seen to be everywhere since airportness is a general feeling, preceding and extending beyond the actual journey. Put simply, 'Airportness is about how air travel gets into our heads and bodies' (Schaberg, 2017a: 6) infiltrating our lives, becoming 'natural to us, expected and accepted' (Schaberg, 2017a: 165).

While acknowledging the contribution of the above transglobal and discursive approaches to the study of aeromobility, it is important to remember that our experiences and imaginings of air travel are dependent on where we are in the system and how and why we are travelling through it (Fuller & Harley, 2004). Although scholars may see air space as 'global transnational space' or as 'discursive space', Cresswell (2006) suggests that the theorists, as the kinetic elite, may be mistaking their own experience for a general global condition. As Darda (2015) argues, travellers tend to move through airports without any thought for their cultural significance. Schaberg, too, observes that, even among critical scholars, there has been a lack of reflection.

> I have often been amazed to find myself at academic conferences in various locations to which thousands of colleagues have flown, thus all having submitted to the regimes and rituals of air travel- and yet the experiences of flight (beyond the occasional story of a delay or lost luggage) become submerged, collectively repressed. (Schaberg, 2015: 170)

I would argue that, despite the scholarly contributions from those taking a discursive approach, we still have limited empirical knowledge about *the lived experience* of the air passenger. Cultural theorists, through textual reading, have exposed the meanings and values of air travel which help us understand the air passenger experience but a critical analysis of this experience also requires us to go beyond representations to consider embodied and affective practice as well as the materialities of air travel.

This book focuses on the air passenger and *the passenger's experience of air travel*. In so doing, it places the traveller centre stage. The subject here is the contemporary, commercial air passenger and their air travel experiences. Cultural change in air transport (technological developments, affordability, availability) and social relations, especially in Western societies, distinguish the experience from that of the past. The air travel experience is situated in the broader field of where air transport is currently positioned in our global, cosmopolitan, modern world. Much of this contemporary understanding emerges through cultural change in how the subject is theorised and researched. The book approaches the object of inquiry from a critical travel and tourism perspective informed by the 'new mobilities' paradigm. It focuses on the mobile subject and how social relations happen on the move both at the airport and in flight. It examines the experiences of different groups of passengers including families with babies, obese passengers, those with impairments and those with a fear of flying and examines their relations with other passengers (and crew). The approach taken views the passenger experience as a socially produced, discursive and embodied practice through which power relations are reflected and reinforced. It acknowledges that the diversity of air passengers within the various temporal and sociocultural/political/technological/physical spaces encountered in air travel ensures there is no singular experience. At the same time, it recognises that if knowledge is socially produced, there will be commonalities of experience, whether it be the anxiety of missing a flight, the exhilaration of take-off, the discomfort of aircraft seats, the boredom of waiting or the emotions of airport farewells and reunions. Above all, it situates the air travel experience within the sociocultural context, a context which also shifts in time and place. The book traces changes in the passenger experience from the time of the jet age to the present including the significant changes which occur when aviation is impacted by a global pandemic. A discussion of the air passenger experience also considers climate change and its inevitable impact on the future of air travel. Central to this collection are the social/mobility justice issues inherent in the experience of mobility.

The critical social science approach taken here is distinguished from the traditional positivist approach of air transport management and tourism management studies with their business, managerial focus on the passenger experience, 'rooted in neo-liberal philosophies and dominated by a drive for industry-oriented solutions which seek to enhance and reinforce the existing systems' (Pritchard *et al.*, 2011: 946). With business and commercial interests the stimuli for traditional management research, the focus has been passenger preferences, expectations, service quality perceptions, purchase decisions, satisfaction and loyalty – knowledge required for an airline to remain competitive. The social science approach adopted in this book is also distinguished from the more traditional health sciences approach to aviation (Bor, 2003, 2007; Bor & Hubbard, 2006; Bricker, 2005; Budd *et al.*, 2011) whose focus has been the *physiological effects* of air travel (such as deep vein thrombosis, air sickness, dehydration, earache, headache and sinus pain) and the *psychological effects* (stress and anxiety including fear of flying). Much of this work, too, is embedded within a positivist paradigm and neoliberal philosophy, employing the medical model with a focus on the individual.

This edited collection fills a number of gaps in the air travel scholarship. *Firstly*, by bringing the *journey* to the fore as a complex and meaningful part of travel and tourism (and thus a subject worth studying), it fills a space in the social research of travel and tourism. As stated earlier, the journey itself, the getting from A to B, has, traditionally, been of less interest to social scientists than the experience at the destination. *Secondly*, the collection contributes to aeromobility studies through its focus on the contemporary passenger and their lived experience including their *in-flight* experience (often neglected in mobility research). *Thirdly*, by taking a critical approach to the subject through incorporating the cultural, mobility and performative turns in social science, the collection expands our understanding of the passenger and the journey and offers an alternative approach to the traditional industry-focused positivist framework in travel and tourism studies. *Fourthly*, by going beyond discourse to consider embodied practice and materialities in the investigation, a more complete picture emerges of the passenger experience than the textual analysis of cultural theorists allows. *Finally*, as a *collection*, relevant research and ideas are brought together in one place.

This edited collection is a response to an invitation from the publishers for a tourism publication on the passenger experience of air travel, following the work on the subject by Jennie Small and Candice Harris. In the call for chapters, the underlying requirement was that the subject be approached from a critical perspective. The authors of this collection come from tourism and hospitality studies but, in taking a social approach, cross over other fields of study. The outcome is a collection which acknowledges the changing social, cultural context in which the passenger experience is produced.

This chapter continues with a review of the historical and cultural changes in the passenger experience of commercial air travel over the last 70 years to understand the emergence of today's 'aerial subject' (Adey, 2010). This is followed by a discussion of the critical tourism/mobility studies approach and, finally, a review of the passenger experience literature framed within this critical approach. The passenger experience of air travel should be of interest to scholars from a broad range of social science disciplines and fields of study interested in mobility: (critical) tourism studies, human geography, sociology, anthropology, cultural studies, (critical) disability studies, to name a few.

The Changing Passenger Experience

Much has been written about air travel over the past century and the sociocultural changes which have transformed air travel from being an extra-ordinary to an 'ordinary' form of transport and experience (see Budd, 2014). The increase in the size and speed of aircraft, the redevelopment and expansion of airports (including the aerotropolis, previously mentioned) and the growth in market size are key features of such changes. Air travel is a sociocultural activity that has evolved from technological innovation, new business models, legislative changes, increasing wealth, education and expectations of the middle classes. The passenger experience also reflects changing relationships with those who work in the industry, the ground staff, flight attendants (Escolme-Schmidt, 2009) and pilot (Millward, 2008).

Taking a mobilities perspective, the passenger experience of flying in the period between the wars has been described by writers, such as Budd (2011), Millward (2008) and Rink (2017). At this time, the novelty of travelling at altitude and at speed for those who could afford it was accompanied by physical discomfort: 'vomit, noise, temperature, food, air quality and the state of ground facilities' (Millward, 2008: 8). However, Budd (2011: 1013) emphasises that accounts of discomfort did not dissuade but 'merely helped reinforce the idea that air travel was adventurous, modern, and progressive, and any bodily discomforts were a price worth paying for speed and progress'. She adds that the inter-war aeromobile body was also affected by the size, appearance and physical configuration of the cabin, the in-flight entertainment, as well as the appearance and behaviour of other passengers. In these early years, the dangers of flying promoted fear and anxiety among passengers as well as excitement and exhilaration to be airborne and view the world from above. Millward (2008: 16) reports 'moments of sublime dislocation' when passengers experienced a dreamlike state, feelings of floating, suspension and disconnection. However, from the accounts of this time, Millward (2008) and Budd (2011) also make the point that, as air travel progressively became normalised, long-haul travel could become boring.

The revolution in commercial air travel came with the introduction in the 1950s of the jet aircraft, especially the Boeing 707, and in 1970, the Boeing 747. Until the 1970s, air travel had been the preserve of the rich, the jetsetters. The lavish experience was reflected in the décor, the on-board service and the fine dress of the passengers (dresses and heels for women, suits and ties for men). As Stadiem (2014) says, 'It was a sky party, and you were honored to be on the guest list' (Introduction, para 6). Travel may have been slower but was, overall, a more luxurious experience than today's, as shown in the following advertisement for Pan Am's Clipper Service; see Figure 1.1.

The 707 became embedded in the cultural consciousness, an aspirational symbol of mobility and the future, as Glancey (2014) describes: 'Hugely popular in its heyday, and a symbol of a new, high-flying age powered by forward-looking technology and design, the 707 featured not just in films and songs, but in fashionable product launches like Jantzen's 1957 "707" swimwear'. For most, air travel was a novel experience and very different from air travel in the digital age, as seen in the mementoes of earlier travel (see Figures 1.2 and 1.3) when: menus doubled as postcards to mail at the next port of call; a *Crossing the Line Certificate* – ('suitable for framing') could be ordered through the airline;

Figure 1.1 A 1951 Pan Am advertisement from The National Geographic Magazine

air tickets were printed; and booklets were provided to passengers advising on all aspects of air travel, including the library and games onboard.

It was not until 1970, with the introduction of the Boeing 747, that air travel became accessible to those other than the super-rich. Being a wide-bodied and more fuel-efficient aircraft, the 747 (or 'Jumbo' aircraft) could carry more passengers and thus reduce costs. Although First Class travel on the 747 was still considered luxury travel for the elite, Economy Class was becoming less so. The 'golden age of travel' was now becoming the era of mass travel and tourism. Stadiem (2014), in his colourful history of the Jet Set, explains that, by now, the Jet Set, as a sociological phenomenon, had had its day. Baby Boomers were rejecting the 'male-supremacist, martini-fuelled, conspicuous- consumption, gray-flannel culture' (Chapter 14, para 57) that had spawned the Jet Set. In Stadiem's words, 'mass overwhelmed class' (Chapter 15, para 22). From the late 1970s, new business models and legislative changes, allowing for the deregulation of airlines (1978 in the United States and the 1990s in Europe), saw the introduction of budget, low-cost airlines, such as Ryanair and EasyJet, which took advantage of technological developments to offer a no-frills (or self-) service policy (both on board and at airports). Having to compete with the budget airlines, full-cost airlines have also had to lower fares and, often, service, especially in Economy. Seat size and legroom have shrunk and the chance of an

Figure 1.2 Menus and 'Crossing the Line' Certificate

empty adjacent seat, or an upgrade, a long distant memory. The service of meals has noticeably changed, from the Silver Service of the past to a plastic tray, and today, often a cardboard box (for which there might be an extra cost). Somewhere along the line, other practices in Economy ceased, such as the pre-dinner drinks service, or the promotional 'gifts' for passengers (for example, Thai Airways orchid corsage for female passengers). High-jackings and the events of 9/11 have also impacted the passenger experience on board (no more visits to the cockpit); see Figure 1.4.

Increased security measures at airports, especially large international airports, have transformed the pre-boarding process and the physical design of the airport, its architecture and public spaces. Public access restrictions have changed the *sociality* of the international airport as a place of 'farewell', preventing family/friends of passengers from 'seeing the passenger onto the plane'. At Sydney International Airport, for

Figure 1.3 Printed tickets and Advice booklet for travellers

example, farewells of the past could be quite an affair 'One passenger – 20 guests' was not uncommon with family and friends congregating in the airport bar for one last drink with the passenger before the boarding call, at which point, family and friends would transfer to the airport balcony to wave their passenger on their way as the passenger crossed the tarmac and boarded the plane. Adey (2008) in his discussion of the special place of the airport (and, in particular, the public balcony) confirms that the meaning of the airport as a social public space has changed in the public consciousness. Schaberg (2016), too, describes changes brought about by technological change – when the jet bridge replaced tarmac boarding in airports and changed the passenger experience. Not only was the glamour and sense of adventure of crossing the tarmac lost for the passenger, but those in the airport were no longer able to see passengers taking their final steps onto the plane or their first steps off. Schaberg asks us to: 'Think of all the turbulent feelings, last

Figure 1.4 A visit to the cockpit in the days before security restrictions (1992 © Jennie Small)

looks, and signs of glee or resignation that occur *right there*, – on the brink and its all kept under wraps' (2016: 146).

However, it would be misleading to imagine that airport architecture, technology and security restrictions fully explain changes to the practice of farewell. The shift in air travel as an exceptional event to one that is more commonplace has, for many, lessened the significance for passengers to 'be seen on their way'.

The meaning of the farewell changes when loved ones are not separated for lengthy periods, made possible today with easier access to air travel. When, in the 1960s, John Denver (Denver & Denver, 1967) (mournfully) sang that he was 'Leaving on a Jet Plane' and didn't know when he'd be back again, flying, for most, was still an exceptional experience.

Along with the arrival of the budget airline, a rising global middle class (educated and able to afford travel) has meant a dramatic increase in those who are travelling by air. According to the International Air Transport Association (IATA) (2020b), 4.5 billion passengers flew on scheduled services in 2019. Prior to the COVID-19 pandemic, the long-term trend of passenger demand has been around 5.5% annual growth (IATA, 2020a) with the International Civil Aviation Organization (ICAO) (2019) forecasting the number of scheduled passengers growing to around 10 billion and the number of departures around 90 million by 2040. Over the past 20 years, the real cost of air travel has more than halved (IATA,

2019). Jetstar (2019) reports that, in 1947, a Sydney to London return trip was £525, equivalent to AUD$35,690 today. In 2019 a Sydney to London return trip on a full-cost airline was around AUD$1800. Such changes have taken place within a globalised world in which aeromobility is encouraged for employment, leisure and maintaining social relations. Air travel has come to be represented as normative. Such changes have led some to refer to the 'democratisation' of air travel. Certainly, the slogan emblazoned on the Air Asia fleet – *Now Everyone Can Fly* – exemplifies this notion. Nonetheless, as Randles and Mander (2009: 97) claim, there are 'some difficulties with the "trickle-down" thesis of flying'. As they explain, 'A far higher penetration of the flying market and indeed a far higher penetration of the frequent flying segment is accounted for by higher income and higher social class groups' (Randles & Mander, 2009: 97). Gössling and Humpe (2020) report that, in 2018, no more than 11% of the world population participate in air travel with 4% at most taking international flights. While 'democratisation' might not accurately describe modern day air travel, the flying public is a more heterogeneous group than in the past with, at times, different expectations of appropriate passenger aerial behaviour.

Our experience of air travel today is often framed within our imaginations of a time past when air travel was exclusive and not so commonplace. These memories often become the yardstick by which today's air travel experience is judged.[1] While there has been a noticeable decline in physical comfort, especially for those in Economy (*Cattle*) Class, in other ways, air travel is more comfortable. Although time at the airport may have increased, time in the air has declined, for example, a Sydney to London flight took 4 days in 1947 (Calder, 2018) compared with around 22 hours today. With non-stop flights from Sydney to London, planned for 2025, the flight duration will be reduced to 20 hours (Visontay, 2022). Flying at higher altitude, planes can avoid turbulence and while those sick bags in the seat pocket are necessary, they are less often used. Air travel on modern planes is quieter and the air quality vastly improved through modern filtration systems and a smoking ban. Where in-flight entertainment is available, the visual and sound quality and choice are more advanced than in the past. Although not always seen as a benefit, developments in technology have revolutionised the passenger air travel experience: online booking and check-in, smartphone boarding passes, e-passports and wifi onboard and at airports, allowing passengers to stay connected to home. Finally, and most importantly, the statistics assure us that air travel is safer today than ever before!

Amidst the developments in air travel, we may ask: Has air travel become as mundane as many other forms of transport? Even back in 1929, Macmillan (as cited in Millward, 2008: 10) believed that frequency of air travel could make passengers blasé: 'one can discern the hardened air traveller. The destination is the thing. But to the novitiate the journey is the real thrill' (Macmillan as cited in Millward, 2008: 10). With air travel becoming more commonplace, does it no longer inspire romance, excitement and mystique? The few studies which have touched on this question have highlighted different passenger experience. On the one hand, are those passengers for whom air travel is mundane and fatiguing. For economy passengers, especially, it can be considered dehumanising. In a study of frequent flyers, Randles and Mander (2009: 106) concluded that, for many, the discomfort, frustrations and stress of air travel meant that it was really just a means to an end: 'a necessary evil; the price to be paid for the more agreeable parts of the holiday'. As they claimed, it is not passengers' love of flying that explains the increase in the numbers on planes. In reference to business travellers, Lassen (2006) similarly concluded: 'instead of being a special activity, international air trips have the same meaning and function for a cosmopolitan professional employee as a bus trip for an industrial worker' (Lassen, 2006: 306). As recognised by Cohen and Gössling (2015), hypermobility for business (and leisure) travellers can have a dark side with physiological, psychological, emotional and social costs.

On the other hand, there is a 'glamorization of hypermobility' (Cohen & Gössling, 2015) framed around aspects which signify network capital. Travelling by air, first or business class, in an aircraft with advanced technology and accumulating frequent flyer points can provide the passenger with that capital. Amongst all air passengers, there are those for whom today's air journey is not tedious but continues to signify mystique, excitement and thrill, for whom the journey is part of the holiday. Randles and Mander (2009: 104) report passenger enjoyment in air travel from being looked after to having time to oneself.

> *On the plane I do like it when you are fed and entertained – it has special associations with going on holiday, you can relax & have first drink 'cheers'! You wait for the drinks and food... it's a fun thing – getting your five containers and packets, it's exciting. (Frequent Flyers Study: Lara)*

> *The journey is part of the holiday ... from the second I leave home I go onto auto-pilot. Eight hours with no-one bothering you .... I can read or think... At the airport I check out the shops, I usually buy something each trip, a cosmetic item or duty free. (Frequent Flyers Study: Judith)*

Fuller (2003) refers to the liberating feeling of 'walking to the departure gate'. She continues, 'There is a certain sublimeness to the felt experiences of becoming – airborne – anonymous – absent'. Schaberg (2017a: 49), referring to the 'extraordinary sensation of takeoff', asks: 'Who can deny the miraculous feeling of takeoff, when the engine whine increases to a roar, your body is pushed back into the seat, and the whole airport becomes a blur, only then to recede into the distance down below?' Yet, he acknowledges that, for the regular traveller, this experience has become humdrum and questions 'how something as magical as flight – and especially that moment of release from the ground – can become so profoundly taken for granted'.

Nonetheless, whether pleasurable or not, the passenger experience still holds meaning, and however habitual or generic air travel may become, it remains a unique form of mobility distinguishable from everyday events. Being up in the air, travelling at speed through space, not only physically disconnects us from the land and life below but can also mentally dissociate us. We can feel remote, untouchable, released from the everyday demands of life (so long as we can avoid advancing technologies which allow onboard communication with home). At the same time, we continue our commonplace behaviours: sleeping, eating, reading, watching movies etc. In his poem, *Back from Australia,* John Betjeman captures the everyday human perspective in this unnatural, inhuman form of transport where we are 'cocooned in time'.

> *Cocooned in Time, at this inhuman height,*
> *The packaged food tastes neutrally of clay.*
> *We never seem to catch the running day*
> *But travel on in everlasting night*
> *With all the chic accoutrements of flight:*
> *Lotions and essences in neat array*
> *And yet another plastic cup and tray.*
> *'Thank you so much. Oh no, I'm quite all right'.* (Betjeman, 1979)
>
>   Reprinted with permission from Hodder & Stoughton,
>   Headline Publishing – Betjeman, J. (1979) Back from Australia.
>   In Lord Birkenhead (ed.) *John Betjeman's Collected Poems*
>   (4th edn, p. 399). London: John Murray Ltd.

A Critical Approach to the Air Travel Experience

Critical of the existing systems, and seeking a deeper understanding of passenger experience, through 'putting social relations into travel' (Sheller & Urry, 2006: 208), the authors in this book take an alternative ideological position from that of the service sector in traditional transport and tourism studies, and mainstream health studies, to consider conceptual approaches from the social sciences, in particular, cultural studies, critical tourism studies, disability studies and mobility studies. With mobility seen as a social practice, a new paradigm is required to study 'aerial life' (Adey, 2010), which Adey and Lin (2014: 61) describe as, 'a culture in its own right'.

The more compelling ideological position is one informed by an approach to social enquiry which assumes a relativist ontological worldview; multiple realities (as opposed to one reality as espoused by positivism) which are produced through language and other social practices. Such a view sees our social world as constructed socially and discursively; produced/emergent from our historical and sociocultural experience (Gergen, 2015). It considers that, through shared social relations, there is an intersubjective notion of the self, or subject. Thurlow and Jawowski (2012: 491), discussing modern tourism, describe it as 'a quintessential example of an industry that is highly semiotically embedded'. As they explain, 'a key part of what is actually "produced" and consumed is the semiotic context of the service itself'. While some argue that life and meaning are more than discourse and representation (we should not privilege cultural readings over everyday, lived practices), others take a broader view, seeing discourse as practice: 'representations are apprehended as performative in themselves' (Dewsbury *et al.*, 2002: 438). As Jensen (2014) explains in his discussion of 'mobile semiotics', the semiotic system interacts with our performance of mobility. Crouch *et al.* (2001: 264) refer to 'embodied semiotics', explaining, 'We cannot and do not want to ignore semiotics, but signs are not constructed only in visual and mental processes, but also produced bodily'.

Inherent in the notion of the embodied subject is the idea that we are actors/performers/doers. It is through the body – through movement, affect and sensations – that we perform, that we practise mobility. All social life can be thought of as performative with spaces and places constituting stages (Edensor, 2000). Technologies and spaces allow the practice of flying to happen but, as Creswell and Merriman (2011) remind us, spaces are not only the context for our mobile practices but are produced through the very act of moving. It is through the corporeal body that movement, places and people are experienced, that we 'create spaces and stories' (Cresswell & Merriman, 2011: 5), that we 'construct emotional geographies' (Sheller & Urry, 2006: 216), that we understand ourselves and others. However, we cannot think of space without considering time; both are entwined in our mobility. Just as mobility is involved in the social production of space, so it is involved in the social production of time. In sum, mobility involves three aspects which are difficult to disentangle, as Cresswell (2010: 19) explains: 'physical movement – getting from one place to another; the representations of movement that give it shared meaning; and, finally, the experienced and embodied practice of movement'.

This alternative approach to the travel experience recognises the material world in our reality, the technologies, objects and things which surround us and with which we interact corporeally. As Haldrup and Larsen (2006: 278) explain, 'things acquire value – *use* value – through being employed in embodied and poetic practices, in and through the sensuous materiality of the body'. Things can be thought of as 'hybrids' of the human and non-human (Franklin & Crang, 2001). This approach sees the material and discursive as interconnected and mutually affecting resulting in a co-production of knowledge. To understand mobility requires recognition of other people and our relational practices. As Bissell (2010: 270) says: 'mobilities are rarely experienced alone or in isolation from other people... In the process of travel, we temporarily submit ourselves to become part of a mobile collective. To become a passenger always involves a "being with"'.

Critical tourism and mobility studies extend the above approach to consider the politics and ethics of travel/mobility. The critical approach requires us to consider and challenge power relations and to question whose interests are served by different paradigms/ideologies. It is concerned with equality, sustainability, social justice and emancipation. With reference to critical tourism studies, Morgan and Pritchard (2015) explain its analysis as 'an ethical and political project dedicated to creating conditions of equality, sustainability, and human freedom'. Mobility in each of its aspects (movement, representation and practice) is political, 'implicated in the production and reproduction of power relations' (Cresswell, 2010: 26) with the politics of each interconnected. Cresswell (2010) asks us to consider: Who moves, furthest, fastest, most often? How is mobility represented? How is mobility practised – embodied? Is it free or forced? While recognising that mobility is central to the modern condition associated with opportunity, freedom and progress (Cresswell, 2006), critical scholars draw attention to the reality that there is a mobility gap (Cresswell, 2006; Hannam *et al.*, 2006; Sheller & Urry, 2006); not all individuals or social groups have 'motility' (the capacity to be mobile). Kaufmann *et al.* (2004: 750) explain the requirements for this capacity: 'access to different forms and degrees of mobility, competence to recognize and make use of access, and appropriation of a particular choice, including the option of non-action'. This capacity for movement is a form of capital through which one can accrue other types of capital, such as 'network capital' which Elliott and Urry (2010: 59) define as 'the capacity to engender and sustain social relations with those people who are not necessarily proximate, which generates emotional, financial and practical benefit...'. As Massey (1993) explains, the mobility and control of some groups can weaken that of others, the already weak. Power differentials are evident not only between those who can choose to be mobile and those who cannot, but also amongst those who are mobile. Power relations are apparent in *how* we move, in our experience of mobility based on class, gender, age, ability, race and ethnicity etc. There are facets of mobility that differentiate people and things into 'hierarchies of mobility' (Creswell, 2010).

In sum, a critical approach is concerned with mobility rights, seeking social transformation and mobility justice to 'even out' mobility capital. It emphasises modes of enquiry which are interpretive, alternative and often radical (Wilson *et al.*, 2008, 2012) as opposed to the traditional approach to the passenger experience which, coming from a positivist position, often prefers modelling and quantitative surveys. Critical social science recognises that embedded in our methodology are assumptions about our social world. It views methodology as: 'inherently political, as inescapably tied to issues of power and legitimacy' (Lather, 1991: 110). It tries to uncover the processes by which meanings are produced and acknowledges the researcher in that construction of knowledge. It requires approaches which engage context, embodied practice and representations (Crouch *et al.*, 2001). The preference has been for qualitative methods, such as interview, ethnography and discourse analysis. However, as Adey (2010: 17) says, 'Bodily perceptions, feelings and sensations unearth a terrain of mobility-in-action that is difficult to portray or represent'. As a consequence, a range of 'mobile' methods, such as mobile participant observation, video ethnography and 'being "mobile with" others' (Sheller, 2013: 50) have been developed, inspired by the transdisciplinary nature of the mobilities field.

A Review of the Literature on the Air Passenger Experience from a Critical Perspective

I turn now to a review of the existing (but limited) literature on the passenger experience of air travel from this alternative, critical position. For the sake of simplicity, the literature has been organised under different headings, however, the components of aeromobility – the movement, the representations of movement, the material and embodied practice are intermeshed and difficult to untangle.

The representation of air travel

Air travel is represented in literature, film, television, song and advertisements (see Van Riper, 2004) and, today, in social media where user-generated representations of air travel abound. As mentioned earlier, Pascoe (2001) and Schaberg (2012) examine the representation of airports in literature and popular culture exposing a rich text of signs and meanings: 'air travel depends on a network of stories and meanings – texts that are interpreted by the everyday practices of flight' (Schaberg, 2012: 11). Schaberg expands:

> airports depend on textuality to a great degree, as much for their straightforward operations (such as the daily performances and narratives that play out all the way from the check-in stand to the departure gate), as for their everyday mysteries and inoperative moments (for instance, how a thousand unique stories can be contained in and canceled out by phrases like 'weather delay' and 'lost baggage').
> (Schaberg, 2012: 2)

In his study of *airportness* – the feel of air travel – Schaberg (2017a) extends his textual reading beyond the airport to all representations of air travel in any cultural format. MacArthur (2012), on the other hand, has focused on one literary form, poetry, to understand the passenger experience, claiming that air travel has been an evocative subject for poets. She describes poetry of the earlier years of flight when the aerial view provided a new way of seeing which was 'meditative, transcendental, rhapsodic, and celebratory' (2012: 266). As air travel has changed so has poetry, with today's verses exposing the tedium of modern-day air travel.

Unsurprisingly, where the onboard experience is featured in airline advertisements, air travel is not represented as tedious, but rather luxurious and comfortable – 'glamourized' (Cohen & Gössling, 2015) and promising so much (Schaberg, 2017b). Those who have commented on contemporary discourse have highlighted the discrepancy between the airline depictions of air travel and the embodied practice of the passenger (at least, the Economy passenger). In a study of Facebook posts of six international airlines, Small and Harris (2019) found that representations of the air travel experience were of Business/First Class travel, with emphasis on comfort and pampering. The Economy passenger onboard experience received little mention. Studying the semiotic landscape of luxury tourism (in particular, Emirates Business Class), Thurlow and Jaworski (2012) claim that what is being promoted is distinction, status and desirability which are imagined and re-imagined by 'all consumer citizens regardless of their power or wealth' (Thurlow & Jaworski, 2012: 492). In earlier studies of the discourse of airline in-flight magazines, Thurlow and Jaworski (2003) and Small *et al.* (2008) highlighted the means by which this genre positioned not only the airlines, but also the passengers themselves as global citizens with an elite status. Small *et al.* (2008), examining the products advertised in Qantas and Air New Zealand in-flight magazines, similarly noted that many of the advertisers were global or multinational companies with a focus on exclusivity, luxury, indulgence, comfort, competition, innovation and a privileging of wealth. The authors concluded that 'travellers are constructed as being rich in time and money, entrepreneurial, leisured, free and happy' (Small *et al.*, 2008: 33). One might say that the air traveller is, thus, socially sorted (Morgan & Pritchard, 2005) from the non-air traveller but with the widening gap between the representation of air travel and practice, passengers are, in effect, socially sorted from each other based on class and wealth (Small *et al.*, 2008).

The representation of an airline as a national symbol is another means by which passenger experience and identity (in this case, nationality and citizenship) may be reaffirmed or subordinated. Here, I look briefly at one example, Australia's national carrier, Qantas. As the airline approached its 100th anniversary, the CEO and Managing

Director, Alan Joyce (Qantas.com, 2020) says, 'The story of Qantas is the story of modern Australia – past, present and future'. Drew (2011: 322) has similarly described the airline as 'an iconic Australian brand whose history is inextricably linked with the nation'. With the flying kangaroo as logo on the tail, *Spirit of Australia* on the fuselage and the long-running commercials and safety videos featuring Australian children's choirs singing, '*I still call Australia home*', there is no doubt for which country the airline is the national carrier. Drew (2011) in his analysis of the discourse of *Qantas Spirit of Australia* commercials, explains that these commercials are appealing to 'a collective consciousness, "an Australian spirit" ostensibly deep within each Australian' (Drew, 2011: 321). It reaffirms Australia's public perceptions of community and self. He further explains that the lyrics of the song and the use of particular (types of) children incite adventure, and freedom (to travel), nostalgia, pride sense of place and a longing for home. Passengers flying the airline (or seeing the airline at foreign airports) may be comforted by the familiar symbols and take 'on board' these meanings. It is not unusual for travellers returning home from the other side of the world to report a sense of comfort on boarding their Qantas flight and hearing the familiar twang of an Australian accent after a long absence from home. Reflecting on his career flying the 747, Qantas pilot, Mark Kelly, (Dye, 2020) says,

> I'm sure so many Baby Boomers recall their first flight going overseas on a 747. When they were coming home they'd get on in London and hear the 'G'day mate' from the captain – just hearing that Australian accent made them feel at home.

In more recent times, passengers express the same sentiments.

> *Hokey as it is, it's a comfort to hear the familiar, especially on the leg home. It's like getting home when you get on the plane.* (Tripadvisor, 2017)

> *… I have to admit that I have felt immediately at home when boarding a Qantas flight and hearing my first Aussie accents after several months overseas!* (Tripadvisor, 2017)

While Qantas, over recent years, has not been devoid of passenger criticism, the airline is still considered by many to hold a special place in the nation's psyche. However, the degree to which Qantas is embedded in the consciousness of Australians will depend not only on representation and performance but also on the airline's ability to represent the diversity of its citizens. While it may not be a conscious act of the producer of images/text to omit certain groups of people from a publication, images nevertheless can suggest who is welcome and who is not. Certainly, in the study of in-flight magazines (Small *et al.*, 2008), discussed above, the images privileged those who were white, able bodied, young, slim-to-medium build, heterosexual and often in corporate professional employment. These findings reflect those of Edelheim (2007) who, in studying the promotional messages in the domestic brochures of Qantas, found that the people portrayed reinforced certain hegemonic views of society: there was a stereotypical portrayal of gender and an absence of certain groups of Australians (ethnicities other than Anglo-Australian, mature travellers, those with a disability and sexualities other than heterosexual). The findings from the previously mentioned study of Facebook posts of six international airlines (Small & Harris, 2019) suggest that little has changed. How the passenger sees themselves, understands their identity, may be constructed from, and reflected in, these socially constructed images and text, although as Edelheim (2007: 14) reminds us, 'no reading of a text is final'.

These representations are situated in the broader discourse which considers mobility and hypermobility as favourable conditions of modernity. Culturally, economically and politically, mobility is perceived more favourably than (what we think of as) immobility (Bissell, 2007). Within this discourse, to travel at fast speed and unimpeded is usually presented as the more desirable option. As Bissell (2007: 280) explains, our acceptance of this may have emerged in part 'from associated economic, business and more generally competitive neoliberal rationales of productivity and a concern that time needs to be utilized more productively in order to be more profitable'. However, as discussed later in this chapter, there are contradictory discourses regarding the desirability of air travel and its impact on the environment: *benign*, according to the airline industry; *damaging*, according to the environmental discourse (Gössling & Peeters, 2007).

The embodied practice of air travel

Air travel is an embodied and affective experience (see Budd, 2011) within a unique material environment of airport and aircraft. The centrality of the body in the air travel experience is highlighted by Veijola and Valtonen (2007) in their accounts of air travel from the perspective of passenger and crew. Jensen and Vannini (2016: 31) further recognise that there is no 'typical' affective atmosphere of a commercial flight since flights will vary depending on the particulars of the situation, such as origin and destination of the flight, time of day and year and composition of passengers and crew. Small and Harris (2012, 2014, 2015) highlight how other passengers and crew contribute to the passenger experience. The type and design of the aircraft, route and duration of flight are also key factors. Jensen and Vannini describe how the aircraft 'stages' a particular experience and atmosphere through the design of its cabin (such as number of rows, orientation of seats, aisle width etc.). The passengers also 'stage' themselves (for example, in seating choice or use of electronic devices), 'thus creating or co-creating the aircraft experience' (Jensen & Vannini, 2016: 29). The authors refer to an atmosphere of *insulation*, designed by the large, modern-day airlines to shield passengers from the discomforts and anxieties of air travel. In contrast is the atmosphere of *suspension* in small, older aircraft where passengers experience the sensation of 'being in the air'. However, Jensen and Vannini (2016: 30) note that there are some relatively stable characteristics of affective experiences on commercial flights:

> feelings of boredom, anxiety, quiescence, dread, excitement, hunger, anticipation, awe and wonder, and bodily discomfort circulate in different measures around the aircraft cabin, affecting passengers and being affected, in turn, by their changing moods, sensations, and states of mind.

At the same time, our experience as passengers is intertwined with regulatory frameworks. The airport and aeroplane can be considered 'enclavic space' (Edensor, 2000) where passenger performances are monitored through surveillance by the authorities and the disciplinary gaze of other passengers. Edensor (2000: 334) describes the 'disciplined rituals' of performance where performance is 'repetitive, specifiable in movement, and highly constrained by time'. We can think of our movements in airports and aeroplanes as being choreographed with our movements purposive and directed along demarcated paths. Edensor (2014), in his discussion of the relationship of rhythm to mobility and sense of place, describes how habitual modes of negotiating mobile space become imprinted in our bodies. He discusses how air travel passengers:

> surrender to the imposed rhythms of air travel, taking the opportunity to read, write, watch a movie, listen to music, eat, drink, chat or sleep, a series of activities that individuals negotiate and improvise within a rigid schedule, abandoning themselves to a different rhythm and temporal structuring. (Edensor, 2014: 166)

Of course, rhythms can be disrupted when running late for a flight or having to wait for a delayed flight. Jet lag also disrupts a passenger's everyday rhythm of sleeping and eating. To perform the air passenger role requires learning and skill if one is to be a 'competent' passenger. For those who frequently fly, the journey may be performed relatively mindlessly (Unger *et al.*, 2016) but for the first-time passenger there is much to learn for this complex performance, from how to book a flight to how to collect baggage at the other end. Nonetheless, the regular remodelling of airports and changes to check-in procedures and security requirements can demand performance re-learning by even the experienced traveller.

The passenger experience of movement and speed

Air travel is an embodied experience involving all our senses including our kinaesthetic sense. We experience the movement of our bodies with the plane's bumps and vibrations especially during turbulence and the sensation of acceleration and speed during take-off and landing. Jensen and Vannini (2016: 33) describe take-off acceleration as appealing to many through its 'almost adrenalin-like rush that is hard to experience elsewhere'. However, aside from take-off and landing, for the most part, it may only be through vision that we register the sensation of movement or speed for, as with the movement of advanced modern trains (Larsen, 2001), aircraft movement can appear smooth and seamless. To the air traveller, this visual register of movement and speed may only occur when closer to the ground as, at high altitude, the sensation of speed is diminished by the absence of proximate points of visual reference (Jensen & Vannini, 2016). As the speed of travel changes so do our space and time relations.

The passenger experience of space and time

Distances that once took months to travel, then weeks, now take hours. As Harvey (1989) says, time and space have become compressed, space has been annihilated by time. Airports, too, as a conduit from one physical location to another 'facilitate the shrinkage of the globe and transcend both space and time' (Gottdiener, 2001: 11). Following the work of Barthes, Schaberg (2016: 89) explains: 'since the jet moves so fast across so much space, the bodily experience of that very same space is diminished, and the excessive speed turns into repose – being reclined in the aircraft seat'. From his textual analysis of airports, he argues that repose is already established at the airport prior to even boarding the plane. For the air traveller, annihilation of space by time can be welcome, especially when air travel is uncomfortable or business requires speedy transport, yet time can also feel 'excruciatingly drawn out, and experienced as profoundly *wasted* time: hours and minutes to be suffered and gotten *through*' (Schaberg, 2016: 89). Flying the same route on different occasions can produce different temporal experiences – on one occasion the flight might seem 'to go fast' (time is experienced as compressed) while on another it 'never ends' (time is experienced as stretched). Even on the same flight passengers will have different experiences. The perception of the utility of travel time will also vary. Here, I suggest that the core ideas in Lyons' (2014) exploration of the meaning and consumption of time in rail travel are likely relevant to air travel. Moving beyond the orthodox view that sees travel time as wasted time, Lyons suggests a positive utility to travel time: travel time can be conceived as a gift. It is a gift to those at the destination, as evidenced in the time the traveller is prepared to give to be co-present. It is also a gift to oneself, the traveller, as it can be experienced as *transition time*, time to adjust between home and destination and, also, *time out* from our different life roles. However, while technological developments in communication may allow travellers (even in the air) to stay connected with others who are not co-present (*connected time*), their unwanted intrusion can result in *infected time*.

Our sense of time is also disrupted in the crossing of time zones. Long-haul passengers flying from West to East are particularly familiar with the experience of jet lag: the desynchrony between the passenger's circadian system and local time cues. However, according to Anderson (2015: 3), we need to go beyond the narrow definition of jet lag and circadian disruption to understand 'the abuse wreaked [sic] on the human body' by high-speed long-haul mobility. He prefers the broader perspective of *travel disorientation* to consider how our sense of place and sense of wellbeing are disrupted by geo-temporal mobility. Included in his state of *travel disorientation* are: geographical dislocation, psychological disorientation and cultural displacement of the passenger. He argues that this disorientation occurs not only at the airport and onboard the aircraft but before we leave home and later, on arrival at the destination.

While compression of space may be welcome, it can disrupt our understanding of 'distance' and sense of location in the world if travel time is no longer perceived as commensurate with distance travelled. Places once considered 'distant' (in terms of mileage) can lose their meaning (as can the act of covering great distances) as travel time declines. The journey becomes too easy and the mystique and romance of distance/remoteness diminishes. Pascoe (2001: 244) quotes the poet, Francis Hope: 'No doubt flying is too fast (as George Orwell thought trains were too fast) for a true flavour of arrival. It merely gives a generalized sense of displacement'. However, he did add, 'But even this is a privilege, and a pleasure'.

The visual gaze from above

The passenger experience of space outside the aircraft involves an interplay of discourses, embodied practice and materialities of the aircraft and the external world. When we fly, we experience new ways of seeing and engaging with the world. The meanings of the place below shift. As Rink (2017: 887) explains, the visual, kinaesthetic and affective sensations work together to 'render the landscape below'. Jensen and Vannini (2016) describe how the type of aircraft will affect the intensity of involvement with the environment through which the aircraft travels. The flight route will determine the landscape that can be viewed while the altitude of the aircraft and the weather will determine if that landscape is visible. Essential, is access to a window from which to view. The speed of the aircraft and distance from the ground will determine how we view what appears to be a moving vista with images moving fast and becoming blurred during take-off and landing and then broadening and slowly moving when travelling at altitude, at which point landscape becomes continental rather than local (Macarthur, 2012). When Sir Charles Johnston wrote *Air Travel in Arabia* (as cited in Crossley-Holland, 1989: 26):

> Then Petra *flashed by* [my italics] in a wink.
> It looked like Eaton Square but pink.

he was unlikely to be travelling at altitude. Rink (2017), studying the aeromobile tourist gaze 'from above' during aerial sightseeing tours of Cape Town, highlights the uniqueness of the perspective (third dimension) informed by verticality. He describes the view from above as 'a totalising one, rendering the city below devoid of its complexity' (Rink, 2017: 882). As G. Sebald writes in *The Rings of Saturn*:

> I watched the shadow of our plane hastening below us across hedges and fences, rows of poplars and canals ... Nowhere, however, was a single human being to be seen. No matter whether one is flying over Newfoundland or the sea of lights that stretches from Boston to Philadelphia after nightfall, over the Arabian deserts which gleam like mother-of-pearl, over the Ruhr or the city of Frankfurt, it is as though there were no people, only the things they have made and in which they are hiding. One sees the places where they live and the roads that link them, one sees the smoke rising from their houses and factories, one sees the vehicles in which they sit, but one sees not the people themselves. (Sebald, 1998: 90–91)

For early travellers, the panoramic view from the air was a novelty and one of the highlights of aerial travel (see Budd, 2009). Millward (2008: 15) writes that, for those flying between the two world wars, the elevated perspective was 'like studying a living map'. Location aids (maps and route plans) provided by the airlines facilitated this impression. To view the earth from above provided a completely different vision of place. Much of the writing on the early years of flying refers to the awe and wonder of viewing the world from the air. However, as air travel became more commonplace, the view from the aircraft, even for these early travellers was not always exciting, it could be disappointing and uninteresting (Budd, 2011; Millward, 2008). While we have personal accounts of flying in the early years, the first-hand experience of today's passenger is less well documented.

Technological advances in aircraft design such as the ability to fly at higher altitude, have meant the landscape below is less visible to today's passengers. As Budd (2009: 86) says: 'aerial skyscapes of space replaced terrestrial landscapes of place'. Wide-bodied jets have meant fewer passengers have access to a window from which to view the land below. Even with a window seat, if seated over the wing, the landscape below may not be visible. Boorstin (1987: 94) relates his experience of a routine flight at 23,000 feet:

> ... far above the clouds, too high to observe landmark or seamark. Nothing to see but the weather; since we had no weather, nothing to see at all. I had flown not through space but through time ... My only problem en route was to pass the time. My passage through space was unnoticeable and effortless. The airplane robbed me of the landscape.

Many modern air travellers would mirror Ruskin's description of rail travellers (Schivelbusch, 1978: 35): 'human parcels who dispatch themselves to their destination ... arriving as they left ... untouched by the space traversed'.

In addition to viewing difficulties, the diminishing novelty of air travel and the competing attraction of non-stop in-flight entertainment (and a flight information video channel) may affect the amount of gazing from the window. The flight information channel has replaced information from the flight deck which in the past might have directed our gaze. On a recent international flight by the author, a rare message from the flight deck reinforced the idea that gazing would be of little interest to the passengers: 'We are passing over Broome, but you are not interested in that. I'm sure you want to watch a movie'. While Budd (2009) describes a different experience, where the captain interrupted the in-flight movie to encourage the passengers to view the glaciers and icebergs below, she similarly observed that the world below held little fascination for the majority of passengers on that flight. Clearly the meaning of the aerial gaze on the landscape below has shifted. Yet, as Schaberg (2017a: 52) observes, airline advertisements continue to feature a 'contented passenger lost in reverie gazing out from the window seat, placid visage caught in a warm glow'.

Budd (2009) highlights the changes in dominant cultural discourses that define what it means to become and be mobile. The discourse of the past which represented air travel as a wondrous, sublime, sightseeing adventure has been replaced by a discourse which sees air travel as 'boring and uncomfortable dead time between departure and arrival, with nothing to see or do' (Budd, 2009: 87), time which defies memory. Budd adds, 'in-flight entertainment systems, personal music devices, and portable gaming consoles are more interesting than the materiality of a flight itself' (Budd, 2009: 87). Being asked to close his window blind so passengers could sleep or watch the entertainment, Bob Brown (ex-leader of the Australian Greens Party) was led to ponder, 'I wonder how many passengers remember what entertained them that night as the Earth passed so spectacularly below' (Gebicki, 2019: 7). At the time, Brown was 'glued to the plane window by the sight of icebergs floating out into the blue Atlantic from the disgorging glaciers of Greenland' (Gebicki, 2019: 7). With the exception of captains, such as the one on Budd's flight who encouraged the passengers to look out the window, the airlines do not seem unhappy to have a compliant planeload of passengers glued to their screens.

However, as evidenced in the contemporary controversy over the practice of some airlines to request closed window blinds during a daytime flight, there are passengers who still want to view the landscape below, for whom the view from the window inspires awe and wonder, for whom the journey begins on departure, not on arrival at the destination. Air travel allows us to view familiar landscapes from a different perspective, and foreign parts that we may never visit. It is an easy consumption of landscape as little effort is required to experience. It is an intimate gaze, which can feel especially so on a night flight when the cabin is in darkness, other passengers asleep, and through our personal window we spy the lights of a remote settlement 'somewhere' in the world. The skyscape, too, can hold our gaze as in Figure 1.5.

Figure 1.5 Cloud formation can still hold interest (2019 © Jennie Small)

In Box 1, below, letter writers to the Traveller section of *The Sydney Morning Herald* refute the argument of another (Mike Weiss) that the aerial gaze is pointless (at least on long-haul flights), defending the raising of blinds. (Another argument for the raising of blinds is the maintenance of circadian rhythms and prevention of jet lag.)

Box 1 Open or Closed Blinds? Letters to the Editor of Traveller (The Sydney Morning Herald, 2019)

DIM VIEWS

Regarding the closing of blinds and dimming of light (Traveller, July 2), I never cease to be amazed by the stupidity of people who travel overseas on long-haul flights. What is one going to see out of a plane window when flying at 39,000 feet? Answer: blue, blue sky and clouds. Have a thought for other passengers as the light shining through the windows at that height is extremely bright... **Mike Weiss, Vermont South, VIC**

(*Source:* Rants & Raves, 2019, August 10: 53)

LIGHTEN UP

I rather object to being called 'stupid', Mike Weiss (Traveller Letters, August 10). I like to see the blue sky, cloud formations and the world far below. I also like to read in the natural light instead of the harsh overhead light, and I don't like being surrounded by darkness for the whole flight. I am not an infant who needs multiple hours' sleep. What about putting on the eyeshades, Mike, and let us all enjoy the ride? **Jenny Mackenzie, Cheltenham, VIC**

Mike Weiss, what utter tosh. As I write, I am at flight level 240 on QR907 flying over some of the most impressive, albeit drought-plagued land, of north-west NSW en route to Doha. I admit we pay for premium class but a daytime flight anywhere overland with a window seat is mind-blowing. It could have been the mountains of Oman, the floods of Bangladesh, the bleak expanse of the Russian Steppes. Get geography and the beauty of our planet which we so need to preserve. **John Moore, Braidwood, NSW**

I totally disagree with Mike Weiss about there being nothing to see 30,000 feet up. My wife and I have enjoyed seeing icebergs while flying Sydney to South Africa, as the flight path dips towards Antarctica; the northern coastline of Africa from Dubai to Casablanca; the land and river patterns from Sydney to Singapore; flying across Africa, India, Balkan countries. There's actually lots to see and windows should stay up during daylight hours. If you want to sleep, wear a blindfold. **Kerry Henry, McMahons Point, NSW**

(*Source:* Rants & Raves, 2019, August 24: 37)

Of course, a passenger's seat selection may be unrelated to their interest in gazing from above. Seat selection may be cost related, influenced by the preference of a travel companion or the ease with which one can exit their seat to move around the cabin (especially on a long-haul flight). For the windowless but interested passenger, the flight information video channel (if available) may have to do.

The diversity of practice

There are recognisable commonalities of experience amongst contemporary air passengers but the multiple forms of difference in the social groups who comprise the passenger body and the material objects/technologies, regulations and other people with whom the passenger comes in contact, can limit generalisation. Passengers may be travelling domestically or internationally, long haul or short haul, solo or with others. They may be frequent or infrequent travellers, on a full-cost or low-cost airline, in first, business or economy class (or in between). They may belong to an Executive club. In addition to class, passengers will differ by age, gender, sexuality, dis/ablebodiness, body shape and size and (especially on an international flight) nationality/culture/ethnicity/race. The experience is also affected by the passenger's physical and mental health. Bor (2007: 208) made the point that 'While engineering developments in air travel have been rapid and spectacular, our species has a certain amount of catching up to do in order to cope better with both the physical and psychological demands of travel'. For certain groups of passengers, flying can trigger intense emotional reactions: separation from loved ones, disrupted routines, disorientation, being out of control, lost luggage and unfamiliar food (Bor, 2007). Passengers also differ in their purpose of travel – holiday, visiting friends and relatives, business/conference, education, migration, health, sport or, as Kloppenburg (2013) discusses, drug smuggling!

A defining difference in the air travel experience is class – class of travel and social class of passenger. As Schaberg (2016: 152) says, 'Air travel… is one of our contemporary social practices that lays absolutely bare how class structure works: you either have lots of room of your own; a smaller amount; your seat is a literal part of your labor; or you aren't even on the plane'. He also cites the 'staggering hierarchy of loyalty levels and elitisms' (2017a: 38) in the boarding order of passengers. Studying Polish migrants to the United Kingdom, Burrell (2011) found the culture of mobility and aeromobility on low-cost air carrier, Ryanair, was integral to the migration experience with airports and aeroplane meaningful social settings for the collective identity of the Polish group. Although the journeys taken on Ryanair were considered particularly emotional – 'the lifeblood of their continued links with friends and family in Poland' (Burrell, 2011: 1028), negative responses were directed at the low-cost airline with the cost-saving policies of its capitalist business model. As Burrell (2011: 1029) concludes:

> The stress and indignity of these flights contrasts starkly with the emotional weight of the experience they are servicing. While these journeys are highly significant for the migrants, their bodies and material possessions are, in effect, just commodities in the airline industry chain.

The powerlessness of the migrants, and their possessions, throughout the travel process led Burrell to remind us that we must not forget the people caught up in the airline's business model.

Passengers can be differentiated by their air travel expertise or 'know how', in other words, their 'skill-kit' (Mertena et al., 2022). The novice passenger, unskilled in air travel, has come to the attention of writers. While Freire-Medeiros and Name (2013) studied the first-time flying experiences of individuals from a Brazilian favela, Hirsh (2017) focused on low-cost aviation in South-East Asia, highlighting the 'less glamorous forms of mobility', such as the movement of students, migrant workers and budget tourists. Included in his study are those travellers referred to as the *'nouveaux globalisés*: people who have just enough money to travel abroad, but who lack the basic knowledge and technical equipment that is needed to fly' (Hirsh, 2017: 260). These are travellers who cannot make online bookings as they do not own a credit card or know how to use a computer. According to Hirsh, their lack of basic knowledge includes such practices as assigned onboard seating. Hirsh (2017) describes the experiences of passengers at AirAsia's low-cost terminal at Kuala Lumpur International Airport which differentiate them from passengers at the Kurokawa-designed main terminal on the other side of the airfield.

> First, the majority are accompanied by children, who make up about a third of the terminal's population. Second, like budget travelers throughout Asia, passengers at the LCCT are slowed down by an inordinate amount of belongings: bulky duffel bags, overstuffed carry-ons, cardboard boxes filled with instant noodles and Milo. Many try to haul more than their own weight in carry-on luggage onto the plane. It's a practice typical of passengers who fly infrequently, and therefore must carry much more luggage; but want to avoid the fees charged for checked or excess baggage. (Hirsh, 2017: 266)

Of greater academic interest has been the experienced (business) traveller who, while not immune from the stress and strain of air travel, enjoys the privileges afforded by special products and services (Cohen & Gössling, 2015). As Lassen (2006: 309) says, the ease with which these travellers are able to traverse airports and international borders demonstrates that 'mobility is intricately tied to relations of power and domination that both produce and shape the forms of mobility (Gogia, 2003)'. With the benefit of 'know how' – where to go and what to do at airports, it appears business travellers are better able to cope with the hassles of air travel and feel a sense of pride in their competence (Gustafson, 2014; Unger *et al.*, 2016). As Gustafson (2014: 70) says, 'Such "travel competence" appears as an important form of mobility capital – a kind of resource, derived from experience and practice that enables or facilitates mobility'. The privileges attached to being a 'business class' passenger (executive lounges, more comfortable seats and better service throughout the whole process) are highly visible in the separate lines for check-in and the location of seating on planes. As Unger *et al.* (2016) describe: 'When "economy" passengers enter the aircraft struggling with their hand bags, they pass through the "business" class where passengers are already settled in their large spacious seats, often with newspapers and drinks in hand'. In addition, the frequent flyer escapes the intensive security within and beyond the airport to which the underprivileged 'kinetic underclass' is subject (Adey *et al.*, 2007).

Faulconbridge (2014) and Lassen (2006) emphasise that aeromobility has become a taken-for-granted social practice for doing business. No longer a special means of travel, it is rather 'a tool for practising an identity on the "global scene"' (Lassen, 2006: 308), a means of accruing network capital (Cohen & Gössling, 2015). Although business travellers may engage in some work while travelling, the flying component of the business trip can often be experienced as 'time off' from work (Gustafson, 2014; Unger *et al.*, 2016). Various material objects affirm status and exclusivity and signify 'belonging in business class'.[2] One such object, according to Hagood (2011) is 'Bose headphones'. By cancelling out noise and producing personal space for the user, they are one means of controlling at least some aspects of the 'misery' of air travel which includes one's (irresponsible) fellow travellers. They allow the user 'to suppress the unfamiliar, idiosyncratic, and potentially uncomfortable' (Hagood, 2011: 578). Hagood (2011: 584) describes the normative self in the discourse of Bose commercials as 'white, male, rational, monied, and mobile'. He continues… 'In this discourse, the rational, normative agent must protect himself from the inchoate sounds of the jet engine, woman, or child' (2011: 585) and, according to neoliberal belief, take individual action within the market rather than look at systemic issues. In studying the hypermobile business traveller, Cohen and Gössling (2015) counteract the glamorous image of business travel alerting us to its 'dark side' – the individual and social health costs. In flight, these include: jet lag, deep vein thrombosis, exposure to germs and radiation. Flying, as a facilitator of business travel, is also associated with poor health at the destination: less regular exercise, poor eating and drinking habits and sleep deprivation. Being away from home for extended periods of time can also cause psycho-social harm – isolation, loneliness, anxiety, depression and guilt with negative impacts also on the wellbeing of those left at home. A follow-up study, which analysed public comments to Cohen and Gössling's (2015) publication, found two key subject positions – the 'flourishing hypermobile' who embraces frequent business travel as a key part of their happiness and identity and the 'floundering hypermobile' for whom frequent business travel causes physiological and psycho-social distress (Cohen et al., 2018).

Passenger gender is also related to the air travel experience, at least for businesswomen (Veijola & Valtonen, 2007; Westwood et al., 2000). Veijola and Valtonen (2007: 26) argue that airline marketing, spatial arrangements and service rituals are 'tailored to *fit the size, form and needs of a male body*' confirming the earlier findings of Westwood et al. (2000) that gender differences are subsumed into a gender-neutral/male norm with no provision for women's specific needs. In the Westwood et al. (2000) study, businesswomen identified a number of areas in which they felt uncomfortable or disadvantaged: having to climb over, or sleep next to, a male passenger on a long-haul flight; inadequate lavatory compartments for freshening up; male-oriented executive lounges and in-flight food options; concerns for personal safety in the lounges at night and on arrival at the destination; and staff attitudes to women. In relation to the latter, the women felt that men were accorded more status, legitimacy and preferential treatment, reflecting 'the dominant male perspective which frames society and the business world' (Westwood et al., 2000: 361). While this study was focused on the businesswoman, many of the findings were no doubt relevant, at the time, to other women passengers. Whether the same disadvantages and discomforts would be found today, is yet to be confirmed. We would want to hear what women have to say before accepting Schaberg's (2017a: 142) claim that 'Gender in flight is not a problem'. He argues that 'airplane lavatories are non-gendered, and this works just fine'. However, it certainly didn't for the women in Westwood's study.

In studying air mobilities, we also need to consider immobilities or 'relative immobilities' (Adey, 2006) in recognition of the many who do not have access to air travel, in turn, hampering their ability to participate in economic and social life. There are any number of reasons for immobility including disability and low income (one still needs a credit card and internet to book a low-cost carrier flight); behind most is a culturally shaped and politically governed system which controls who can travel and how they travel (Sheller, 2018). Even amongst those who travel by air, there are differences and inequalities in the ease, comfort and speed with which they move through the air spaces. As discussed above, the kinetic elite are advantaged over the budget passenger, as the male passenger has been over the female passenger. Encounters with airport security and immigration may differ depending on the passenger's nationality/culture/race. For those with disability who engage in air travel, there are many reported examples of disadvantage and discrimination (Chang & Chen, 2012; Darcy, 2012; da Silva *et al.*, 2017; Davies & Christie, 2017; Major & Hubbard, 2019; Poria *et al.*, 2010). Lin (2014, 2016) extends our understanding of aeromobility injustice by going beyond the inequalities structured along social axes, such as class, gender, disability etc., to consider 'an institutional and macrostructural form of discrimination in aerial movement' (Lin, 2019: 50) which impacts entire nation states, especially in the Global South. Here, he is referring to the workings of international regimes relating to air traffic rights, aeronautical expertise and aviation security (such as passport standards) which advantage some nations and disadvantage (maroon) others, thus affecting if and how their citizens can move. Discussion of aeromobility justice also needs to consider those who fly but for whom such travel is not a choice, those who are forced to fly. As with other forms of mobility, aeromobility both produces and reproduces social inequalities.

To fly or not to fly?

The argument for expanding access to air travel needs to be considered alongside the urgent environmental plea for the kerbing of air travel due to its contribution to global warming. The contradictory discourses of mobility associated with modernity, freedom and morality (Doughty & Murray, 2016) increasingly confront both scholar and passenger. Such environmental concerns have led researchers to investigate passenger beliefs, attitudes and behaviours in relation to flying. That a gap has been found between passenger attitude and behaviour suggests that voluntary kerbing of air travel or carbon offsetting (Ritchie *et al.*, 2020) is unlikely. Indeed, it is estimated that less than 10% of air travellers voluntarily purchase carbon offsets (Ritchie *et al.*, 2020). Young *et al.* (2014: 51) refer to 'flyers dilemma' – 'where an individual's self-identity as an environmentally-responsible consumer conflicts with the environmental impacts of frequent air travel'. To understand passenger resistance to change, we need to recognise the social and cultural capital which is accrued from travelling away from home (Urry, 2002) and which is facilitated by flying (Randles & Mander, 2009). Whether or not we call it the 'democratisation' of air travel, the opening up of air travel to greater numbers of individuals has meant 'the transformation of many people's desire for air travel into a consumer expectation, a norm, or even a "right"' (Shaw & Thomas, 2006: 209) whether it be to visit new places, connect with family and friends, engage in activities or conduct business. It has raised expectations that are difficult to diminish. Some have labelled excessive air travel, 'binge flying' and likened it to an addiction (Cohen *et al.*, 2011).

In contrast to the individual-focused psychological studies (Davison *et al.*, 2014; Oswald & Ernst, 2020) and the commercial-oriented studies which have looked at the green image of airlines and passenger perceptions, willingness to pay and airline choice (Choi & Ritchie, 2014; Hagmann et al., 2015; Hinnen et al., 2017; Mayer et al., 2012), critical research argues that there can be too much emphasis on individual responsibility which deflects from corporate responsibility (Kroesen, 2013). Young et al. (2014) make this point in their critique of the 'binge flyer' concept. They explain that in equating flying behaviour as an addiction, the behaviour is pathologised and the problem located with the individual, thereby ignoring the 'social, institutional and economic forces that produce excessive consumption in the first place' (Young et al., 2014: 55) and to which the individual aspires. Situating the problem with the individual exempts industry and government from taking responsibility for the issue from which they profit: 'The failings of Western consumerism are insidiously dressed up as the failings of the individual' (Young et al., 2014: 58). Since capital takes no responsibility for the consequences of its production, it is the individual who bears the dilemma of flying. As Young et al. (2014: 61) claim, 'the "flyers' dilemma" is, in fact, integral to the reproduction of capital'. Kroesen (2013) argues that the consumption discourse can be self-contradictory – 'legitimizing consumption on the one hand (consumption is good) and delegitimizing it on the other (consumption leads to environmental destruction)'. Hares et al. (2010) refer to the somewhat contradictory nature of UK Government policy regarding air travel: on the one hand, commitment to ensuring that the aviation industry takes responsibility for its climate change emissions and, on the other hand, stressing the critical role of international aviation in the economy and the need to expand airport capacity.

In studying industry representations of air travel and the environment, Gössling and Peeters (2007) identified four major industry discourses: the energy efficiency of air travel with marginal CO_2 emissions; the importance of air travel which would prevent restriction; the minimisation of fuel use and optimism for new technology to solve the problem; and the view that air travel is treated unfairly compared with other forms of transport. Clearly, any passenger awareness of aviation's environmental impact has not originated from the airline industry. Agreeing with Gössling and Peeters (2007) that we need to move beyond individual responsibility, Becken (2007) asserts that, with the assistance of scientists, governments need to take the lead role to work with the airlines. As she argues:

> A social movement such as this will also require renegotiating the current trends towards hypermobility and the positively biased social representation of air travel in particular. Initiatives need to take explicit account of the fact that tourists' behaviour cannot be reduced to individual decision making, but has to be dealt with in the context of the society tourists live in. (Becken, 2007: 365)

The Structure of the Book

The chapters that follow continue with a critical approach, expanding on the passenger experience of air travel as discussed above. In Chapter 2, Erwin Losekoot and Jennie Small examine the passenger experience of the airport and the changing cultural interpretations of this space. While some writers have considered these dead spaces or non-places, the authors argue that they are meaningful social, ritualised places. They are experienced as spaces of liminality and transition, mobility and immobility, surveillance and consumption. Passengers share these spaces with others. The frequent redevelopment of airports means that our experience of an airport may be ever changing. In Chapters 3 and 4, Jennie Small explores the online discourse on passenger behaviour in flight. Air travel means being mobile with others and here we see how passengers' embodied practice can disrupt that of others, or as Edensor (2000: 331) says, 'disrupt the stage' through questionable performance of the passenger role. Chapter 3 focuses on contested onboard behaviour related to: crying babies, larger-sized passengers, companion animals and air rage. Chapter 4 continues the discussion of passenger–passenger relations by exploring the discourse on passenger appearance and dress and how the 'look' of passengers contributes to others' flight experience. The chapter then turns to passenger discourse on the appearance of flight attendants, in particular, older (female) flight attendants. It situates the contemporary discourse within the industry's historical production of the sexualised 'flight attendant body', indicating that, while there has been a positive change in attitudes to female flight attendants, this change is only partial. In exploring passengers' relations with others, moral issues are raised in connection with rights and responsibilities, inclusion and exclusion, power and resistance. Central to the discourse is a cultural change in passenger focus from concern for the collective to that of the individual. These chapters demonstrate that air travel is an embodied, affective experience related to place and *others* inhabiting that place.

Chapters 5 and 6 focus on a developing recognition of immobilities/'uneven mobilities' (Sheller, 2008; 2013) in air travel, establishing that not all individuals are equally mobile in the 21st century. Central to the discussion are passengers with disability. In Chapter 5, Simon Darcy, Jennie Small and Barbara Almond explore the general subject of disability before turning their attention to those air travellers who have a mobility disability. They identify the significant challenges, constraints and issues which occur at all stages of travel for these passengers. Chapter 6 by Jennie Small, Alison McIntosh, Barbara Almond and Simon Darcy continues the discussion but here examines those passengers with *non*-mobility disabilities – vision impairment, hearing impairment, cognitive impairment (including dementia, autism and epilepsy) and mental health conditions. As some of these are hidden disabilities, there are additional challenges in meeting the needs of such passengers. The discussion exposes the ways in which those with disability are 'othered' in society. It is clear that one cannot think of the passenger experience of those with a disability without recognising that meaning goes beyond the discursive. The passenger experience is clearly embodied as exhibited in the physical discomfort of the passenger with mobility impairment being lifted into their seat or the passenger with hearing impairment missing auditory announcements from the flight deck. It is an emotional and affective experience as passengers interact with the material artefacts of air travel, other people with whom they come into contact and the systems which make up air travel. Chapter 7 by Jennie Small and Cheryl Cockburn-Wootten extends the discussion on mental health conditions to consider those who experience extreme stress and anxiety from flying – who have a *fear* of flying. Once again, we need to go beyond the discursive to appreciate that such a fear is experienced cognitively, emotionally and behaviourally; it is experienced bodily. The chapter contrasts a more traditional mental health perspective with an alternative critical approach which takes us beyond a neoliberal focus on individual responsibility and management of fear to consider the wider societal and organisational framing which has constructed the activity of air travel. Underlying these chapters is the moral issue of mobility justice – air transport should be inclusive and accessible for all.

The above chapters have interrogated the passenger meaning of air travel and argued for greater accessibility for those who may be currently excluded or disadvantaged. However, a discussion of the passenger experience cannot ignore the concerning environmental impact of aviation and emerging cultural change in attitudes to flying. In Chapter 8, James Higham and Martin Young advance the discussion by confronting the unavoidable and thorny issue of the sustainability of air transport, drawing into question the social desirability of air travel as a form of leisure consumption. However, their review of the international research highlights that the environmental urgency is not reflected in passenger behaviour; there is a disconnect, a 'flyers' dilemma' between passengers' environmental attitudes and their behaviour. This may be experienced as denial or, emotionally, as guilt or anxiety. Arguing from a critical perspective, the authors claim that such a dilemma cannot be resolved by individuals acting independently. A reformulation of 'flyers' dilemma' is required which takes into account the structural issues underlying the dilemma. In other words, state and industry action is needed.

In the process of completing this book, the unthinkable happened in 2020 – a global pandemic – COVID-19 – which changed our understandings of the passenger experience of air travel. Chapter 9 by Jennie Small concludes the collection drawing on media reports and early published scholarly works which advance our understanding of the passenger experience during this time. The representations of air travel, the embodied and affective practice and materialities which make up the experience can only be understood within the frame of the pandemic. Government decisions as to who could, and who could not, travel at this time accentuate the political nature of mobility. The chapter concludes with a discussion of the inherent competing social justice issues in air travel – mobility justice and environmental justice. The chapters highlight the passenger experience within the culturally changing wider society. They also reflect cultural change in theoretical and methodological approaches to the study of air travel.

Summary

This book looks at what happens when people are on the move. As Cresswell and Merriman (2011: 5) recognised, mobile worlds that might once have been considered dead, 'come alive when they become the focus of our attention'. Like other mobilities, air travel has its own set of practices and normative regulating principles (Jensen, 2009). In studying the passenger experience of air travel, we need to consider the embodied experiences of the passengers, their emotional and affective states and the technologies, materialities of air travel that make up that experience: the trolleys, check-in terminals, immigration desks, security conveyer belts, hoists to embark a passenger with mobility disability, aircraft seats, overhead bins, in-flight entertainment, lighting, temperature and so on, even down to the safety card (Barry, 2017). In travelling by air, we are part of the 'mobile public' (Bissell, 2010), our experiences are intersubjective as we share time, airport and aircraft spaces with embodied others and their practices. We also need to consider the discourse and texts, the representations of air travel that give air travel its meaning. As Adey (2010: 10) says, one should not discard representations or ignore the power of the imagination, these 'are bound up in the production of aerial subjectivities, in the production of aerial life itself'. We cannot dissociate experiences from their wider political, economic, cultural and social contexts which are forever changing. Bissell and Adey (2011: 1008) refer to the 'containerised subjectivity' of the passenger who is '"cocooned" not only within tangible spaces and infrastructures, but also within sophisticated and bureaucratic systems of governance and control', clearly evident during the COVID-19 global pandemic. We need to consider who is included and who is excluded from the experience of air travel if we wish for a more just society. Finally, and crucially, we must work towards a sustainable future.

Notes

(1) Shared nostalgia was witnessed in Sydney in July 2020 when Sydneysiders took up vantage spots to farewell the last Qantas 747 as it did a circuit of the city (on its way to retirement in the Mohave Desert). Similar to Adey's sightseers/enthusiasts who

frequented the Liverpool airport balcony, up to the mid-1980s, the Sydney enthusiasts could be said to have 'watched in a social way' (Adey, 2008: 40) as they shared information from their modern spotting equipment (flight tracking apps) and their fond memories of travelling on the 747 over the past half century.
(2) Of course, not all travelling for business will be 'Business Class' passengers and not all in Business Class will be business travellers.

References

Adey, P. (2006) If mobility is everything then it is nothing: Towards a relational politics of (im)mobilities. *Mobilities* 1 (1), 75–94. DOI: 10.1080/17450100500489080.

Adey, P. (2008) Architectural geographies of the airport balcony: Mobility, sensation and the theatre of flight. *Geografiska Annaler. Series B, Human Geography* 90 (1), 29–47. https://doi.org/10.1111/j.1468-0467.2008.00274.x.

Adey, P. (2010) *Aerial Life: Spaces, Mobilities, Affects*. Chichester: Wiley-Blackwell.

Adey, P. and Lin, W. (2014) Social and cultural geographies of air transport. In L. Budd and A. Goetz (eds) *The Geographies of Air Transport* (pp. 61–71), Abingdon, Oxon: Routledge.

Adey, P., Budd, L. and Hubbard, P. (2007) Flying lessons: Exploring the social and cultural geographies of global air travel. *Progress in Human Geography* 31, 773–791. https://doi.org/10.1177%2F0309132507083508.

Anderson, J. (2015) Exploring the consequences of mobility: Reclaiming jet lag as the state of travel disorientation. *Mobilities* 10 (1), 1–16. https://doi.org/10.1080/17450101.2013.806392.

Augé, M. (1995) *Non-places: An Introduction to Supermodernity*. London: Verso.

Barry, K. (2017) The aesthetics of aircraft safety cards: Spatial negotiations and affective mobilities in diagrammatic instructions. *Mobilities* 12 (3), 365–383. https://doi.org/10.1080/17450101.2015.1086101.

Becken, S. (2007) Tourists' perceptions of international air travel's impact on the global climate and potential climate change policies. *Journal of Sustainable Tourism* 15 (4), 351–368. https://doi.org/10.2167/jost710.0.

Betjeman, J. (1979) Back from Australia. In Lord Birkenhead (ed.) *John Betjeman's Collected Poems* (4th edn) (p. 399). London: John Murray Ltd.

Bissell, D. (2007) Animating suspension: Waiting for mobilities. *Mobilities* 2, 277–298. https://doi.org/10.1080/17450100701381581.

Bissell, D. (2010) Passenger mobilities: Affective atmospheres and the sociality of public transport. *Environment and Planning D: Society and Space* 28, 270–289. https://doi.org/10.1068%2Fd3909.

Bissell, D. and Adey, P. (2011) Guest editorial: Introduction to the Special Issue on Geographies of the Passenger. *Journal of Transport Research* 19, 1007–1009. DOI: 10.1016/j.jtrangeo.2011.06.002.

Boorstin, D. (1987) *The Image: A Guide to Pseudo-events in America*. New York: Atheneum.

Bor, R. (ed) (2003) *Passenger Behaviour*. Aldershot: Ashgate.

Bor, R. (2007) Psychological factors in airline passenger and crew behaviour: A clinical overview. *Travel Medicine and Infectious Disease* 5 (4), 207–216. DOI: 10.1016/j.tmaid.2007.03.003.

Bor, R. and Hubbard, T. (eds) (2006) *Aviation Mental Health; Psychological Implications for Air Travel*. Aldershot: Ashgate.

Bricker, J. (2005) Development and evaluation of the air travel stress scale. *Journal of Counseling Psychology* 52 (4), 615–628. https://doi.org/10.1037/0022-0167.52.4.615.

Budd, L. (2009) The view from the air: The cultural geographies of flight. In P. Vannini (ed.) *The Cultures of Alternative Mobilities: Routes Less Travelled* (pp. 71–90). Farnham: Ashgate.

Budd, L. (2011) On being aeromobile: Airline passengers and the affective experiences of flight. *Journal of Transport Geography* 19, 1010–1016. https://doi.org/10.1016/j.jtrangeo.2010.06.017.

Budd, L. (2014) The historical geographies of air transport. In L. Budd and A. Goetz (eds) *The Geographies of Air Transport* (pp. 9–24). Abingdon, Oxon: Routledge.

Budd, L., Warren, A. and Bell, M. (2011) Promoting passenger comfort and wellbeing in the air: An examination of the in-flight heath advice provided by international airlines. *Journal of Air Transport Management* 17, 320–322. https://doi.org/10.1016/j.jairtraman.2011.02.015.

Burrell, K. (2011) Going steerage on Ryanair: Cultures of migrant air travel between Poland and the UK. *Journal of Transport Geography* 19, 1023–1030. https://doi.org/10.1016/j.jtrangeo.2010.09.004.

Calder, S. (2018) How UK-Australia journey went from 28 days to 17 hours in 100 years. *The Independent*, 22 March. See https://www.independent.co.uk/travel/news-and-advice/uk-australia-flight-time-travel-100-years-change-london-perth-direct-a8268311.html (accessed April 2021).

Chang, Y. and Chen, C. (2012) Meeting the needs of disabled air passengers: Factors that facilitate help from airlines and airports. *Tourism Management* 33 (3), 529–536. https://doi.org/10.1016/j.tourman.2011.06.002.

Choi, A. and Ritchie, B. (2014) Willingness to pay for flying carbon neutral in Australia: An exploratory study of offsetter profiles. *Journal of Sustainable Tourism* 22 (8), 1236–1256. https://doi.org/10.1080/09669582.2014.894518.

Cohen, S. and Gössling, S. (2015) A darker side of hypermobility. *Environment and Planning A* 47 (8), 1661–1679. https://doi.org/10.1177/0308518X15597124.

Cohen, S., Hanna, P. and Gössling, S. (2018) The dark side of business travel: A media comments analysis. *Transportation Research Part D: Transport and Environment* 61, Part B, 406–419. https://doi.org/10.1016/j.trd.2017.01.004.

Cohen, S., Higham, J. and Cavaliere, C. (2011) Binge flying: Behavioural addiction and climate change. *Annals of Tourism Research* 38, 1070–1089. https://doi.org/10.1016/j.annals.2011.01.013.

Cresswell, T. (2006) *On the Move: Mobility in the Modern Western World*. Abingdon, Oxon: Routledge.

Cresswell, T. (2010) Towards a politics of mobility. *Environment and Planning D* 28, 17–31. https://doi.org/10.1068/d11407.

Cresswell (2011) Mobilities 1: Catching up. *Progress in Human Geography* 35 (4), 550–558. https://doi.org/10.1177/0309132510383348.

Cresswell, T. and Merriman, P. (2011) Introduction: Geographies of mobilities – practices, spaces, subjects. In T. Cresswell and P. Merriman (eds) *Geographies of Mobilities: Practices, Spaces, Subjects* (pp. 1–15). Farnham: Ashgate.

Crossley-Holland, K. (ed.) (1989) *The Oxford Book of Travel Verse*. Oxford: Oxford University Press.

Crouch, D., Aronsson, L. and Wahlström, L. (2001) Tourist encounters. *Tourist Studies* 1 (3), 253–270. https://doi.org/10.1177/146879760100100303.

Cwerner, S. (2009) Introducing aeromobilities. In S. Cwerner, S. Kesselring and J. Urry (eds) *Aeromobilities* (pp. 1–21). Abingdon, Oxon: Routledge.

Darcy, S. (2012) (Dis)embodied air travel experiences: Disability, discrimination and the affect of a discontinuous air travel chain. *Journal of Hospitality and Tourism Management* 19 (1), 91–101. https://doi.org/10.1017/jht.2012.9.

Darda, J. (2015) Airport memory: Recalling Vietnam from the terminal in Andrew Pham's travel writing. *Criticism* 57 (2), 191–210. https://www.jstor.org/stable/10.13110/criticism.57.issue-2.

da Silva, T., de Souza, J., da Silva, L., Figueiredo, J. and Menegon, N. (2017) Passengers with disabilities in the Brazilian air transport: Different actors and similar perspectives. *Gestão & Produção* 24 (1), 136–147. https://doi.org/10.1590/0104-530x1681-15.

Davies, A. and Christie, N. (2017) An exploratory study of the experiences of wheelchair users as aircraft passengers – implications for policy and practice. *IATSS Research* 41 (2), 89–93. https://doi.org/10.1016/j.iatssr.2017.05.003.

Davison, L., Littleford, C. and Ryley, T. (2014) Air travel attitudes and behaviours: The development of environment-based segments. *Journal of Air Transport Management* 36, 13–22. http://dx.doi.org/10.1016/j.jairtraman.2013.12.007.

Denver, John and Denver, John, 'Leaving on a Jet Plane' (1967) *Vocal Popular Sheet Music Collection*. Score 1517. https://digitalcommons.library.umaine.edu/mmb-vp-copyright/1517.

Dewsbury, J., Harrison, P., Rose, M. and Wylie, J. (2002) Introduction: Enacting geographies. *Geoforum* 33, 437–440. https://doi.org/10.1016/S0016-7185(02)00029-5.

Doughty, K. and Murray, M. (2016) Discourses of mobility: Institutions, everyday lives and embodiment. *Mobilities* 11 (2), 303–322. https://doi.org/10.1080/17450101.2014.941257.

Drew, C. (2011) The Spirit of Australia: Learning about Australian childhoods in Qantas commercials. *Global Studies of Childhood* 1 (4), 321–331. http://dx.doi.org/10.2304/gsch.2011.1.4.321.

Dye, J. (2020) Qantas Boeing 747 jumbo jet retirement: Veteran pilot says goodbye to 'Queen of the skies', *Traveller*, 18 July. See https://www.traveller.com.au/qantas-boeing-747-jumbo-jet-retirement-veteran-pilot-says-goodbye-to-queen-of-the-skies-h1pfl1 (accessed December 2020).

Edelheim, J. (2007) Hidden messages: A polysemic reading of tourist brochures. *Journal of Vacation Marketing* 13 (1), 5–17. DOI: 10.1177/1356766706071202.

Edensor, T. (2000) Staging tourism: Tourists as performers. *Annals of Tourism Research* 27 (2), 322–344. https://doi.org/10.1016/S0160-7383(99)00082-1.

Edensor, T. (2014) Rhythm and arrhythmia. In P. Adey, D. Bissell, K. Hannam, P. Merriman and M. Sheller (eds) *The Routledge Handbook of Mobilities* (pp. 163–171). London: Routledge.

Elliott, A. and Urry, J. (2010) *Mobile Lives*. Abingdon, Oxon: Routledge.

Escolme-Schmidt, L. (2009) *Glamour in the Skies: The Golden Age of the Air Stewardess*. Cheltenham: The History Press.

Faulconbridge, J. (2014) The executive. In P. Adey, D. Bissell, K. Hannam, P. Merriman and M. Sheller (eds) *The Routledge Handbook of Mobilities* (pp. 376–387). London: Routledge.

Franklin, A. (2014) Tourist studies. In P. Adey, D. Bissell, K. Hannam, P. Merriman and M. Sheller (eds) *The Routledge Handbook of Mobilities* (pp. 74–84). London: Routledge.

Franklin, A. and Crang, M. (2001) The trouble with tourism and travel theory? *Tourist Studies* 1 (1), 5–22. https://doi.org/10.1016/S0160-7383(99)00082-1.

Freire-Medeiros, B. and Name, L. (2013) Flying for the very first time: Mobilities, social class and environmental concerns in a Rio de Janeiro Favela. *Mobilities* 8 (2), 167–184. DOI: 10.1080/17450101.2012.655974.

Fuller, G. (2003) Life in transit: Between airport and camp. *borderlands* 2 (1). See http://www.borderlands.net.au/vol2no1_2003/fuller_transit.html (accessed September 2020).

Fuller, G. and Harley, R. (2004) *Aviopolis A Book about Airports*. London: Black Dog Publishing.

Gebicki, M. (2019) Rites: What travel has taught me. *Traveller*, 12 January, p. 7.

Gergen, K. (2015) *An Invitation to Social Construction* (3rd edn). London: Sage.

Glancey, J. (2014) Boeing 707: The aircraft that changed the way we fly, *BBC*, 20 October. See https://www.bbc.com/culture/article/20141020-the-plane-that-changed-air-travel (accessed July 2020).

Gössling, S. and Humpe, A. (2020) The global scale, distribution and growth of aviation: Implications for climate change. *Global Environmental Change* 65, November 2020, 102194. https://doi.org/10.1016/j.gloenvcha.2020.102194.

Gössling, S. and Peeters, P. (2007) 'It does not harm the environment!' An analysis of industry discourses on tourism, air travel and the environment. *Journal of Sustainable Tourism* 15 (4), 402–417. https://doi.org/10.2167/jost672.0.

Gottdiener, M. (2001) *Life in the Air: Surviving the New Culture of Air Travel*. Lanham, Maryland: Rowman & Littlefield.

Gustafson, P. (2014) Business travel from the traveller's perspective: Stress, stimulation and normalization. *Mobilities* 9 (1), 63–83. http://dx.doi.org/10.1080/17450101.2013.784539.

Hagmann, C. Semeijn, J. and Vellenga, S. (2015) Exploring the green image of airlines: Passenger perceptions and airline choice. *Journal of Air Transport Management* 43, 37–45. https://doi.org/10.1016/j.jairtraman.2015.01.003.

Hagood, M. (2011) Quiet comfort: Noise, otherness, and the mobile production of personal space. *American Quarterly* 63, 573–589.

Haldrup, M. and Larsen, J. (2006) Material cultures of tourism. *Leisure Studies* 25 (3), 275–289. https://doi.org/10.1080/02614360600661179.

Hannam, K., Sheller, M. and Urry, J. (2006) Editorial: Mobilities, immobilities and moorings. *Mobilities* 1 (1), 1–22. https://doi.org/10.1080/17450100500489189.

Hares, A., Dickinson, J. and Wilkes, K. (2010) Climate change and the air travel decisions of UK tourists. *Journal of Transport Geography* 18 (3), 466–473. https://doi.org/10.1016/j.jtrangeo.2009.06.018.

Hart, M. (2015) Threshold to the Kingdom: The airport is a border and the border is a volume. *Criticism* 57 (2), 173–189. https://doi.org/10.13110/criticism.57.2.0173.

Harvey, D. (1989) *The Condition of Postmodernity: An Enquiry into the Origins of Cultural Change*. Oxford: Blackwell.

Hinnen, G., Hille, S. and Wittmer, A. (2017) Willingness to pay for green products in air travel: Ready for take-off? *Business Strategy and the Environment* 26 (2), 197–208. https://doi.org/10.1002/bse.1909.

Hirsh, M. (2017) Emerging infrastructures of low-cost aviation in Southeast Asia. *Mobilities* 12 (2), 259–276. https://doi.org/10.1080/17450101.2017.1292781.

International Civil Aviation Organization (2019) *Annual Report 2019. The World of Air Transport in 2019*. See https://www.icao.int/annual-report-2019/Pages/the-world-of-air-transport-in-2019.aspx (accessed March 2022).

International Air Transport Association (IATA) (2019) *More connectivity and improved efficiency – 2018 airline industry statistics released*, Press Release No. 45, 31 July. See https://www.iata.org/en/pressroom/pr/2019-07-31-01/ (accessed July 2020).

International Air Transport Association (IATA) (2020a) *Slower but Steady Growth in 2019*. Press Release No: 5, 6 February. See https://www.iata.org/en/pressroom/pr/2020-02-06-01/ (accessed March 2022).

International Air Transport Association (IATA) (2020b) *Safety Report 2019*. 56th Edition, 1 April. See https://libraryonline.erau.edu/online-full-text/iata-safety-reports/IATA-Safety-Report-2019.pdf (accessed March 2022).

Jensen, O. (2009) Flows of meaning, cultures of movements – Urban mobility as meaningful everyday life practice. *Mobilities* 4 (1), 139–158. https://doi.org/10.1080/17450100802658002.

Jensen, O. (2014) Mobile semiotics. In P. Adey, D. Bissell, K. Hannam, P. Merriman and M. Sheller (eds) *The Routledge Handbook of Mobilities* (pp. 566–574). London: Routledge.

Jensen, O. and Vannini, P. (2016) Blue sky matter: Toward an (in-flight) understanding of the sensuousness of mobilities design. *transfers* 6 (2), 23–42. https://doi.org/10.3167/TRANS.2016.060203.

Jetstar (2019) Making history. *Jetstar Magazine*, August, 107.

Kasarda, J. and Lindsay, G. (2011) *Aerotropolis: The Way We'll Live Next*. London: Penguin.

Kaufmann, V., Bergman, M. and Joye, D. (2004) Motility: Mobility as capital. *International Journal of Urban and Regional Research* 28 (4) 745–756.

Kloppenburg, S. (2013) Mapping the contours of mobilities regimes. Air travel and drug smuggling between the Caribbean and the Netherlands. *Mobilities* 8 (1), 52–69. https://doi.org/10.1080/17450101.2012.747766.

Kroesen, M. (2013) Exploring people's viewpoints on air travel and climate change: Understanding inconsistencies. *Journal of Sustainable Tourism* 21 (2), 271–290. https://doi.org/10.1080/09669582.2012.692686.

Larsen, J. (2001) Tourism mobilities and the travel glance: Experiences of being on the move. *Scandinavian Journal of Hospitality and Tourism* 1 (2), 80–98. https://doi.org/10.1080/150222501317244010.

Larsen, J. (2014) Distance and proximity. In P. Adey, D. Bissell, K. Hannam, P. Merriman and M. Sheller (eds) *The Routledge Handbook of Mobilities* (pp. 125–133). London: Routledge.

Lassen, C. (2006) Aeromobility and work. *Environment and Planning A* 38, 301–312. https://doi.org/10.1068/a37278.

Lather, P. (1991) *Getting Smart: Feminist Research and Pedagogy within/in the Postmodern.* New York: Routledge.

Lin, W. (2014) The politics of flying: Aeromobile frictions in a mobile city. *Journal of Transport Geography* 38, 92–99. http://dx.doi.org/10.1016/j.jtrangeo.2014.06.002.

Lin, W. (2016) Re-assembling (aero)mobilities: Perspectives beyond the West. *Mobilities* 11 (1), 49–65. https://doi.org/10.1080/17450101.2015.1101904.

Lin, W. (2019) Aeromobility justice: A global institutional perspective. In N. Cook and D. Butz (eds) *Mobilities, Mobility Justice and Social Justice* (pp. 41–53). Abingdon, Oxon: Routledge.

Lyons, G. (2014) Times. In P. Adey, D. Bissell, K. Hannam, P. Merriman and M. Sheller (eds) *The Routledge Handbook of Mobilities* (pp. 154–162). London: Routledge.

MacArthur, M. (2012) One world? The poetics of passenger flight and the perception of the global. *Publications of the Modern Language Association of America* 127 (2), 264–282. https://doi.org/10.1632/pmla.2012.127.2.264.

MacCannell, D. (1976) *The Tourist: A New Theory of the Leisure Class.* London: The Macmillan Press.

Major, W.L. and Hubbard, S.M. (2019) An examination of disability-related complaints in the United States commercial aviation sector. *Journal of Air Transport Management* 78 (July), 43–53. https://doi.org/10.1016/j.jairtraman.2019.04.006.

Massey, D. (1993) Power-geometry and a progressive sense of place. In J. Bird, B. Curtis, T. Putnam, G. Robertson and L. Tickner (eds) *Mapping the Futures: Local Cultures, Global Change* (pp. 59–69). London: Routledge.

Mayer, R., Ryley, T. and Gillingwater, D. (2012) Passenger perceptions of the green image associated with airlines. *Journal of Transport Geography* 22, 179–186. https://doi.org/10.1016/j.jtrangeo.2012.01.007.

Mertena, I., Kaaristo, M. and Edensor, T. (2022) Tourist skills. *Annals of Tourism Research* 94, 103387. https://doi.org/10.1016/j.annals.2022.103387.

Millward, L. (2008) The embodied aerial subject: Gendered mobility in British inter-war air tours. *The Journal of Transport History* 29 (1), 5–22.

Morgan, N. and Pritchard, A. (2005) Security and social 'sorting': Traversing the surveillance–tourism dialectic. *Tourist Studies* 5 (2), 115–132. https://doi.org/10.1177/1468797605066923.

Morgan, N. and Pritchard, A. (2015) Critical tourism studies. In J. Jafari and H. Xiao (eds) *Encyclopedia of Tourism.* Switzerland: Springer. https://doi.org/10.1007/978-3-319-01669-6_41-1.

Oswald, L. and Ernst, A. (2020) Flying in the face of climate change: Quantitative psychological approach examining the social drivers of individual air travel. *Journal of Sustainable Tourism* 29, 68–86. https://doi.org/10.1080/09669582.2020.1812616.

Pascoe, D. (2001) *Airspaces.* London: Reaktion Books.

Poria, Y., Reichel, A. and Brandt, Y. (2010) The flight experiences of people with disabilities: An exploratory study. *Journal of Travel Research* 49 (2), 216–227. https://doi.org/10.1177/0047287509336477.

Pritchard, A., Morgan, N. and Ateljevic, I. (2011) Hopeful tourism: A new transformative perspective. *Annals of Tourism Research* 38, 941–963. https://doi.org/10.1016/j.annals.2011.01.004.

Qantas.com (2020) *Celebrating 100 years of the spirit of Australia.* See https://www.qantas.com/au/en/100-years-of-the-spirit-of-australia.html (accessed July 2020).

Randles, S. and Mander, S. (2009) Aviation, consumption and the climate change debate: 'Are you going to tell me off for flying?' *Technology Analysis and Strategic Management* 21 (1), 93–113. https://doi.org/10.1080/09537320802557350.

Rants & Raves (2019) *The Sydney Morning Herald, Traveller*, 10 August. p. 53.

Rants & Raves (2019) *The Sydney Morning Herald, Traveller*, 24 August, p. 37.

Rink, B. (2017) The aeromobile tourist gaze: Understanding tourism 'from above'. *Tourism Geographies* 19 (5), 878–896. https://doi.org/10.1080/14616688.2017.1354391.

Ritchie, B.W., Sie, L., Gössling, S. and Dwyer, L. (2020) Effects of climate change policies on aviation carbon offsetting: A three-year panel study. *Journal of Sustainable Tourism* 28 (2), 337–360. https://doi.org/10.1080/09669582.2019.1624762.

Schaberg, C. (2012) *The Textual Life of Airports: Reading the Cultural Life of Flight*. New York: Continuum.

Schaberg, C. (2015) Introduction. *Criticism* 57 (2), 169–171. https://www.jstor.org/stable/10.13110/criticism.57.issue-2.

Schaberg, C. (2016) *The End of Airports*. New York: Bloomsbury.

Schaberg, C. (2017a) *Airportness: The Nature of Flight*. New York: Bloomsbury.

Schaberg, C. (2017b) Ecological disorientation in airline ads and DeLillo's *Zero K*. *ISLE: Interdisciplinary Studies in Literature and Environment* 24 (1), 75–91. https://doi.org/10.1093/isle/isw090.

Schivelbusch, W. (1978) Railroad space and railroad time. *New German Critique* 14, 31–40. DOI: 10.2307/488059.

Sebald, W. (1998) *The Rings of Saturn* (M. Hulse, trans.). New York: New Directions (original work published 1995).

Shaw, S. and Thomas, C. (2006) Discussion note: Social and cultural dimensions of air travel demand: hyper-mobility in the UK? *Journal of Sustainable Tourism* 14 (2), 209–215. https://doi.org/10.1080/09669580608669053.

Sheller, M. (2008) Mobility, freedom and public space. In S. Bergmann and T. Sager (eds) *The Ethics of Mobilities: Rethinking Place, Exclusion, Freedom and Environment* (pp. 25–38). Aldershot: Ashgate.

Sheller, M. (2013) Sociology after the mobilities. In P. Adey, D. Bissell, K. Hannam, P. Merriman and M. Sheller (eds) *The Routledge Handbook of Mobilities* (pp. 45–54). London: Routledge.

Sheller, M. (2018) Theorising mobility justice. *Tempo Social* 30 (2), 17–34. DOI: 10.11606/0103-2070.ts.2018.142763.

Sheller, M. and Urry, J. (2006) The new mobilities paradigm. *Environment and Planning A* 38 (2), 207–226. https://doi.org/10.1068/a37268.

Small, J. and Harris, C. (2012) Obesity and tourism: Rights and responsibilities. *Annals of Tourism Research* 39 (2), 686–707. https://doi.org/10.1016/j.annals.2011.09.002.

Small, J. and Harris, C. (2014) Crying babies on planes: Aeromobility and parenting. *Annals of Tourism Research* 48, 27–41. https://doi.org/10.1016/j.annals.2014.04.009.

Small, J. and Harris, C. (2015) The older flight attendant: Treasured or dreaded? In E. Wilson, and M. Witsel (eds) *Rising Tides and Sea Changes: Adaptation and Innovation in Tourism and Hospitality: Proceedings of the 25th Annual CAUTHE Conference*, Gold Coast, Queensland, 2–5 February 2015 (pp. 713–716). Gold Coast, Qld: Southern Cross University.

Small, J. and Harris, C. (2019) Hardly disruptive! Airline representations and Facebook. *Proceedings of the 29th Annual Conference Council for Australasian University Tourism and Hospitality Education (CAUTHE)*. Cairns: University of Central Queensland.

Small, J. Harris, C. and Wilson, E. (2008) A critical discourse analysis of in-flight magazine advertisements: The 'social sorting' of airline travellers? *Journal of Tourism and Cultural Change* 6 (1), 17–38. http://dx.doi.org/10.1080/14766820802140422.

Stadiem, W. (2014) *Jet Set: The People, the Planes, the Glamor, and the Romance in Aviation's Glory Years* [e-book]. New York: Ballantine Books.

Thurlow, C. and Jaworski, A. (2003) Communicating a global reach: Inflight magazines as a globalizing genre in tourism. *Journal of Sociolinguistics* 7 (4), 579–606. https://doi.org/10.1111/j.1467-9841.2003.00243.x.

Thurlow, C. and Jaworski, A. (2012) Elite mobilities: The semiotic landscapes of luxury and privilege. *Social Semiotics* 22 (4), 487–516. http://dx.doi.org/10.1080/10350330.2012.721592.

Tripadvisor (2017) *Qantas. Nice Service*. See https://www.tripadvisor.com.au/ShowTopic-g1-i10702-k10152106-o10-Qantas_Nice_Service-Air_Travel.html (accessed July 2020).

Unger, O., Uriely, N. and Fuchs, G. (2016) The business travel experience. *Annals of Tourism Research* 61, 142–156. http://dx.doi.org/10.1016/j.annals.2016.10.003.

Urry, J. (2002) Mobility and proximity. *Sociology* 36 (2), 255–274. https://doi.org/10.1177/0038038502036002002.

Van Riper, A. (2004) *Imagining Flight: Aviation and Popular Culture*. College Station, Texas: Texas A&M University Press.

Vannini, P. (2009) The cultures of alternative mobilities. In P. Vannini (ed.) *The Cultures of Alternative Mobilities: Routes Less Travelled* (pp. 1–18). Farnham: Ashgate.

Veijola, S. and Valtonen, A. (2007) The body in tourism industry. In A. Pritchard, N. Morgan, I. Ateljevic and C. Harris (eds) *Tourism and Gender: Embodiment, Sensuality and Experience* (pp. 13–31). Wallingford, Oxfordshire: CABI.

Visontay, E. (2022) Qantas announces plans for non-stop flights from Sydney to New York and London. *The Guardian*, 2 May. See https://www.theguardian.com/business/2022/may/02/qantas-non-stop-flights-australia-to-new-york-london-from-sydney-melbourne-airbus-a350-1000 (accessed May 2022).

Westwood, S., Pritchard, A. and Morgan, N. (2000) Gender-blind marketing: Businesswomen's perceptions of airline services. *Tourism Management* 21, 353–362. https://doi.org/10.1016/S0261-5177(99)00069-2.

Wilson, E., Harris, C. and Small, J. (2008) Furthering critical approaches in tourism and hospitality studies: Perspectives from Australia and New Zealand. *Journal of Hospitality and Tourism Management* 15 (1), 15–18. https://doi.org/10.1375/jhtm.15.15.

Wilson, E., Small, J. and Harris, C. (2012) Editorial introduction: Beyond the margins? The relevance of critical tourism and hospitality studies. *Journal of Hospitality and Tourism Management* 19 (1), 1–4. https://doi.org/10.1017/jht.2012.2.

Young, M., Higham, J. and Reis, A. (2014) 'Up in the air': A conceptual critique of flying addiction. *Annals of Tourism Research* 49, 51–64. http://dx.doi.org/10.1016/j.annals.2014.08.003.

2 The Airport Experience

Erwin Losekoot and Jennie Small

Had one been asked to take a Martian to visit a single place that neatly captures the gamut of themes running through our civilization – from our faith in technology to our destruction of nature, from our interconnectedness to our romanticizing of travel – then it would have to be to the departures and arrivals halls that one would head. (de Botton, 2009: 13)

Introduction

Being 'up, up and away' can be an exhilarating and exciting experience. However, the act of flying in an aeroplane is bracketed or bound by something which is often a far less uplifting experience – the progress through an airport. As airports are places of departure, transit and arrival, the experience can vary depending on the stage of travel. It may be a place of farewell, a place to bide time or a place of greeting. During the PhD research of one of the authors (Losekoot, 2015), an airport police officer tried to explain what was so special about an airport. He took the researcher to a place at Auckland Airport where he could see both the departure gate and the arrivals gate and observed, 'It's funny – you can stand in one spot and see one area embedded with sadness and another area embedded with happiness, within sight of each other. Where else do you get that?'. Emotions are on display in all corners of an airport. Adey (2009: 278) warns that 'airports are remarkably emotional places of dread, boredom, fear, excitement, sadness and terror. Airports have atmospheres of tension, a stressed feeling' with much of our time in airports concerned with waiting, queuing and negotiating crowds (Burrell, 2011). The aircraft itself can be a sanctuary after the chaos of the airport (Pascoe, 2001). Unfamiliarity with an airport and the airport process (check-in, immigration controls, security measures and boarding) can be stressful for passengers especially if there are wayfinding difficulties (see Figure 2.1) and time pressures to make the flight. Passenger fatigue and language issues can further contribute to airport stress. As Fuller and Harley explain, the passenger needs to know 'the techno-cultural dialect of English - the international language of the airport' (2004: 31).

Figure 2.1 'You are here' – even the signage can add to the sense of disorientation (Shanghai Airport, 2017© Erwin Losekoot)

How the passenger experiences the airport has much to do with its representations (Pascoe, 2001), as well as its physical manifestations. Passenger knowledge and skill as an air traveller also contribute to the experience. The experience of the competent frequent-flying business traveller (with associated privileges) (Unger *et al.*, 2016) can be contrasted with those whom Hirsh (2017), in his study of Low-Cost Carrier passengers in South-East Asia, calls the '*nouveaux globalisés*' (Hirsh, 2017: 260), those who 'lack the basic knowledge and technical equipment that is needed to fly'. Experience of the airport can also be contingent on whether one is departing, in transit or arriving at the airport and whether the airport is domestic or foreign. Although airports are often associated with stress, Adey (2009) also suggests, airports can be exciting places as one anticipates the journey ahead or arrives in a foreign destination. They can still hold an allure. In the words of Fuller and Harley (2004: 41), 'The airport is still the site of take-off, a dramatic ascent into the vertical realm, with all its attendant tropes of power and transcendence. The modern airport still offers that *frisson* of danger that characterized the very early year of aviation…'. While writers may highlight passenger boredom, frustration, dislocation or solitariness at the airport, Merriman (2004) reminds us that such feelings are not inevitable.

The quotation at the start of this chapter from British philosopher Alain de Botton, suggests airports encapsulate negative and positive aspects of modern life. This chapter examines the growing academic interest in the airport experience, beginning with the history of airports before discussing the nature of modern airports which contribute to the airport experience. How one experiences an airport is related to how that space is understood. The chapter explores the academic discussion on the airport as a place or non-place, a liminal space or space of transition, a space of mobility or immobility, a space shared with others, a space of surveillance and a space of consumption. It draws on literature from various fields of study including hospitality studies, sociology, anthropology, geography, mobility studies, transport studies and tourism management. In so doing, it demonstrates the complexity that is the modern airport experience for airline passengers. While the airport may be a symbol of global, postmodern nomadism, as social and cultural theorists propose, travellers may have a less grand view.

The Changing Airport

Airports have changed a great deal in the 100 years since the Wright brothers flew their first plane in North Carolina, USA. Today's aerotropolis (Kasarda & Lindsay, 2011) cannot be compared with airports of the past. Once airports were the backdrop to glamorous travel with customers dressed in evening clothes and sipping cocktails. Then, airports sought to match this glamour with their architecture, as in Idlewild, New York (later to be renamed JFK International Airport). Gradually, however, the focus changed to being an efficient transportation hub. As Gordon (2008: 85) explains, 'by the mid-1930s, airport buildings started to look less like temples and more like outgrowths of modern technology and urbanism'. The focus shifted to efficiency and speed; good airports were ones that passengers could get through quickly with minimal delay and inconvenience. Over time, travellers and journalists started to complain about crowding, expensive concessionaires, dirty terminals, delays and 'ordeal-by-loudspeaker' (Graham, 2001: 145). Some post-war airport redevelopments (for example, Schiphol airport which re-opened in July 1945) were rebuilt as symbols of national pride and recovery. Further changes occurred in the 1970s with the emergence of the hub airport to cater for the new wide-bodied planes. As Adey (2007) explains, the size of these airports meant that passengers now took a much longer time to negotiate their way through the terminal. It also meant that their waiting times for connecting flights were extended. Together with these redevelopments, there was also a shift in focus from airports as public service infrastructure projects to market-led commercial organisations. In more recent times we have seen increased surveillance and security checks alter the nature of the airport and the passenger experience.

The need to respond to global and local markets has meant that airports are constantly re-invented and rebuilt, leading TWA veteran pilot, Hal Blackburn, to make a comment that is still relevant today: 'To the best of my knowledge I never landed on a completed airport' (Graham, 2001: 167). Airports are, as Fuller and Harley (2004: 114) explain, 'metastable' – stable in their instability. The constant changes and improvements in airports across the world can create an unsettling sense of impermanence for travellers (Adey, 2006a, 2006b). English architecture critic, Reyner Banham, may have had this in mind when he compared airports to a 'demented amoeba' (Gordon, 2008: 225). It is very difficult to get to know an airport unless a traveller is one of the 'road-warriors' who spend many days a year travelling, with much time spent in airports.

Finally, the increased focus on security, as a result of hijackings (400 hijackings involving 75,000 passengers between 1969 and 1978), has led to a focus away from a hospitable and welcoming experience. As Gordon (2008: 236) said, 'post-hijack terminals were heavy and grounded, whereas earlier ones had been light and soaring. Transparency had suddenly become a liability at the airport'. The events of 11 September 2001 have further changed the nature of airports to places of high surveillance and security.

The physical environment of an airport plays a major role in the airport customer experience. Sir Winston Churchill is reported to have said 'we shape our buildings and afterwards, they shape us' (Ezeh & Harris, 2007: 59). He is thought to have been referring to the British Houses of Parliament and the behaviour of politicians within, but his comment is also relevant to how people feel or behave in other buildings – such as airports. In 1988 Douglas Adams (author of *The Hitchhiker's Guide to the Galaxy*), opened one of his books with a rather brutal description of the emotional effect of airport architecture on the users. He writes:

> It can hardly be a coincidence that no language on earth has ever produced the expression 'as pretty as an airport'. Airports are ugly. Some are very ugly. Some attain a degree of ugliness that can only be the result of a special effort. This ugliness arises because airports are full of people who are tired, cross, and have just discovered that their luggage has landed in Murmansk ... and architects have on the whole tried to reflect this in their design. They have sought to highlight the tiredness and crossness motif with brutal shapes and nerve-jangling colours. (Adams, 1988: 1)

Certainly, many of the airports servicing low-cost carriers would not be considered attractive. Commenting on low-cost aviation in South-East

Asia, Hirsh (2017: 266) said of Air Asia's airport in Kuala Lumpur: 'the airport terminal is difficult to distinguish from the adjacent long-distance coach terminus'. However, new or remodelled international airports of the 21st century (especially those servicing full-cost airlines) might be considered 'pretty' by some passengers. International airports such as those at Doha and Dubai, with their soaring ceilings and vast halls of glass, might be seen by some as harking back to the heyday of airport opulence and the 'temples' of yesteryear. Hirsh (2017: 265) compares Air Asia's airport to the main passenger terminal at Kuala Lumpur International Airport with its 'triumphal arches'; see *The Art of the Airport: The World's Most Beautiful Airports* by Eiselin et al. (2016), which profiles 21 airports – 'cathedrals of the jet age'.

One unintended consequence of the constant remodelling starting back in the 1960s has been a growing 'sense of sameness' (Graham, 2001: 214) which may be comforting or re-assuring for some but the cause of disorientation for others. Smith (1962) and Gordon (2008) use the term 'airportness' to refer to the distinctive architectural character of airports. While some airports are iconic structures built by internationally acclaimed architectural firms such as that of Sir Norman Foster (Stansted Airport, Heathrow Airport, Hong Kong International Airport and Beijing Airport), many airports suffer from this mundane sameness that adds to the sense of alienation, anonymity and exhaustion that many travellers feel as they travel through the space. German philosopher, Heidegger (1953), discussed the difference between a structure being a 'building' or a 'dwelling' – the latter being one that provides shelter, comfort, and a sense of belonging. Airports are transient places for most people, but the question arises whether a passenger in an airport could 'feel at home' if the airport is experienced by them as homogeneous and sterile. Speaking of the changes to airports in the wake of terrorist attacks, Gordon (2008: 221) says 'departure lounges became shadowless holding tanks, saturated with Muzak and fluorescent lighting. The experience was ersatz and vacuum-sealed from beginning to end'. Yet, while the familiarity that emerges within the modern-day airport is tedious in experience, it is also 'sublime in its promise' (Fuller & Harley, 2004: 81). Perhaps less sublime is the airport traveller's experience of going from gate to plane which New Zealand poet, Kevin Ireland (2007), in his poem, 'Airport Blues', likens to sausage meat being squeezed into the sausage skin.

This rather pessimistic view of the airport experience is reinforced by those who perceive the airport as a 'non-place'. That it is perceived as a transitional or liminal space also differentiates it from other places. However, as we shall see later in this chapter, there are others, for example, from mobility studies, who disagree with these interpretations of airports.

Airports as Places or Non-places

New Zealand urban planner, James Lunday, warned 'an arch enemy of place, it seems, is subjugation by sameness' (Lunday, 2009: 12). This point is also made by Augé (1995: xii) who reflects:

> The same hotel chains, the same television networks are cinched tightly round the globe, so that we feel constrained by uniformity, by universal sameness, and to cross international borders brings no more profound variety than is found walking between theatres on Broadway or rides at Disneyland.

Before discussing Augé's (1995) views, as expressed in his book, *Non-places: An Introduction to Supermodernity*, we should turn to geographer Edward Relph's seminal discourse in the 1970s on 'place and placelessness'. Relph (2008) argues that, through places, we have a link to the past. Places may also have a specific geographical location – they are truly unique. However, in the case of transport networks, such as airports, 'standardisation dominates and uniqueness is subservient' (Relph, 2008: v). Relph argues that although a sense of place is essential for humans to be who they are, we have lost our sensitivity to the significance of a sense of place which has led to the development of sites (referred to as 'standardized landscapes') which have no links to the history and culture of their geographical location. He thus defines 'placelessness' as 'the weakening of distinct and diverse experiences and identities of place' (Relph, 2008: 6).

Following Relph, Augé (1995) argues that airports share these characteristics. He focuses particularly on the impact of speed, claiming that the role of airports is for 'the accelerated circulation of passengers and goods' (Augé, 1995: 63) thereby making an airport a 'non-place'. He explains:

> If a place can be defined as relational, historical and concerned with identity, then a space which cannot be defined as relational, or historical, or concerned with identity will be a non-place. The hypothesis advanced here is that supermodernity produces non-places, meaning spaces which are not themselves anthropological places, and which ... do not integrate the earlier places. (Augé, 1995: 63)

He sees a difference between 'geometrical spaces' such as a crossroad (or an airport) and an 'anthropological/sociological space' which is a place which has meaning to people (perhaps because of what has happened there). He credits de Certeau (1984) with the concept of a 'non-place', although he in turn claims to have borrowed the term from Merleau-Ponty. Non-places are spaces that people pass through at great speed – too fast to understand where somewhere is, what happened there or why it is important. Non-places are spaces without social bonds or social emotions (Augé, 1996) where one may feel detached and alienated. This lack of ability to relate to the location is what creates non-places such as airports. Augé suggests that airports, like roads, railway stations and even luxury hotel chains and holiday camps are just as much non-places as transit or refugee camps, where people find themselves in a state of limbo – legally, politically and emotionally. The only difference is the comfort in which people wait.

Nonetheless, not all view airports as placeless 'non-places'. Merriman (2004) argues that feelings that have been associated with 'non-places', such as alienation and detachment, are also experienced in those spaces we consider 'a place', such as home or office, making the concept of a 'non-place' irrelevant. An airport can have meaning and sociality. It can fit with Augé's definition of 'a place' – 'relational, historical and concerned with identity' (Augé, 1995: 63). The social complexity of airports is reason to refute the idea that an airport is a non-place (Cresswell, 2006; Hannam *et al.*, 2006). Airports often have complex histories, geographies and materialities which may change over time and may be experienced differently by their heterogeneous users. Airport management may design experiences which give meaning to an airport, As seen in Figure 2.2, the invitation for the customer to play the piano allows for the co-creation of experience. The traveller interacts

Figure 2.2 'Share your talent' – co-creating the airport customer experience (Schiphol Airport, Amsterdam, 2018 © Erwin Losekoot)

with the airport organisation to co-create value and meaning of the airport as place.

Varley *et al.* (2020) while not dismissing the concept of non-places, claim that 'intentionality' has the potential of liberating place experience. The authors explain that 'all space holds the potential for becoming place and non-place, even for the tourist passing through' (Varley *et al.*, 2020: 9). They describe three approaches of passengers to the airport. They may accede/give in to the airport as (non-) place, they may consume it, embracing it as a place for what it is, appreciating its functionality as a (non-) place or conquer, resist the (non-) place. They conclude that these three approaches 'suggest that (non-) place experiences are bendable *and* bounded' (2020: 9). Gottdiener (2001: 61) sees airports as a new kind of space offering 'portals to the realms of both place and placelessness'. In defence of Augé, Merriman (2004) explains that non-places were never considered to exist in a pure form. Explaining Augé, Merriman (2004: 149) says, 'Place and non-place are always relational, contingent and continually folded into one another'.

While some may argue whether airports are places or non-places, for others, viewing airports as a transitional or liminal space has been a means to understanding the passenger experience of airports.

Airports as Spaces of Liminality and Transition

Pascoe refers to the airport as a 'time-free' zone, 'nothing other than an infinite loop' where past and future are effaced, leaving only the relativity of the present (2001: 34). Derived from the Latin word, 'limen' meaning threshold, Turner (1969) used the term 'liminal space' to identify that period of time when one is between places, 'between the mundane and the extraordinary' (Pritchard & Morgan, 2006: 764). For the passenger, the airport is a transitory space. While Turner's ethnographic interest was in rituals and pilgrimage, writers have seen parallels with passenger transition through an airport. Turner (1969) suggests that people move through three phases – the separation of an individual from the group of which they are a part, a stage of ambiguity during which their status is not clear, and then finally, a re-assimilation into society. This description similarly describes the process of moving through an airport. In the first phase, the passenger leaves behind their non-travelling family and friends; see Figure 2.3.

In the second phase, identity and status are verified at passport control and security points to make sure one is 'sterile' (the word security personnel use to describe those who have 'passed' their checks). Huang *et al.* (2018), examining the phenomenological experience of passengers in international airports, explain that once passengers have gone through security and moved from landside to airside, they enter a restricted zone – a liminal space which is a more relaxed and safe space.

Figure 2.3 Liminal line – where travellers must say farewell and start on their journey alone (Auckland International Airport, 2013 ©Erwin Losekoot)

The liminal nature of the space (the restrictive nature of the space and the temporary community that is formed) 'allows passengers to interact with fellow passengers from all walks of life' (Huang *et al.*, 2018: 8). The authors explain that a characteristic of the liminal phase is the absence of social class distinctions and, although privileges for some passengers still exist in the lounges, distinctions are reduced. 'Liminality is derived from passenger watching and assistance offering to strangers, whereby a sense of communitas is felt in a secure and often facilitating environment' (Huang *et al.*, 2018: 11). However, the authors found that, for frequent travellers, the airport was experienced as a 'personal space' with less interaction with strangers as they used the airport as a mobile office. The airport also offered those travelling alone, quality alone time, especially if out of phone and internet contact.

The third, final phase of movement through the airport, re-assimilation, occurs on arrival. Many airports symbolise the transitional nature of an airport, through physical signage or design. For example, in the Arrivals Hall at Auckland International Airport there is a *Tomokanga*, a wooden, carved Māori gateway, which was presented to the airport by the local tribe or *iwi*. It symbolises the transition from one space to another. For returning New Zealand residents, it signifies a move from 'the unknown' to 'the known' and, for visitors to New Zealand, it denotes arrival at the unknown, a place of difference.

When one is 'between places' the rules and conventions and even one's previous identity may no longer count – something which can be a great release to some. This liminal state can be seen to be at once liberating and exciting but also frightening and unsettling, or even boring (being forced to wait and not having any control over what happens next). Pritchard and Morgan (2006: 765) explain that individuals experience liminal spaces differently:

> Differentially empowered, socially positioned and embodied people interact to construct and consume spaces and whilst liminal places are typically associated with freedom, our gender, race, sexuality and embodiment all combine to constrain or empower our every experience and perception of such places.

While history has constructed the mobilities of Western citizens as a sign of progress, others' mobility can be depicted as threatening and thus denied or limited (Khoshneviss, 2017). For these other groups, anticipation and interactions with a country's immigration and security gatekeepers can be a heightened emotional experience. Putting the politics of mobility in the colonial context, Khoshneviss highlights the anxieties of Iranian students entering American airports where the fear of hostile treatment and deportation is very real.

> Airports are the example of a liminosphere par excellence where both spatial and temporal aspects are intensely and relentlessly at play. Going through airports as purely liminal spaces is, in general, a wearing experience, and even more strenuous to unwelcome travelers. (Khoshneviss, 2017: 315)

The Iranian passengers were found to be aware of the significance of their body and performance contradicting the view that the time in the airport is 'dead time'.

> This performance on the front stage, as a form of agency, is an elaborate tactic. It is the performance of accountability. It is an extra effort that envisions all possible scenarios. The travelers in the liminal stage, in their 'dead time' think through different strategies and choose mechanisms capable of offsetting possible conflicts. Additionally, to avoid incongruity and emotional entanglement, they may rationalize their tactics and internalize the treatment they receive. (Khoshneviss, 2017: 317)

Khoshneviss highlights the porous nature of transition, the interdependency of the three stages through which passengers travel–departure, liminality and integration. Each stage could affect the other. As Khoshneviss (2017: 320) says: 'The transition is a venue in which past, present, and future, space and time, interact to shape the traveler's experience'. If the student does not integrate into American society, they may stay in a permanent liminal state during their time there.

While acknowledging that airports act as thresholds, Gottdiener (2001), rather than referring to them as liminal spaces, prefers to think of them as transitional spaces or gateways. They act 'as the conduit from one physical location on the planet to another, they facilitate the shrinkage of the globe…'. Transcending space and time, he sees airports as personifying the 'great escape' and for such reason 'air transportation possesses the aura of romance and exoticism, of possibility, difference, and a new chance for daily living' (Gottdiener, 2001: 11).

However, as with the criticism of airports as non-places, the idea of airports as transitional or liminal spaces can also be problematic from the perspective of the mobilities paradigm. As explained by Abranches (2013: 508), the idea that these spaces:

> materialise a lack of identity or are located betwixt and between spatial identities has been criticised in academic literature in two ways: on the one hand, its failure to grasp the networks of connections that they are tied into; on the other, its lack of success in understanding the circulation of people, material and ideas, not as fleeting, temporary and ephemeral, but as an integral part of the performance and sense of space and place.

Airports as Spaces of Mobility and Immobility

The above discussion leads to a consideration of mobilities and immobilities in airports. To explain, the mobilities paradigm does not distinguish places as fixed and people as mobile, but rather recognises that, in today's world, everything is on the move – people, objects and information 'contingently brought together to produce certain performances in certain places at certain times' (Hannam *et al.*, 2006: 13). Everything is circulating in a 'networked society' (Urry, 2004). Even the airport itself is mobile as exemplified, for example, by the constant refurbishments and activities taking place. Airports are thus not static but dynamic, facilitating this movement of people and objects domestically and internationally. Nonetheless, we may still *experience* 'immobility' in an airport in what appears locational or structural fixedness or the behaviour of passengers, for example, those quietly waiting in queue. Adey (2006b: 84) explains this immobility as illusion: 'when we say that something is immobile, we are normally saying this in relation to ourselves or something else'. In other words, immobilities are 'relative' as they are understood in relation to mobilities. Airports are mobile places, but, as Adey (2007) argues, airports are designed with areas of 'immobility' or '*relative* immobility' to 'hold' passengers in specific spaces. Adey (2008: 439) explains that airline passengers are embodied 'and have important physical and emotional relationships with the airport terminal building'. Airports in the design and building of spaces attempt to predetermine the situational context that passengers will inhabit and thus 'hope to shape and bend people's motions, feelings and emotions' (Adey, 2008: 447).

Through the creation of observation points for passengers: the positioning of windows (shopfront and those which allow passengers to look out on the action of the apron) and the siting of information and television screens, airports manage passenger spectatorship. At Terminal 4, Heathrow Airport, passengers are invited to take a lift to an Observation Deck to 'View Heathrow'; see Figures 2.4 and 2.5. The positioning of passengers is also an opportunity for retail spending. Airports also spatially position passengers so they can observe others (Adey, 2007). As Gottdiener says, '"People watching" is ... rated highly as a time-killer' (2001: 48); see Figure 2.6.

For many passengers, airports are associated with boredom and waiting. DeLillo (1982: 7) in his novel, *The Names*, argues that airport waiting is 'dead time':

> This is time totally lost to us. We don't remember it. We take no sense impressions with us, no voices, none of the windy blast of aircraft on the tarmac, or the white noise of flight, or the hours waiting. Nothing sticks to us but smoke in our hair and clothes.

Figure 2.4 Entry to Observation Deck, Terminal 4, Heathrow Airport (London, 2019 © Jennie Small)

56 The Passenger Experience of Air Travel: A Critical Approach

Figure 2.5 View of Apron from Observation Deck, Terminal 4, Heathrow Airport (London, 2019 © Jennie Small)

Figure 2.6 Positioning of window and seating allow observation of other passengers making their way to their departure gate (Sydney International Airport, 2020 © Jennie Small)

Figure 2.7 Waiting... Check-in (Sydney International Airport, 2020 © Jennie Small)

In the words of Gottdiener (2001: 48), 'Air terminals reek with the tedium of killing time'. In an airport, all passengers are in transit, forcibly waiting (Rowley & Slack, 1999), as evident in the familiar scenes in Figures 2.7 and 2.8.

However, Bissell challenges the view that waiting is 'an inert and immobile experience' (Bissell, 2007: 285). Rather than using velocity as a differentiator, he prefers to use embodied action/inactivity. This is not dead time; much of what happens in waiting involves corporeal attentiveness and engagement whether it be deciding what to do while waiting, gazing around or experiencing feelings associated with waiting, such as impatience or fatigue. Bissell (2007: 277) concludes that 'waiting as an event should be conceptualised not solely as an active achievement or passive acquiescence but as a variegated affective complex where experience folds through and emerges from a multitude of different planes'. The response of passengers to the experience of waiting (whether it be calmness or anxiety, irritation, frustration) may be conveyed to others and infect their experience of waiting. While most people transit through an airport with a few hours' delay, others may spend longer. In an unusual case, Mehran Karimi Nasseri (immortalised by Tom Hanks in the movie *The Terminal*) spent 18 years living at Paris Charles de Gaulle airport between 1988 and 2006 because of a problem confirming his identity.

Figure 2.8 More waiting at Departure Gate (Sydney International Airport, 2020 © Jennie Small)

Airports as Spaces Shared with Others

As Kellerman (2008: 176) says, airport terminals imply 'a simultaneous mix of social separation and blending'. On the one hand, passengers are expected to keep social distance from each other, for example, when going through security checkpoints. Pütz (2012) employed Goffman's idea of 'civil inattention' to describe the ability of passengers when going through security to ignore the fact that those immediately around them are being searched for dangerous items, asked to empty their bags or take off clothing (shoes, belts etc.) in front of complete strangers. He makes the point that, in our 21st century society, it is considered rude to admit to noticing such experiences so, by turning these into 'non-events', we avoid feeling embarrassed or uncomfortable. Pütz (2012: 155) says it is 'a display of good intentions and the mutual right to mind one's own business' (similar to behaviour on a plane where one might not speak to one's neighbour despite the intimate activities of sleeping and eating in close proximity for 10 to 15 hours). Pütz (2012) also argues that everyone wants security processes to be conducted as quickly and smoothly as possible and the fastest way to get through the process is to ignore what is going on around one. Gottdiener (2001: 35) makes a similar point when he explains 'the airport norm is one of *non-interaction*. People are *expected* to keep to themselves in airports'.

If airports are considered similar to coach terminals, this may be 'as a way of avoiding information overload' (Pearce, 1980: 935).

Although, for the most part, other people in airports 'fade in and out of our consciousness with a swiftness that defies memory' (Gottdiener, 2001: 31), airports may also be sites for social transactions with staff and fellow passengers, an opportunity to feel part of a community, even if only for a few hours. In the airport this might be observed in a variety of ways of stranger interaction: children playing together in a ball pit, business people sharing a drink in a departure lounge/champagne bar, mobile phone users sharing chargers and adaptors or passengers social networking in an airport community forum (Wattanacharoensil et al., 2016). The opportunity for social interaction increases with the (enforced) shared experience of a delayed flight. Gottdiener (2001: 30) provides an example of passengers on a delayed flight sharing information with other passengers: 'by 3:00 am we had all pretty much introduced ourselves to each other and created a temporary community'. Anderson (2006) speaks of 'imagined communities' to describe a diaspora of people who have a (perceived) shared heritage. One can think of passengers temporarily stranded at an airport as such a community, even if only as long as the storm or technical failure lasts. Small and Harris (2014) use the term 'micro-community' to describe the people who find themselves sharing a flight for a defined period of time and Rowley and Slack (1999) identify the same phenomenon with the term, 'transient community'. Pearce (1980, 2005) refers to 'familiar strangers' (Simmel, 1950) to describe our fellow travellers (those we do not personally know but with whom we have something in common simply by sharing the journey). He describes the benefits of being attentive to these strangers at airports: they can provide guidance, help in times of stress and assist us pass the time through conversation.

As a space of urban anonymity, the airport can be seen to offer the possibility for inventing the self (Gottdiener, 2001). Gottdiener also claims that 'the anonymity of the airport milieu is supercharged with eroticism, with sexual innuendo, and with promise… Gazing at strangers in a crowded terminal is an erotic activity' (2001: 38). Yet, Crang (2002: 573) argues that this approach 'risks falling for the manipulated image of airports'. As he says, 'It may speak to a globe-trotting semiotician, but says little to the family with overtired children delayed by lack of connecting buses in Majorca'. And, in the words of Schaberg (2016: 166), 'There is almost nothing so abject as parenting at the airport – whether seeing it, doing it, or being subject to it. And the delayed family at the airport is an exasperated diaspora indeed'. Passengers clearly practice mobility in different ways. Yet, whatever the social transactions with other passengers, they are usually temporary as we end up boarding our separate flights to different destinations.

They are the temporary communities which perhaps can turn an airport from a processing facility into a memorable and positive emotional experience. Opportunities for interaction with other passengers may depend on the spaces occupied: executive lounge, play area, bar, café, smoking room, waiting areas etc.

The other passengers with whom we share the airport, beyond the commonality of being fellow air travellers, can be differentiated in terms of their purpose of travel, class of travel and travel group as well as their ethnicity, religion, nationality, gender, age, sexuality, dis/ablebodiness etc. All travellers come together in this space; see Figure 2.9. The diversity of passengers implies that 'not all passengers in terminals are mobile in quite the same way' (Cresswell, 2006: 222). Cresswell (2006) describes how the comfort of mobility and the production of identity may depend on passenger citizenship. In his study of Schiphol Airport, he describes the ease with which European Union citizens can pass through the checkpoints compared with non-European Union citizens who wait in slowly moving lines. Discussed above, Khoshneviss (2017) similarly observed difficulties of Iranian students at American airports. As Cresswell (2006: 224) says, 'very few places are more finely differentiated according to a kinetic hierarchy than an international airport'.

One group of passengers at the top of this hierarchy is the business traveller. Referred to as the 'kinetic elite', they are able to move more easily through the airport (Sheller, 2008), conduct business and stay in touch with their organisations while 'on the road' due to the airport and

Figure 2.9 The mixing of cultures (Qatar International Airport, 2018 © Erwin Losekoot)

onboard facilities and services provided. Moving from city to city or country to country, they arrive, plug in their laptops and continue what they were working on thousands of kilometres away. Regular executive business travellers (and quite a number of academics) find themselves spending a considerable amount of their time in airports. Gordon (2008: 250) suggests that 'the postmodern concourse would become the oasis (or village green) for that restless, floating class of airport nomads and "departure lounge lizards"'. The aim of executive departure lounges is to give a sense of opulence, sophistication and success, with luxury brands, pleasant physical environments (temperature, sound and layout) 'conveying the message that the passenger was a valued customer' (Rowley & Slack, 1999: 368). Chua *et al.* (2017: 652) point out that 'an airline lounge is an experiential place that involves the creation of travelers' experiences'. Airport lounges are extremely symbolic places, demonstrating that one has 'made it' as well as being purely functional places to rest, eat, wait and work. Having lounge access removed is a sad day for many regular travellers! Much thought has been given how to make the inevitable airport wait as relaxing or productive as possible. It is suggested that the availability and quality of an airport executive lounge are influential factors in a passenger's choice of airline (Chua *et al.*, 2017; Lee *et al.*, 2017). Lee *et al.* (2017: 2902), in their study of airport lounge experiences, found that 'to some air travellers, patronizing a lounge is regarded as a form of self expression' matching their self-image (reliability, intelligence and success). However, they also found that lounge visitation was not all about work and business with 80% of respondents saying they visited the lounge mainly for relaxation, confirming the findings of Unger *et al.* (2016) that, for business travellers, the lounge is not just a work-place. Coming back to the idea of airports as emotional places, Urry (2004: 35) suggests that 'this mobile life is felt by mobile workers to be lonely', even by those 'digital nomads' who seem to cope in this environment.

Not all groups of passengers consider that their needs are met at airports. Examples of groups of passengers who have fought for inclusion at airports are persons with disability (see Chapters 5 and 6). Mothers of infants have also argued for the right to have a designated, comfortable space in which to feed their infants other than the public lavatory. Certainly, passengers who do not fit the destination image of the acceptable passenger may be subjected to more surveillance and security than other passengers.

Airports as Spaces of Surveillance and Control

Many of the changes to the airport environment over the years concern issues of security. The airport, especially the international airport, is a political place, an 'environment of "authorities"' (Kellerman, 2008: 161).

The increased requirement for security, however, may work against the liberating experience of the airport as a liminal space (as some propose). The airport may no longer imbue the passenger with that uplifting, anticipatory feeling of going 'up, up and away'. As stated by Schaberg (2017: 22), security checkpoints are 'epicenters of embarrassment, stress and insecurity… the rude counterbalances to all the progress and uplift of travel'. In reference to body scans at airports, Tulloch points out that 'The vulnerability of women to insensitive and sometimes downright sexist searches is rarely highlighted' (Tulloch, 2022: 6). Turner (1969: 359), in his discussion of liminal space, describes the rituals he observed and the people undergoing a transition in society by saying, 'their behavior is normally passive or humble; they must obey their instructors implicitly, and accept arbitrary punishment without complaint. It is as though they are being reduced or ground down to a uniform condition'. In a similar way, it could be argued that during their progress through an airport, people are stripped of their rights. Adey (2009: 276) quotes British author Salman Rushdie as describing 'this line, at which we must stand until we are allowed to walk across and give our papers to be examined by an officer who is entitled to ask us more or less anything'. A similar point is made by de Botton (2009: 275) in his book, *A Week at the Airport*:

> A noiseless, unchecked progress through the detectors allow one to advance into the rest of the terminal with a feeling akin to that one may experience on leaving church after confession or a synagogue on the Day of Atonement, momentarily absolved and relieved of the burden of one's sins.

Reflecting on changes over time in the treatment of passengers, Gordon (2008) considers that, where they were once treated as royalty, now they are all considered suspicious until they have been cleared by security and no longer present a risk. He describes the behaviour expected of passengers:

> The ritual of passenger processing has become more like an exercise in obedience training. A 'good' passenger waits patiently in line with boarding pass and passport ready for inspection, walks through the scanning portal when ordered to do so, and never, but never, talks back, complains or questions the authority of airport personnel. (Gordon, 2008: 262)

Schaberg (2012) explains that bodies are in a complex relation to airport screening: passenger bodies are screened by other bodies (security agents) and also by metal detectors and scanners. He adds:

> Screening is also performed by a more abstract 'body' – the TSA or even the larger post-9/11 security regime: this is a collective gaze at once more ubiquitous and less visible than any individual agent brandishing a magnetic sensing wand or wearing blue latex gloves. (Schaberg, 2012: 71)

Airports are contested spaces, alive with officials whose job it is to ensure that things do *not* happen, such as the importation of drugs or other contraband, the introduction of disease, the entry of illegal persons or the departure of those fleeing the justice system. This has led some to suggest that airports share many characteristics with prisons and other 'total institutions' such as asylums (Goffman, 1961; Morgan & Pritchard, 2005). Gordon (2008: 238) makes the point that 'both the airport and the cell block used similar kinds of logic'; both prisoners and passengers move through a series of checkpoints where they are searched, and their identity is confirmed. He concludes with the comment, 'only the duration of incarceration differed'. Kellerman (2008: 166) sees international airport terminals as 'the most authoritarian facility designed for the use of free civilians'. While we might expect that travellers experience their home airport as less threatening and stressful than foreign airports, this can shift when off-shore airport borders are constituted (security officials from the foreign country are stationed at the home airport to apply their immigration rules before passenger departure, rather than on arrival). It is important for airport security staff to be aware of the impression they create for passengers and, while still being thorough, they should do everything in their power to reduce passengers' feelings of stress, discomfort and inconvenience (De Barros *et al.*, 2007). The paradox of airports is noted by Morgan and Pritchard (2005) and Sharma (2009) with Sharma (2009: 139) describing a journey through a US airport, 'where one is hailed by the aromas of duty free perfume and chocolates in one moment and then processed by US Homeland Security in the other and where VIP lounges and detention rooms can be found on the same blueprint'. While the discussion so far might seem to paint an overwhelmingly negative picture of airport experiences, Morgan and Pritchard (2005) also point out that heightened surveillance can be comforting for many tourists and travellers.

Although one might reasonably expect that *everyone* is required to comply with the same rules in an airport, this is often not the case. Morgan and Pritchard (2005: 124) use the term 'asymmetric surveillance' to describe 'travel elites who now not only demand higher levels of service but also expect to be insulated from much of this often invasive scrutiny'. While royalty, heads of state and 'Commercially Important Persons' (as they are sometimes referred to) do not use the same doors, lounges and car parks as the rest of the travelling public, there are means through which others can buy their way out of some of the 'normal' airport processes, for example, at Los Angeles International Airport, The Private Suite (private terminal) or, at Amsterdam Schiphol Airport, 'Privium' with its fast-track eye-scan facility (Lee *et al.*, 2017; Rowley & Slack, 1999; Straker & Wrigley, 2016). As Cresswell (2006) says, allowing Privium passengers to pass through unmolested frees up security officials to monitor the non-Privium passengers: 'The speed of some is logically related to the slowness of others' (Cresswell, 2006: 240). For those who can afford such privileges, the airport experience can be a very different experience from that of the masses!

Airports as Spaces of Consumption

Increasingly, airports have become sites of consumption with shopping malls, entertainment and other leisure facilities (Losekoot, 2015). They can become a tourist attraction in themselves; see Figure 2.10. Rowley and Slack (1999) also suggest that a further role of airport retailers is communicating messages, values and even cultural interpretation of a destination. While some may argue that 'the main reason for people being at the airport is that they have to catch a plane and not because they have to do some shopping' (Geuens *et al.*, 2004: 621), airport policymakers no longer see the transportation of passengers and goods as the sole purpose of an airport. Straker and Wrigley (2016) note that the increased requirement for airports to deliver non-aeronautical revenue makes retail a survival strategy, not an optional extra. Thompson (2007) pointed out that airport shopping is one of the fastest growing niche retail markets and there is no evidence

Figure 2.10 Pop-up Bounce trampoline park at Dubai International Airport (2019 © Jennie Small)

Figure 2.11 Luxury brands at Sydney International Airport (2020 © Jennie Small)

of it changing as people spend ever longer periods of time in airports. Duty free and luxury brand shops dominate the large international airports with brand exposure, the 'raison d'être' for their existence; see Figures 2.11 and 2.12.

Perng *et al.* (2010), in their study of Taiwan's Kaohsiung airport, noted that good retail facilities with quality service and a wide range of products led to an enjoyable and satisfying emotional experience for travellers: 'once passengers have their boarding passes, their tension is relieved and replaced by excitement' (at the prospect of 'retail therapy') (Perng *et al.*, 2010: 279). Those travelling alone were more likely to spend on large luxury items, whereas those travelling in groups purchased low-cost merchandise. Geuens *et al.* (2004) suggest that the unique environment of an airport retail operation attracts different shopper types and shopping needs. In their study of passenger behaviour at Brussels Airport, they found that 'airport shopping will be more influenced by experiential, travel-related and atmospheric factors than by functional factors' (Geuens *et al.*, 2004: 621). Interestingly, the authors found no significant difference in shopping habits between business and leisure travellers while Fodness and Murray (2007) argued that purpose of trip was very significant in satisfaction with airport shopping facilities. Shopping at airports is complex because of the variety of

Figure 2.12 Luxury brands at Sydney International Airport (2020 © Jennie Small)

customers: different classes of travellers, languages and amount of time (too much or too little). With pressure to find that perfect gift, restrictions with luggage and concern about customs requirements at the destination (or connecting airport), shopping at airports can be a stressful as well as an enjoyable experience. For frequent airport visitors, familiar with certain airports, consuming may become a ritual with passengers having their own shopping routines (Huang *et al.*, 2018). Even the act of shopping (or window shopping) as a familiar performance may allow some passengers to feel at home in an otherwise alien public space. Adey (2010: 7) makes the point that brand names can 'provide a welcome familiarity in a space that is often disorientating'. While not all passengers can afford the high-priced goods of the luxury stores which dominate most large international airports, the retail *atmosphere* of wealth and privilege may allow the passenger, at least for the time in its presence, to take on a different identity and see themselves as one of the world's elite. On the other hand, the luxury stores and brands may alienate other passengers, emphasising their lack of success compared with others (Small *et al.*, 2008).

Conclusion

In drawing this discussion to a close, it is worth reflecting on the journey we have taken. Starting with an overview of the history of airports and their changing nature, the chapter notes the unsettling effect of constant rebuilding and renovation of airports. The emotions experienced by passengers can be related to the architecture of airports which in many cases is one of sameness and sterility. Whether the airport is a place or non-place has been debated and the transitional nature of an airport highlighted. Those arguing for the liminality of an airport have proposed that the airport can be a place of freedom from daily life or a very lonely and disorientating environment. Overall, airports are considered emotional places beyond the obvious signs of sadness and joy that accompany the farewells and the welcomes. The requirement for airports to remodel their physical and technological environment to meet new security threats has led to a feeling for many that an airport is an ordeal to be endured, not an experience to be enjoyed. It has been noted that some of the technology commonplace in airports would not be out of place in a prison (but, for the passengers, there is the consolation of duty-free shopping!). Airports are spaces that are shared with others, and usually, many others. While the airport norm is considered one of 'non-interaction', opportunities arise for passengers to come together in temporary or transient communities, if only because a snowstorm has grounded a flight. Yet, it would be wrong to imagine intermingling among all passengers. The executive lounge is not open to all. As Cresswell (2006: 223) indicates, the politics of mobility are ever present, especially, at the international airport:

> The suggestion that airports erase class and nationality seem, frankly, bizarre in an instrumental space where you are literally divided into classes and so frequently asked to show your passports as evidence of where you come from and where you are allowed to go.

Schaberg (2016: 192), in his concluding chapter of *The End of Airports*, says:

> Airports are strange spaces. Neither here nor there, airports nevertheless evoke strong associations and ambivalent feelings. For many people, airports have a certain pull: they announce something special to come. For others, airports are repellent: tedious, drab, dull – simply the worst places imaginable.

When airports work, they go unnoticed but when they fail, 'they infuriate, they madden' (Schaberg, 2016: 168).

The monitoring and micromanaging of bodies is a prime concern of airports. McNeill (2009: 219) suggests that airport management must make improvements because 'the airport itself has shifted from being a lay-over to a new central place' and this has an impact on the passenger experience of air travel in the modern age. Through ever more immersive consumer retail, entertainment and food and beverage offerings, airport management provides distractions for the passenger from the ordeals and uncertainties inherent in air travel. Attempts are made to give airports a 'sense of place'.

There is an interesting juxtaposition of surreal sameness (global food and beverage and retail brands) and efforts by airport management to create a unique identity for the gateway to their country, to present its local colour. Some airports have worked very hard to create an engaging experience – at check-in, during the wait to take off, during transit or on arrival. For example, Amsterdam's Schiphol airport has a mini national museum so travellers can relax and admire paintings by famous Dutch artists. They also provide a library with real books and a 'sitting room' with sofas and a fireplace. Korea's Incheon airport has musical performances which move around the airport like a Disney parade to entertain travellers. Las Vegas has slot (poker) machines. Melbourne, Australia's Tullamarine airport displays native artwork and, as already mentioned, Auckland airport has the Māori carved gateway or 'Tomokanga' to greet visitors. Auckland also uses the traditional koru design and has a recording of native birds, such as the Tui, playing for visitors as they walk down the airport corridors, with their panoramic New Zealand landscape photographs. Gordon (2008) explains that while some airport experiences may not be authentic, playing to stereotypes (clogs in Amsterdam, slot machines in Las Vegas, Harrods department store in London), they at least alleviate and distract travellers from the possibility of travel boredom and monotony. They also enhance cultural attachment to place (Wattanacharoensil et al., 2016). Indeed, from the air traveller's perspective, the association of airports with the destination leads to the perception of the airport 'as an internal component of tourism experience' (Wattanacharoensil et al., 2017: 124). Retail shops sell last-minute souvenirs of the destination to departing travellers; see Figure 2.13.

The mobility literature suggests that there will always be a need to travel, and that technology has fuelled this need and desire, rather than lessening it, as was once the expectation (Urry, 2002, 2004). Air travel has accelerated some people's lives (those who belong to the global elite) while those lacking the right passport, nationality or bank balance (McNeill, 2009) remain at home or travel by slower means. They do not use airports, at least not in the role of traveller. Even amongst the global elite, there are groups whose airport needs are not met and who can feel disenfranchised. A critical approach to the study of airports acknowledges that not all users of an airport are treated with the same respect and privilege as others. It is also worth noting that airports, too, differ depending on their role as domestic or international airports, level of importance and location in the world. Abranches (2013), from her study of Bissau Airport in Guinea-Bissau in West Africa, argues that much of the scholarly work on airports has focused on those which are 'symbols of progress and technological achievements in modernity' (Abranches, 2013: 508), such as Changi or Dubai International Airports, and ignored those which do not fit this prototype.

Figure 2.13 Sydney International Airport promoting Australian way of life-sheepskins, kangaroo skins, boomerangs with a touch of Chinese culture-lanterns for Chinese New Year (2020 © Jennie Small)

Airports will continue to play a critical role in economic, social and political developments around the globe and, in a mobile society, the passenger experience of departure, transit and arrival is worthy of ongoing academic study. Adey (2007, 2009), Sharma (2009) and Morgan and Pritchard (2005) claim that more and more places are becoming like airports, and more and more of the technology and processes developed and trialled at airports are becoming part of our everyday experiences of living in a 'surveillance culture' in which we exist in a panopticon of surveillance cameras (Morgan & Pritchard, 2005); another reason for observing carefully what happens at airports around the world.

References

Abranches M. (2013) When people stay and things make their way: Airports, mobilities and materialities of a transnational landscape. *Mobilities* 8, 506–527. https://doi.org/10.1080/17450101.2012.705510.

Adams, D. (1988) *The Long Dark Tea-Time of the Soul*. New York, NY: Simon & Schuster.

Adey, P. (2006a) Airports and air-mindedness: Spacing, timing and using the Liverpool airport, 1929–1939. *Social and Cultural Geography* 7 (3), 343–363. https://doi.org/10.1080/14649360600714998.

Adey, P. (2006b) If mobility is everything then it is nothing: Towards a relational politics of (im)mobilities. *Mobilities* 1 (1), 75–94. https://doi.org/10.1080/17450100500489080.

Adey, P. (2007) 'May I have your attention': Airport geographies of spectatorship, position, and (im)mobility. *Environment and Planning D: Society and Space* 25, 515–536. https://doi.org/10.1068/d69j.

Adey, P. (2008) Airports, mobility and the calculative architecture of affective control. *Geoforum* 39, 438-451. https://doi.org/10.1016/j.geoforum.2007.09.001.

Adey, P. (2009) Facing airport security: Affect, biopolitics, and the preemptive securitisation of the mobile body. *Environment and Planning D: Society and Space* 27, 274–295. https://doi.org/10.1068/d0208.

Adey, P. (2010) *Aerial life: Spaces, Mobilities, Affects.* Chichester: Wiley-Blackwell.

Anderson, B. (2006) *Imagined Communities.* London: Verso.

Augé, M. (1995) *Non-places: An Introduction to Supermodernity.* London: Verso.

Augé, M. (1996) Paris and the ethnography of the contemporary world. In M. Sherringham (ed.) *Parisian Fields* (pp. 175–181). London: Reaktion.

Bissell, D. (2007) Animating suspension: Waiting for mobilities. *Mobilities* 2, 277–298. https://doi.org/10.1080/17450100701381581.

Burrell, K. (2011) Going steerage on Ryanair: Cultures of migrant air travel between Poland and the UK. *Journal of Transport Geography* 19, 1023–1030. https://doi.org/10.1016/j.jtrangeo.2010.09.004.

Chua, B-L., Lee, S., Kim, H-Y. and Han, H. (2017) Investigating the key drivers of traveler loyalty in the airport lounge setting. *Asia Pacific Journal of Tourism Research* 22 (6), 651–665. https://doi.org/10.1080/10941665.2017.1308392.

Crang, M. (2002) Between places: Producing hubs, flows, and networks. *Environment and Planning A* 34, 569–574. https://doi.org/10.1068/a34154.

Cresswell, T. (2006) *On the Move: Mobility in the Modern Western World.* London: Routledge.

de Barros, A., Somasundaraswaran, S. and Wirasinghe, S. (2007) Evaluation of level of service for transfer passengers at airports. *Journal of Air Transport Management* 13, 293–298. https://doi.org/10.1016/j.jairtraman.2007.04.004.

de Botton, A. (2009) *A Week at the Airport.* New York, NY: Vintage Books.

de Certeau, M. (1984) *The Practice of Everyday Life* (S. F. Rendall, trans.). Berkeley, CA: University of California Press.

DeLillo, D. (1982) *The Names.* New York: Vintage.

Eiselin, S., Frommberg, L. and Gutzmer, S. (2016) *The Art of the Airport.* London: Frances Lincoln.

Ezeh, C. and Harris, L. (2007) Servicescape research: A review and research agenda. *The Marketing Review* 7 (1), 59–78. https://www.ingentaconnect.com/contentone/westburn/tmr/2007/00000007/00000001/art00005.

Fodness, D. and Murray, B. (2007) Passengers' expectations of airport service quality. *Journal of Service Marketing* 21 (7), 492–506. https://doi.org/10.1108/08876040710824852.

Fuller, G. and Harley, R. (2004) *Aviopolis A Book about Airports.* London: Black Dog Publishing.

Geuens, M., Vantomme, D. and Brengman, M. (2004) Developing a typology of airport shoppers. *Tourism Management* 25, 615–622. https://doi.org/10.1016/j.tourman.2003.07.003.

Goffman, E. (1961) *Asylums.* London: Penguin Books.

Gordon, A. (2008) *Naked Airport: A Cultural History of the World's Most Revolutionary Structure.* Chicago, IL: University of Chicago Press.

Gottdiener, M. (2001) *Life in the Air: Surviving the New Culture of Air Travel.* Oxford: Rowman & Littlefield.

Graham, A. (2001) *Managing Airports: An International Perspective.* Oxford: Butterworth-Heinemann.

Hannam, K., Sheller, M. and Urry, J. (2006) Editorial: Mobilities, immobilities and moorings. *Mobilities* 1, 1–22. https://doi.org/10.1080/17450100500489189.

Heidegger, M. (1953) *Being and Time: A Translation of Sein und Seit* (J. Stambaugh, trans.). Albany, NY: State University of New York.

Hirsh, M. (2017) Emerging infrastructures of low-cost aviation in Southeast Asia. *Mobilities* 12 (2), 259–276. https://doi.org/10.1080/17450101.2017.1292781.

Huang, W., Xiao, H. and Wang, S. (2018) Airports as liminal space. *Annals of Tourism Research* 70, 1–13. https://doi.org/10.1016/j.annals.2018.02.003.

Ireland, K. (2007) *Airports and Other Wasted Days*. Christchurch, New Zealand: Hazard Press.

Kasarda, J. and Lindsay, G. (2011) *Aerotropolis: The Way We'll Live Next*. London: Penguin.

Kellerman, A. (2008) International airports: Passengers in an environment of 'authorities'. *Mobilities* 3 (1) 161–178. https://doi.org/10.1080/17450100701797406.

Khoshneviss, H. (2017) Accountability in a state of liminality: Iranian students experiences in American airports. *Mobilities* 12, 311–323. https://doi.org/10.1080/17450101.2017.1292028.

Lee, S., Chua, B-L., Kim, H-Y. and Han, H. (2017) Shaping and enhancing airport lounge experiences: The application of brand personality and image congruity theories. *International Journal of Contemporary Hospitality Management* 29 (11), 2901–2920. https://doi.org/10.1108/IJCHM-12-2015-0672.

Losekoot, E. (2015) Factors influencing the airport customer experience: A case study of Auckland International Airport's customers. PhD Thesis, Auckland University of Technology, New Zealand. Available at: http://hdl.handle.net/10292/8739.

Lunday, J. (2009) Beyond the burbs: An urban design essay. Paper presented at the Second International Urban Design Conference, Queensland, Australia (2–4 September).

McNeill, D. (2009) The airport hotel as business space. *Geografiska Annaler: Series B, Human Geography* 91 (3), 219–228.

Merriman, P. (2004) Driving places: Marc Augé, non-places, and the geographies of England's M1 motorway. *Theory, Culture & Society* 21 (4/5), 145–167. https://doi.org/10.1177/0263276404046065.

Morgan, N. and Pritchard, A. (2005) Security and social 'sorting'. *Tourist Studies* 5 (2), 115–132. https://doi.org/10.1177/1468797605066923.

Pascoe, D. (2001) *Airspaces*. London: Reaktion Books.

Pearce, P.L. (1980) Strangers, travelers, and Greyhound terminals: A study of small-scale helping behaviors. *Journal of Personality and Social Psychology* 38 (6), 935–940.

Pearce, P. (2005) *Tourist Behaviour: Themes and Conceptual Schemes*. Clevedon: Channel View Publications.

Perng, S-W., Chow, C-C. and Liao, W-C. (2010) Analysis of shopping preference and satisfaction with airport retailing products. *Journal of Air Transport Management* 16, 279–283. https://doi.org/10.1016/j.jairtraman.2010.02.002.

Pritchard, A. and Morgan, N. (2006) Hotel Babylon? Exploring hotels as liminal sites of transition and transgression. *Tourism Management* 27, 762–772. https://doi.org/10.1016/j.tourman.2005.05.015.

Pütz, O. (2012) From non-places to non-events: The airport security checkpoint. *Journal of Contemporary Ethnography* 41 (2), 154–188. https://doi.org/10.1177/0891241611426431.

Relph, E. (2008) *Place and Placelessness*. London: Pion Limited.

Rowley, J. and Slack, F. (1999) The retail experience in airport departure lounges: reaching for timelessness and placelessness. *International Marketing Review* 16 (4/5), 363–375. https://doi.org/10.1108/02651339910281901.

Schaberg, C. (2012) *The Textual Life of Airports: Reading the Cultural Life of Flight*. New York: Continuum.

Schaberg, C. (2016) *The End of Airports*. New York: Bloomsbury.

Schaberg, C. (2017) *Airportness: The Nature of Flight*. New York: Bloomsbury.

Sharma, S. (2009) Baring life and lifestyle in the non-place. *Cultural Studies* 23 (1), 129–148. https://doi.org/10.1080/09502380802016246.

Sheller, M. (2008) Mobility, freedom and public space. In S. Bergmann and T. Sager (eds) *The Ethics of Mobilities: Rethinking Place, Exclusion, Freedom and Environment* (pp. 25–38). Aldershot: Ashgate.

Simmel, G. (1950) *The Sociology of Georg Simmel*. (H. Woolf, trans.). New York: Free Press of Glencoe.
Small, J. and Harris, C. (2014) Crying babies on planes: Aeromobility and parenting. *Annals of Tourism Research* 48, 27–41. https://doi.org/10.1016/j.annals.2014.04.009.
Small, J., Harris, C. and Wilson, E. (2008) A critical discourse analysis of in-flight magazine advertisements: The 'social sorting' of airline travellers? *Journal of Tourism and Cultural Change* 6 (1), 17–38. https://doi.org/10.1080/14766820802140422.
Smith, G.E.K. (1962) *The New Architecture of Europe*. Hammondsworth, Middlesex: Penguin.
Straker, K. and Wrigley, C. (2016) Translating emotional insights into digital channel designs: Opportunities to enhance the airport experience. *Journal of Hospitality and Tourism Technology* 7 (2), 135–157. https://doi.org/10.1108/JHTT-11-2015-0041.
Thompson, B. (2007) Airport retailing in the UK. *Journal of Retail & Leisure Property* 6 (3), 203–211. https://doi.org/10.1057/palgrave.rlp.5100067.
Tulloch, L. (2022) Why some women dread airport scans. *The Sydney Morning Herald, Traveller,* 23 July, p. 6.
Turner, V. (1969) *The Ritual Process: Structure and Anti-structure*. Chicago, IL: Aldine Publishing.
Unger, O., Uriely, N. and Fuchs, G. (2016) The business travel experience. *Annals of Tourism Research* 61, 142–156. http://dx.doi.org/10.1016/j.annals.2016.10.003.
Urry, J. (2002) Mobility and proximity. *Sociology* 36 (2), 255–274. DOI: 10.1177/0038038502036002002.
Urry, J. (2004) Connections. *Environment and Planning D: Society and Space* 22, 27–37. https://doi.org/10.1177/0038038502036002002.
Varley, P., Schilar, H. and Rickly, J. (2020) Tourism non-places: Bending airports and wildscapes. *Annals of Tourism Research* 80, 102791. https://doi.org/10.1016/j.annals.2019.102791.
Wattanacharoensil, W., Schuckert, M. and Graham, A. (2016) An airport experience framework from a tourism perspective. *Transport Reviews* 36 (3), 318–340. https://doi.org/10.1080/01441647.2015.1077287.
Wattanacharoensil, W., Schuckert, M., Graham, A. and Dean, A. (2017) An analysis of the airport experience from an air traveler perspective. *Journal of Hospitality and Tourism Management* 32, 124–135. http://dx:doi.org/10.1016/j.jhtm.2017.06.003.

3 Passenger–Passenger Interaction

Jennie Small

Introduction

> A tall, middle-aged airline passenger finds himself cramped in the dreaded center seat, 'E,' flanked by a heavy smoker on one side and a mother with a crying baby on the other. Trying to make himself as comfortable as possible, the passenger finds both armrests are already being used. The fan above his seat is broken and there's no room to cross his legs. Later while departing the plane, the disgruntled passenger snarls at the flight attendant when she asks, 'How was your flight?' (Martin & Pranter, 1989: 5)

Although smoking is no longer permitted on aeroplanes, much of the experience above will resonate with passengers today (at least those in the Economy section of the plane). The passenger's experience of air travel is not only the consequence of the duration of the flight, the comfort of the seats, the safety record of the airline, the quality of the meals and in-flight entertainment but also the interaction with those with whom the passenger shares the journey, both airline personnel and other passengers. Other passengers may comprise those familiar to us (our travel companion/s) or strangers, yet we know little about their influence on our comfort (Patel & D'Cruz, 2018). This chapter explores the practice of mobility with a focus on passenger-to-passenger behaviour and the ways in which other passengers (strangers) can affect our experience. On a plane, we share the space with those travelling to the same destination while at the airport we cross paths with many different airline groups. Before exploring the air travel experience, the chapter considers the concept of 'customer-to-customer interaction' from the position of the service sector. It then considers these interactions from a critical perspective incorporating the 'new mobilities' approach, thus extending our understanding of air travel as an embodied, affective experience in which the passenger interacts with the materialities of air travel.

Customer-to-Customer Interaction

Thirty years ago, Martin and Pranter (1989) published their seminal work on customer-to-customer relationships in service environments where they addressed a gap in the marketing and management literature: the overlooked role and influence of customers on the satisfaction or dissatisfaction of *other* customers in many service environments. Arguing that customers affect the experiences of other customers, they claimed: 'to a large extent other customers in the service environment *are* part of the service' (Martin & Pranter, 1989: 6). Whether interaction is direct or indirect, other customers are part of the scene. Previous disregard for the customer–customer relationship is thought to be due to the belief that the service provider could do nothing to enhance the compatibility amongst consumers, that these interactions were 'inevitable and uncontrollable' (Pranter & Martin, 1991: 44). Since then, service researchers have expanded on the idea of customer-to-customer interaction and consider the means by which providers can enhance and manage the relationship between customers.

Compatibility amongst consumers is considered by many to be the key to customer satisfaction, and the inverse, incompatibility, the key to dissatisfaction. Martin and Pranter (1989) identified characteristics which they considered relevant to compatibility, claiming that 'instances of extreme compatibility or incompatibility are almost always associated with services or environments that exhibit several of seven interrelated characteristics, although compatibility remains a relevant issue whenever at least one of these characteristics exists' (Martin & Pranter, 1989: 10). In their study of compatible and incompatible behaviours that consumers experience in the marketplace, the authors found that, while most consumers had no difficulty providing a specific list of dissatisfiers, identifying satisfiers was more challenging. It is clear that the understood rules (explicit or implicit) of appropriate customer behaviour in one service situation differ from those in other environments. Martin and Pranter (1989: 12) make the point that 'Behaviours are also situation-specific to the extent that they vary in frequency, duration, and association with other customer behaviors'. What might be considered acceptable or unacceptable behaviour is, additionally, culturally and individually specific. Martin (1995: 302) explains that 'the heart of the customer compatibility construct seems to rest in the individual's subjective interpretation and evaluation of other customers, regardless of the attendant behaviours'. Implied in satisfaction/dissatisfaction are varying degrees of personal tolerance and psychological comfort (Martin, 1995).

Service environments, including travel and tourism operations, vary in the extent to which customer-to-customer interaction is significant for positive customer experience and business success. For some businesses, interaction may be the core service. A coach tour, cruise, resort such as Club Med, facilitates and encourages interaction amongst its passengers/guests to enhance the experience of the users. Transport (such as air), less an attraction itself and more a means of transporting the passenger from A to B, is not in the business of encouraging positive interaction – however, it may want to discourage negative interaction. Air travel certainly has the potential for incompatible behaviour, exhibiting a number of (in)compatibility-relevant characteristics, as identified by Martin and Pranter (1989): customers are in close proximity to each other; the service environment attracts a heterogeneous customer mix; customers must occasionally wait for the service; and customers are expected to share time, space or service utensils with one another. The relevance of other characteristics: 'verbal interaction among customers is likely' and; 'customers are engaged in numerous and varied activities', may depend on the type of flight (such as long haul/short haul) and the passenger. Whether there is verbal interaction may depend on the chattiness of passengers or the necessity for assistance. While activities might not be as numerous and varied as in some other tourism environments, they are still evident in the flight experience in terms of the passenger who wants to sleep/read; look out the window/watch the movie; recline the seat/have legroom.

A Critical Approach

A critical approach expands our understanding of travelling with others. It directs us to view air travel as a corporeal, embodied experience as our body interacts with the materialities of air travel including other passenger bodies. Bissell (2010), with a focus on passenger mobilities, moves beyond vocal forms of communication amongst passengers to examine nonrepresentational modes of communication and comprehension – affective environments – 'a pull or a charge that might emerge in a particular space which might (or might not) generate particular events and actions, feelings and emotions' (2010: 273). In a group setting there can be, what Tarde (as cited in Thrift, 2008) refers to as, 'imitative contagion', a spread of feelings which are infectious 'through gesticulation, bodily movements, motor co-ordinations and repetitions, as well as all the technologies of the body that now exist' (Thrift, 2008: 231). While Bissell's (2010) study was focused on passengers in a railway carriage, his observations might equally apply to airline passengers. Viewing the practices and demeanour of proximate passengers can generate an affective atmosphere that primes the passenger to behave in a particular way. Depending on the stage of flight, the affective environment might change. Affects related to excitement and expectancy might characterise the space of the aircraft at take-off/landing/mealtime. The affective environment of an

18-hour flight may be different from that of a one-hour flight. Delays will also create a different affective environment. Describing the affective environment of a train making an unexpected stop, Bissell describes possible changes in the disposition of passengers. Negative affects borne out of frustration might appear through involuntary facial movements, raised eyebrows and pursed lips. Bissell (2010: 276) adds:

> This transmission of affect between bodies literally changes their biochemical properties: the release of adrenaline and particular neurotransmitters, tensed muscles, quickening heartbeat, the sinking feeling in the stomach, flushed face, beads of sweat forming on the forehead, all of which again change the capacity of the passenger to affect and be affected.

Going beyond conversational interaction to consider affective environments 'forces us to think through "the social" as not being reduced to or taken to be the product of particular individuals' (Bissell, 2010: 276). For those who are aggrieved by other passengers' behaviour, frustration is transmitted through contagion. As Hemmings (2005: 552) explains, 'It is transferred to others and doubles back, increasing its original intensity'. Bissell claims that responses are more complex than merely intrusion of personal space. 'Far from the formation of collectives, such events demonstrate the ability of affects to splinter and distance passengers' (Bissell, 2010: 279). According to Brennan (as cited in Bissell, 2010: 279) 'the act of directing negative affects to the other severs my kin tie with her by objectifying her. I make her into an object by directing these affects toward her, because the act marks her with affects that I reject in myself ... I assume that she does not feel as I do'. There are many anxieties associated with air travel and many sources of those anxieties that prompt passengers to behave in particular ways. For example, when it comes to body size of passengers, it is not only the physical intrusion of a larger sized person on a passenger's space that might cause anxiety but also the rhetoric in the West and the nonrepresentational messages about obesity that influence the passenger response.

Air Passenger-to-Passenger Interaction

Interaction between passengers, including airline passengers, may be positive and lead to satisfying experiences. Certainly, in other service environments this has been the case. As Harris and Baron (2004) found in their study of conversations between strangers on British trains, conversations can have a stabilising effect and reduce dissatisfaction by relieving passenger anxiety concerning the service, providing an opportunity for passengers to display their knowledge about the service and adding value through enjoyment to a service experience which might otherwise be boring. Pearce (2005) adopts Simmel's (1950) 'familiar stranger' concept (that person who is mentally recorded as sharing our space/experience) in explaining traveller–traveller relationships and the positive role this person can play. Employing an example of passengers on an international flight, Pearce identifies the benefits in being attentive to one's fellow passengers. They may provide guidance. Certainly, when exhausted and in transit and having to move from one Gate to another for an onward flight, awareness of fellow passengers can assist in navigation. They may also help one pass the time in conversation or be a source of help in times of trouble. Nonetheless, competing needs for space or resources or the exhibition of socially transgressive behaviour can create conflict. Most references to airline passenger-to-passenger interaction (albeit in the media) refer to dissatisfaction, born out of incompatibility associated with the heterogeneity of passengers.

Airline passengers differ from each other in numerous ways, many of which are relevant in a consideration of customer compatibility/incompatibility (Martin & Pranter, 1989). Passengers may have different preferences in how to pass the time while on the plane or they may differ in past experiences of flying, often giving rise 'to incompatible frames of reference' (Martin & Pranter, 1989: 11). They may have conflicting value systems, different perceptions of crowding and personal space and 'personality-related differences in traits such as generosity, self-consciousness, self-esteem and patience' (Martin & Pranter, 1989: 11). Demographic characteristics, such as age, gender, (Martin, 1996) or culture, may also differentiate customers in their satisfaction or dissatisfaction with other customers' behaviour. Nicholls (2005) identified physical characteristics of other customers as one situational factor which may intensify customer–customer interactions. Other barriers to compatibility may be prejudicial beliefs and attitudes to other groups of passengers. Aeroplanes and airports are for a large part, mixed-culture settings with consequent differences in values, expectations and attitudes to that which is considered appropriate behaviour in public settings. In a study of Polish passengers travelling in similar circumstances, Burrell (2011) found that, even while Polish ethnicity and migration status allowed for a collective identity to emerge, the passengers were markedly heterogeneous in what they considered appropriate passenger behaviour. There was much criticism by some of their fellow countrymen/women in terms of their drinking behaviour, pushing and shoving etc. especially during periods of waiting at the airport and onboard. While much of the research on customer-to-customer interaction has stressed the relationship between compatibility and satisfaction of customers, Nicholls (2019) draws attention to the evidence that, in some contexts, tourist dissimilarity can be a source of 'value added', yet this may be less relevant for air travellers.

Passenger-to-passenger interaction in air travel is a neglected area of academic research. What we know about interaction is mainly via the media and focused on passenger interaction (direct and indirect) with strangers. We know little about passenger-to-passenger interaction with our travel companions – partner, family, friends, sports groups etc. Reports on interaction tend to be post experience and outside the service setting.

Contested behaviours

While most passengers on planes are well mannered, there are a considerable number of reported undesirable incidents between passengers. Airline analyst, Robert Kokonis (Harris, 2017) believes that bad behaviour on planes has increased as air travel has become more commonplace – when flying is no longer a special occasion. As Small and Harris (2019) explain:

> The 'democratisation' of air travel has meant passengers have become more heterogeneous with the consequence that the 'etiquette' of air travel is often contested. In a confined space for sometimes up to 18 hours, passengers observe each other and interact, some transgressing what others consider socially appropriate behaviour.

The most concerning behaviours are drunkenness and disorderly behaviour which pose safety risks and are punishable by law. However, there are many other behaviours which transgress our unwritten codes of etiquette and, while less serious, are still annoying and distressing to other passengers and flight attendants who may have to address the behaviour. Bissell (2010) posits that while certain behaviours, such as a passenger smoking, are illegal, other behaviours, such as pressing the feet against the back of the seat, might actually generate more intense aggravation 'precisely because there might be less justification for retaliation' (2010: 281). He explains that, unless the passenger says something to the 'violator' and the behaviour ceases, the passenger may be in a permanent state of expectancy (and stress) waiting for the behaviour to start up again. He also adds that passenger annoyance may continue long after the event.

From an informal study of travel writers and frequent flyers by CNN (Busch, 2017) a list of annoying behaviours was compiled, commencing with the least to most irritating: 'Overhead bin abuse', 'taking ages to choose a movie', 'compulsive leg-shaking', 'boarding before group number is called', 'babies crying', 'getting huffy over bathroom visits', 'yapping on cell phone', 'scarfing smelly food', 'loud talking', 'establishing armrest hegemony', 'poaching the empty middle seat', 'coughing, sneezing, germ sharing', 'playing games without turning sound off', 'rolling huge suitcases up aisle', 'people behind you trying to disembark first', 'neglecting personal hygiene', 'bare feet', 'hogging the toilet', 'reclining the seat' and 'kicking/bumping/shoving the seat back'. In another investigation of 'worst flight passengers', Expedia (2018) describes its online survey as 'A deep dive into travel behavior from 35,000 feet to 350 square feet'. From its survey of 18,229 respondents across 23 countries, it similarly found the worst passenger to be 'The Seat Kicker/Bumper/Grabber' (51%). This was followed by 'The Aromatic Passenger' (43%), 'The Inattentive Parent' (39%), 'Personal Space Violators' (34%) and 'Audio Insensitive' (29%). In a study of personal space invasion, Lewis *et al.* (2017) found invasion could be a physical or sensory encroachment (noise, smells or eye contact) leading to feelings of annoyance, discomfort, irritation and anger and a variety of coping strategies, such as asking the person to stop, ignoring the situation, moving away, reclaiming the space, listening to music, watching a film, reading a book, sleeping or even offering to help as a means to improve the situation. Schaberg (2017: 59) argues that we should pay special attention to armrests. They are not minor partitions, 'never a simple matter of neutral ground; they are subtle barometers of power differentials ... They can become sites of passive aggression, intense contestation, and simmering wrath ...'.

Social media channels have become a popular means by which people can interact and express their views on air travel and those with whom they share that space. In 2013, one US flight attendant, annoyed by rude behaviour of some passengers, developed a blog which focused on shaming passengers (Harris, 2017). It quickly morphed into an Instagram site (passengershaming) which, by the start of 2021, had 1.3 million followers (passengershaming, 2021) and 511,880 followers on Facebook (Passenger Shaming, 2021). It even has its own merchandise store. These Facebook and Instagram sites were the focus of a study (Small & Harris, 2019) of socially transgressive behaviour posted over a six-month period (June to December 2018). Taking a discursive approach, the researchers identified the types of behaviours 'shamed' in the posts, the themes and categories and the number of comments each theme attracted. Taking the view that 'discourse builds objects, worlds, minds and social relations' (Wetherell *et al.*, 2001: 16), they considered how the Instagram and Facebook posts actively construct knowledge and social relations.

The underlying finding was that shameful behaviours were 'disgusting' or 'an insult to human dignity'. The cited behaviours included: placing dirty feet on the tray table or another passenger's seat, placing a child on a potty in the aisle, allowing children to draw on the tray table or wall of the plane, giving oneself a pedicure in flight and refusing to sit near an elderly woman of colour. Those posting the comments were offended both by the behaviour itself and the inherent sense of entitlement and disregard for fellow passengers exhibited by the 'perpetrator'. Public shaming allowed those posting to discipline and enforce cultural skills for 'appropriate' air travel behaviour. However, the researchers noted evidence of bullying, harassment and class distinction in the posts. They concluded:

> The posts while engaging in the rhetoric of criticism, are in fact complicit in maintaining a discourse that elevates the complainant whose 'rights' have been violated. A focus on the passengers in terms of 'violators' and 'violated' also serves to excuse the airline in failing to prevent or manage the violations. (Small & Harris, 2019)

Crying babies

While behaviours highlighted on Passenger Shaming sites may reflect the more extreme forms of bad behaviour, another behaviour that is often encountered on planes (and seen by many as annoying) is crying babies. To explore the public discourse on this topic, Small and Harris (2014) employed Critical Discourse Analysis (Fairclough, 1993) to review 1420 comments posted on newspaper and television online sites. Their analysis highlighted the contested nature of the issue: annoyance at being disturbed by crying babies (especially on long-haul flights) versus tolerance of the situation, with the dispute centred on the rights and responsibilities of passengers. The more tolerant position on crying babies held that all people (including families with babies) have a right to travel on planes (as public transport). Those distressed by crying babies were advised to use noise cancelling headphones or travel first class where they would be less likely to encounter babies/young children. Complaining passengers should 'put things into perspective':

> *It's a glorified bus travelling at 0.8 the speed of sound with an ambient noise level of around 100 decibels, not a night at the opera. Get over yourself...* (as cited in Small & Harris, 2014: 34)

Some posts appealed for sympathy for the parents.

> *Can you actually not see the embarrassment and pain on the parents' faces as they try to calm the little ones? Poor kids, having to fly. And poor parents, having to endure the horrible stares and total lack of empathy...* (as cited in Small & Harris, 2014: 33)

Commiseration for the parents was absent in the less tolerant comments; parents were seen as *the source* of the problem for not attending to and managing the situation. As the 2018 Expedia survey had found, 'The Inattentive Parent' was third on its list of 'worst flight passengers'.

> *It is so frustrating when you have to sit and watch the ineptitude of some of the parents. Some of them just don't have a clue and my heart goes out to the child. It is the parents who need a good slap.* (as cited in Small & Harris, 2014: 31)

The discourse exposed the aeroplane as a microcosm of today's Western individual-based, neoliberal society. Indeed, in the confines of the plane societal attitudes could be magnified. Inherent in the discourse were those familiar judgements and criticisms of parenting today (Cui et al., 2019) as too child-focused, permissive, entitled and favouring the individual as opposed to the collective. The comments also questioned the suitability of air travel for the baby. Parents of today were compared with those of previous generations who, out of consideration for others, would manage their children or even forego their air travel. Today's parents were seen as less thoughtful.

> ... the parents, do not want to be limited in their plans and movements by the fact that they have a child. So it's a loud me! me! me! by the parents, and the child comes a distant second, where everybody else's [other passengers'] concerns do not rate at all. The self-absorption of this generation of parents knows no bounds. (as cited in Small & Harris, 2014: 32)

However, comments were less critical when parents at least *appeared* to attend to the child, thus demonstrating some consideration for fellow passengers.

> ... At least show others that you make effort... My empathy will surely follow if you have done all you can and the baby [is] still crying. Show a courtesy to others, have an apologetic look rather than just staring & challenging at other annoyed passengers... (as cited in Small & Harris, 2014: 32)

Even those comments that endorsed the right of parents to travel with an infant were not without conditions. The needs of other passengers must be respected. This might mean not travelling First or Business Class – privileged spaces where the occupants were seen as having more rights than others (such as families with babies).

The general stress of travel for parents (Backer & Schänzel, 2012; Small, 2005) can be exacerbated by air travel. The close proximity of passenger to passenger means that passengers are under the observation of others – what is private becomes public. Inability to avoid surveillance and the disciplinary gaze can be difficult for parents. The findings from a Gatwick Airport study (Traveller.com.au, 2011) highlight the power of the gaze on travelling families.

> More than half of parents have been made to feel bad when their child cries or misbehaves on holiday, and four in ten have found themselves on the receiving end of 'evil stares' from other holidaymakers... In addition, children misbehaving or crying when on the plane scares parents the most, with 62 per cent admitting this is the part of travelling they fear above all else.

As Sedgley *et al.* (2017) found, travelling with a child on the autistic spectrum can be particularly challenging for parents.

Prevalent in the online comments analysed by Small and Harris (2014) were many suggestions to address the issue of crying babies: from parental management of the situation (give the baby something to suck, administer drugs, distract the infant or bribe the older infant/child), to airline management (establish family-only flights or separate, soundproofed areas for families with children). In a recent study of 4000 travellers by Airfarewatchdog (Matousek, 2018), more than half felt that families with children under the age of 10 years should be required to sit in a separate section of the plane. Indeed, the response from some international Asian airlines including Malaysia Airlines, AirAsia, Scoot Airlines and IndiGo was the introduction of a 'child-free' zone.

Yet, the silence from most airlines on the issue of crying babies maintains the image of an 'aeroplane as a luxury, privileged space which is harmonious and unproblematic' (Small & Harris, 2014: 37). Since the airlines do not compensate passengers disturbed by babies and children's behaviour, Judge (2011) argues that the airline authorities and cabin crew are 'complicit in the antisocial behaviour of the "perpetrators"' (Judge, 2011: 5). Judge (2011) suggests a range of measures that a responsible airline could take: relocation of passengers, provision of noise-cancelling headphones, guidelines (when checking in, boarding or seated), use of air points as reward or punishment, 'noise detectors' of disruptive noise and interactive social media empowering passengers during the flight to voice their feelings about the disruption. Other means by which airlines could assist parents would be the provision of information on ways of dealing with a crying child and extra assistance in the travel process. The steps taken by some Middle Eastern airlines to introduce Sky Nannies/Flying Nannies is one means of addressing some of the problems faced by parents on planes. However, while it is left to passengers to manage the situation, the underlying message of the discourse is a plea for consideration and respect for the collective: for parents to make an effort to silence their child and for other passengers to recognise that this is public transport.

Passenger size – obesity

Fourth on Expedia's (2018) survey list of 'worst flight passengers' was 'Personal Space Violators'. Violation can occur when a passenger takes up 'too much' space in the overhead luggage bin or intrudes on another passenger's seating space. With allocated space limited (especially in Economy Class), passengers may fiercely defend their space. In recent years, the size of passengers has made headlines, raising issues over policies for the transport of overweight/obese passengers, such as weighing passengers or requiring passengers to purchase two seats. According to the World Health Organization (2020), 'In 2016, more than 1.9 billion adults, 18 years and older, were overweight. Of these over 650 million were obese'. Since 1975, world obesity has nearly tripled. At the same time, aircraft seat size is not increasing. Despite this rising issue, obesity has been a neglected topic in travel and tourism studies. Two exceptions are the research by Small and Harris (2012) and Poria and Beal (2017) on passenger obesity and air travel. Underlying both studies was the principle of inclusion; the assumption that everyone has a right to travel. Both studies took a qualitative approach with Poria and Beal (2017) studying passenger experience through in-depth interview with self-identified obese people while Small and Harris (2012) used Critical Discourse Analysis to examine online comments on eleven web and blog sites focused on obesity and air travel. The findings of both studies highlight the problem of seat size and ensuing physical discomfort for larger passengers. Cited in Small and Harris (2012: 694) was the comment below from one larger passenger:

> *I love to travel ... But being obese does rob me of some of that joy ... Airplane seats are notoriously narrow. Flying Delta is downright painful. And even if I do get my giant ass wedged in between the armrests, there's the matter of the seat belt.*

Negotiating the aisle and toilets were also found to present physical difficulties for obese passengers as was opening the tray table, especially for women with larger breasts (Poria & Beal, 2017).

Both studies concluded that, while physical features of the aircraft could lead to bodily discomfort, most of the discomfort experienced was psychological, a consequence of the social environment. Under the gaze of other passengers, the obese passengers experienced shame, embarrassment and humiliation as they interpreted the meaning of the gaze.

> *... one of the things [about air travel] I hate the most is... The Walk of Shame! – It's exactly like it sounds. When I get on the plane... I have to make the walk to my seat in complete shame. Everyone is already seated and watching as I maneuver* [sic] *my way past every seat ... just about everyone is hoping that I'm not going to sit next to them!* (as cited in Small & Harris, 2012: 694)

Both studies reported passenger embarrassment if a seat belt extender was required, especially when the belt was bright yellow in colour (Small & Harris, 2012). Discreet and respectful treatment by flight attendants could go some way to alleviating the unpleasant experience for the larger passenger. Other factors which could moderate an otherwise unpleasant air travel experience were: shorter-haul flights (inconvenience to others was minimised as was use of toilet and tray table), a direct flight (the need to walk a distance or rush for a connecting flight was avoided) and being seated next to an empty seat (both physical discomfort and embarrassment were lessened) (Poria & Beal, 2017).

Analysis of the online discourse (Small & Harris, 2012) found that some travellers who were overweight/obese chose to buy two seats in order to travel in comfort. However, not all could afford to do so or resented the need to purchase the second seat. Some had no choice in the matter; the airline required it. Further strategies to minimise discomfort of obese passengers, by avoiding the gaze of other passengers, were reported by Poria and Beal (2017): boarding first and deplaning last, sitting at the back of the plane, bringing a snack to get around the need for the tray table and not drinking in order to avoid using the toilet.

Small and Harris (2012) found in their analysis of the website discourse that despite the difficulties for overweight/obese passengers, the loudest complaints about travel and obesity emerged from passengers who were *not* overweight/obese. They, too, felt they were physically impacted – by reduced seat space – when sitting next to a larger passenger. Their emotional response was anger and disgust towards the overweight/obese passenger for 'invading' their personal space and thus impacting on their comfort and right to the airline seat for which they had paid.

> *I think my rights were violated. I had to fly in the middle seat next to someone who was probably 500 lbs... the woman could not put the armrest down, she took up a good portion of my seat... she was touching me (from shoulder to toe), but worst of all her arm and shoulder were resting on me. I couldn't get out of the seat because she couldn't get up without help. I pay for a whole seat and I don't think it's fair that a large person beside me pays the same amount but uses a bit of my seat as well when the fat spills over... I'm not against large people but I don't sit in their seat. Why should they sit in mine.* (as cited in Small & Harris, 2012: 695)

The association of larger bodies with sweatiness and smell was evident in the online discourse: '*I don't want my thighs and arms to have to touch some gigantic person who's sweaty. YUCK!*' (as cited in Small & Harris, 2012: 695). The online comments also associated overweight/obese passengers with safety concerns in the event of an emergency evacuation or when armrests were raised to accommodate the passenger's larger size. Questions of fairness underpinned the comments concerning weight of luggage versus weight of passenger.

> *If I can't use my lack of body weight to off set some Luggage weight then yes I am all for 'pay by the pound' travellers.* (as cited in Small & Harris, 2012: 695)

Small and Harris (2012) found that negative feelings were exacerbated if the flight were long, the ticket price high or obesity seen as a matter of choice. While there was some recognition that people who were tall or broad shouldered could also impinge on others' space, hostility was not directed at them. When it came to the question of who was responsible for the problem, opinion was divided: the 'thin' passenger (who should 'get over it'), the obese passenger (who should travel business/first class or buy two economy seats) or the airline (which should increase the seat size, weigh passengers with luggage or require larger passengers to purchase two seats).

Much of the debate here and views expressed reflect that of contemporary Western society in relation to the body and its size – the degradation of fatness. While one can understand that the smaller body would wish to receive the full product/seat for which they paid, the discourse often moved beyond 'entitlement to space' to expose stigma, prejudice and disgust towards the overweight/obese body that was not evident when other bodies (broad shouldered or tall) encroached on seat space. The message is that the passenger does not want to be *touched* by an overweight/ obese body. Clearly, it is not just the physical dimension of size which is relevant here but the socially constructed meaning of size in contemporary neoliberal societies. A study of reactions to obesity (Vartanian, 2010) similarly identified others' disgust response. Vartanian (2010) offers two explanations. One relates to the perceived association of obesity and lack of hygiene and disease related concepts (Puhl & Brownell, 2001). The other relates to the breach of today's moral value for the 'thin ideal'. Poria and Beal (2017), from their interviews of the flight experiences of American obese passengers, offer a further explanation for society's stigma: the perceived association of obesity and financial exploitation. They explain: obesity leads to unemployment and it is the taxes of the non-obese in society which pay the unemployment benefits in addition to health insurance and medical treatment. As the body of media research indicates, the dominant individualising framings of obesity emphasise personal responsibility and self-control (Atanasova & Koteyko, 2017). Such representations of obesity in neoliberal society contribute to the aversion response.

While airlines are quiet on the issue with few stated policies, the matter clearly requires addressing as populations increase in body size. Lack of space raises health and safety questions for all passengers, especially when the flight is long haul. Cases of litigation have occurred in the United States and United Kingdom and the potential for more remains. Mobility justice demands that all passengers are made to feel welcome, not subjected to feelings of stigma and shame nor subjected to physically unsafe and uncomfortable seating space. According to Small and Harris (2014), if social justice concerns do not persuade the airlines to reconsider the needs of overweight/obese passengers in terms of facilities (such as seats, toilets, tray tables, airport carts) and procedures (for example, boarding and seat allocation – window or aisle, front or back of plane), then perhaps the economic value of this growing market could prompt them into action.

Companion animals

While not yet appearing in the above cited lists of annoying behaviours, an emerging debate, and one that is becoming an issue between passengers, surrounds the carriage of animals on planes. The problem is not so much with 'service animals' (trained to assist a passenger with a disability), but rather 'emotional support animals' which require no training. Although such animals have the benefit of providing comfort and companionship to their owner in flight, the arguments against their carriage in the cabin concern other passengers – stress, allergy and further health and hygiene issues. Safety is an issue with reports of other passengers having been bitten by emotional support animals. And, for those with a genuine service animal, 'Many resent their work animals being lumped in with emotional support animals, whom they consider poseurs' (Calder, 2018). There is also the argument that it is unethical to take emotional support animals on a plane as flying can cause stress in those animals untrained for flying (Calder, 2018). The recent surge in the number of passengers wanting to take an emotional support animal in the cabin of the plane (a 77% increase in one year for United Airlines; see Calder, 2018) has led the airlines to develop policies to restrict animals, especially when passengers have used the guise of 'emotional support animal' to bring their pet on board. Many have argued that the situation has got out of hand especially when the animal has been a peacock or a goat. The CEO of United Airlines, Oscar Munoz, reported the case where a passenger had brought a support animal for an emotional support animal! (Brandt, 2018). However, a rule change by the US Department of Transportation in December 2020 has determined that US airlines will no longer be required to transport emotional support animals and only dogs qualify as service animals. As Association of Flight Attendants President, Sara Nelson, said, 'The days of Noah's Ark in the air are hopefully coming to an end' (BBC News, 2020).

To understand the debate about animals on planes requires an appreciation of the changing nature of the relationship of humans and animals in the West where pets are treated more and more like humans. For many, pets (especially dogs) have become an integral member of the family (Carr, 2017) accompanying their owner in their leisure travel. With increasing societal focus on mental health and the role animals can play in human health, the issue of companion animals on planes becomes complicated. Once again, rights become contested between those who wish to travel with an animal and those who object, for any number of reasons, to animals on aircraft.

In addition, the rights of the animal become part of the discussion. Carr (2014: 138) considers the emerging focus on the 'rights and welfare of dogs based on their existence as sentient beings rather than as objects'. Here, we see different arguments about animal rights: on the one hand, the right to be a companion, not a pet and, on the other hand, the right of the animal to escape the reported discomfort/trauma of flying.

While the passenger behaviours discussed above, such as crying babies, space intrusion and companion animals, may be annoying (or unhealthy), there are other behaviours that are disruptive, dangerous, threaten flight safety and carry legal consequences.

Air rage

Air rage is defined variously but the basic understanding is reflected in the Cambridge English Dictionary's definition: 'Sudden angry and violent behaviour by a passenger on an aircraft during a flight' (air rage, n.d.a). Other definitions identify the target of the rage (other passengers or airline employees) or the safety implications for others onboard, while the Oxford English Dictionary refers to the cause: 'provoked in a passenger on board an aircraft by the stress associated with air travel' (air rage, n.d.b). Thought to be coined in the 1990s by the news media (Hunter, 2016), the concept of air rage makes for 'good' media stories as evident in the headline: 'Gin-crazed mum punched stewardess and bit plane passenger who tried to stop her after downing bottle of Bombay Sapphire' (Cox, 2017). Broader terms for unacceptable behaviour are Disruptive Airline Passenger Behaviour (DAPB) and Unruly Passenger Behaviour (UPB) which may include behaviours that are not violent but still interfere with passengers and crew. The International Air Transport Association (IATA) (2019) describes three levels of unacceptable passenger behaviour.

> Level 1: Disruptive behaviors which are mainly verbal in nature such as failure to follow crew instructions or violation of a safety regulation...
>
> Level 2: Physically abusive or obscene behaviors, verbal threats of physical violence, tampering with emergency or safety equipment...
>
> Level 3 and 4: Life-threatening behavior or attempt to breach cockpit door.

McLinton *et al.* (2020: 34) cite the issues that 'bedevil the accuracy of DAPB estimates' – under-reporting, selective reporting and the adequacy of staff training and reporting mechanisms. As stated by Timmis *et al.* (2018), there is no globally comprehensive single-source database for the reporting of disruptive passenger behaviour. The most comprehensive dataset is that collected by IATA, yet not all airlines are represented. IATA (2019) reported 8731 unruly passenger incidents on board aircraft in 2017, a small decrease from the previous three years. Nonetheless, the issue is seen as significant with an increase in the absolute number of DAPB incidents over the last decades with the most common DAPB incident being verbal abuse, followed by physical abuse (McLinton *et al.*, 2020). While the proportion of more serious incidents is small, there is some debate as to whether such numbers are increasing (Bradley, 2017; IATA 2019) or are stable (McLinton *et al.*, 2020). A major Australian airline estimated it dealt with approximately 30 unruly passenger incidents per month (Goldsmid *et al.*, 2016). 'The severity of these incidents varied; they included cases of onboard smoking, failure to comply with instructions, failure to fasten seatbelts, intoxication, and offensive and disorderly conduct' (Goldsmid *et al.*, 2016: 1). As IATA (2019) explains,

> Unruly passengers are a small minority but their actions can have a disproportionate impact on others. Other flyers can have their journey disturbed and inconvenienced as a result of delays, missed connections and diversions. This can impact holidays and important business meetings.

Witnessing unruly behaviour, especially when it escalates to air rage, can make other passengers fear for their own safety; once airborne there is no means of escaping the situation.

IATA (2019) confirms that passenger alcohol and drug use is one of the main issues with consumption occurring 'prior to boarding or onboard from their own supply without knowledge of the crew'. In their review of the academic DAPB research from 1985 to 2020, McLinton *et al.* (2020: 38) conclude that 'the most commonly attributed causes of DAPB are alcohol … and illegal smoking, medications and drugs, and poor customer service' (see Hunter, 2006). Other reported causes of DAHB are passenger characteristics, changes in travel mores, airport stressors, such as waiting and flight delays (see DeCelles *et al.*, 2019) and stressors once onboard. Onboard stressors, such as invasion of personal space due to shrinking seat size and legroom in Economy (Whitley & Gross, 2019) (as discussed in the section *Passenger size – obesity*), may incite anger and action against the passenger (Vredenburgh *et al.*, 2015). However, Tsang *et al.* (2018) report differences amongst passengers in their acceptance of Unruly Passenger Behaviour, for example, when it came to personal space intrusion, Asian passengers were found to be more tolerant than non-Asian passengers. A study by DeCelles and Norton (2016) published in the *Proceedings of the National Academy of Sciences* (and later contested by Crede *et al.*, 2016 and Giner-Sorolla, 2016) suggests an antecedent of air rage is 'status inequality', experienced by passengers when there is a first-class section on a plane. They explain:

> the modern airplane reflects a social microcosm of class-based society, making inequality salient to passengers through both the physical design of the plane (the presence of a first class cabin) and, more subtly, the boarding procedure (whether economy passengers must pass through the first class cabin).

To investigate how the public attributes meaning to air rage, Small and Harris (2018) examined public reaction (365 responses) to a 2017 online media article on air rage in *The Washington Post* ('Air rage incidents are on the rise. First-class sections aren't helping'). Along with more traditional explanations for air rage, the article introduced the aforementioned 'status inequality' as a possible trigger. Small and Harris found that the majority of public comments associated air rage with the stress of air travel. In a number of comments, other passengers were considered a factor contributing to passenger stress through intrusion on space whether that be overhead locker space or seat space by larger passengers. Passenger status inequality was identified by some as an explanation. In other comments, blame was squarely attributed to the raging passenger for their lack of emotional self-control. However, there was little mention of alcohol consumption that other sources have identified as an antecedent of air rage. Included in the comments was advice to the travelling public as to how to avoid a stressful situation – 'travel first class'; 'take an analgesic, eye mask, headphones etc.' with the warning, 'you get what you pay for'.

While many comments saw responsibility for air rage as residing with the individual, others referred to air rage as a social problem; the behaviour was symptomatic of broader society that was declining in civility. In many ways, the findings confirmed those from previously cited studies. The airline industry featured prominently in the public comments as the trigger for air rage. The basis of the rhetoric was airline 'greed', exemplified in the treatment of passengers (notably, Economy passengers), particularly in regard to the physical environment of the plane: the on-board crowding, small seat size, restricted legroom and resulting discomfort. Comments on limited space also extended to the overhead bins. Criticism was directed at the practice of charging passengers for every service and the stressful check-in and boarding procedures. Unfriendly service and perceived over-reaction to passenger 'incidents' by flight attendants and other airline staff were also seen as contributory factors to air rage.

The focus of this chapter is passenger–passenger interaction, but it must not be forgotten that air rage also has an impact on the air crew. Dahlberg (2001: xii) refers to air rage as 'a form of workplace violence'. As Hu *et al.* (2017) state, passengers' misbehaviour can 'transform cabin crew from service providers into authority figures, increasing their stress levels and even leading to emotional exhaustion' (2017: 1794), which can impact on their job performance, reduce job satisfaction and exacerbate the prospects of resignation. It can become a vicious cycle. The causes of air rage are multi-faceted but one thing is clear, an understanding of the practice of air rage and its effect on others requires us to consider the materialities of the modern aircraft, airline procedures and service, as well as the sense of entitlement of some passengers within today's competitive, neoliberal environment. An understanding of the discourse on air travel is also warranted. Certainly, incidents of air rage highlight a gap between the experience of air travel and its representation by the airlines as a safe, comfortable means of travel.

Discussion and Conclusion

As Grove and Fisk (1997: 87) observe, 'Few problems are more significant than the problem of "getting along" with other people'. The unique environment of an aeroplane with a heterogeneous group of customers in a confined space at 35,000 feet means conditions are ripe for passenger conflict and stress, with behaviours, that might be ignored and insignificant in other environments, becoming problematic in the air. This chapter shows how passengers affect and are affected by the other passengers with whom they share the air-travel space. In doing so, it confirms that air travel is not simply movement, '"dead time" in which nothing happens' (Cresswell, 2010: 18), but rather is imbued with complex meaning.

The chapter has taken a critical approach exposing the discourse/ideologies which shape the meaning of the passenger experience. While the passenger in flight may feel cocooned and disconnected from their home environment, this does not mean that social relations from home are put on hold. There are blurred boundaries between our flying practices and our non-flying practices. Along with their everyday objects and home routines, airline passengers also bring their constructions of social relations. To grasp the experience of passenger-to-passenger interaction, as reported in this chapter, requires an understanding of changing societal discourses on personal space, parenting, obesity, health and beauty, hygiene, violence and human/animal relationships etc. These discourses intersect with those of air travel as a form of transport. Even here, there is no singular discourse. The lingering discourses and imaginations from the past which position air travel as luxurious, glamorous and elite collide with the contemporary discourse of air travel as a democratised space and 'just another mode of public transport'. How one views that space affects perceptions of entitlement to that space. Central to the passenger discussion is the moral question of rights: the rights of the individual passenger (the focus of neoliberal societies) versus those of the collective (Small & Harris, 2014). Associated with rights is a consideration of responsibilities and the personal characteristics of an individual, such as discipline and self-respect, believed necessary to be a responsible member of the passenger collective. Through their moral judgements, passengers were often seen to differentiate themselves from other passengers. As Brennan (as cited in Bissell, 2010) explains, when we direct negative comments, we objectify the other with the result that we sever ties. Central to the discourse was the perceived cultural change in the morality of others in the 21st century.

However, we need to go beyond a discursive approach to understand the passenger experience. The material reality of the aircraft cannot be ignored: the physical size of the seats, the ambient temperature, the lighting. Certainly, sufficient passenger space is a critical factor affecting comfort/discomfort. This is particularly critical for passengers who are obese where insufficient space can have serious health effects, and prevent efficient evacuation, the consequences of which can be fatal for both obese and non-obese passengers. Ergonomic design intersects with passenger behaviour. Nicholls (2010: 94) provides an example of the use of the overhead locker: 'an air passenger loading hand-luggage into a plane's overhead locker will have a different ergonomic experience depending on whether a co-passenger has folded their coat or laid it out across the entire locker'. The studies reported in this chapter confirm that air travel is an embodied experience. Passenger-to-passenger interaction is about the interaction of bodies. Through our senses we experience the crying baby or the smelly passenger or the touch of the larger body. The discourse/ideologies shape the meaning of our embodied experience in this material context (and, in turn, is itself shaped by our embodiment). We see that passengers are not merely passive consumers of discourse. They are not just consuming places (airports and aircraft) but also actively producing them in their interaction with others. Also, through the performance of making their voices heard (the posting of comments, circulating tales and photographs) they become producers reframing the passenger experience through generating, reinforcing and violating certain myths about the air travel experience (Haldrup & Larsen, 2010).

In sum, the sociality of mobilities is more than discourse; affective atmospheres emerge 'through the complex interplay of technologies, matter, and bodies' (Bissell, 2010: 284). Affective modulations and their force transcend individual bodies taking 'the onus of responsibility and primary ethical agency away from individual passengers towards a more collective rendering of responsibility that envelops humans and non-humans within the emergence of affective atmospheres' (Bissell, 2010: 286). Although Bissell was discussing rail travel, the same can be said for those in the air as passengers turn to gaze at the parents of the crying baby or the obese passenger making their way down the aisle, or move away from the dirty feet placed on the bulkhead.

Airports and aircraft are recognised as spaces of surveillance and discipline, an 'environment of "authorities"' (Kellerman, 2008: 161) with passengers subject to international, national and industry laws and regulations. Yet, surveillance and discipline are not limited to the immigration or security officer at the airport or the cabin crew onboard but, as the above examples indicate, extend to the other passengers with whom the space is shared. The words and behaviour (and *imagined* gaze) of other passengers can be just as powerful in disciplining and affecting passenger experience. Power relations are complex in the air travel space; it is not always clear with whom the power lies. For example, in the debate concerning overweight/obese passengers, does the power reside with the larger passenger 'impinging' on the neighbouring passenger, the thin (but indignant) adjacent passenger, surrounding passengers through their gaze, the flight attendant providing the seat belt extender or the airline in its design of the aircraft cabin? We can think of power as imminent, everywhere and relational with opportunities for resistance (Small & Harris, 2014) as indicated in the issues discussed. Bissell recognises that any collective rendering of responsibility does not absolve the passenger. These are spaces of negotiation 'with the capacity to redraw our ethical orientation, and potentially enhance our affective capacities' (Bissell, 2010: 286).

Yet, neither should the airline be absolved. Reflective of today's neoliberal practice, the findings above highlight the individualisation of responsibility, with passengers often having to manage the issues themselves. The airlines, too, have responsibilities in managing interactions between passengers. Although there are certainly airline policies and crew who enforce behaviours in the interests of collective comfort, the many passenger complaints reflect the view that the airlines need to do more. Intervention might involve segregation of passengers (such as families with infants or children), amended boarding/deplaning procedures, increased staff training and education of passengers. The internal design of the cabin – restricted legroom and diminishing size of airline seats – often featured as the perceived cause for passenger–passenger conflict. Yet, it is unlikely that airlines will be open to making spatial changes which will satisfy the Economy passenger. As Sloterdijk (as cited in Thrift, 2006) claims, the challenge for designers of planes and those who manage passenger behaviour is to create spaces with good 'ventilation', which, at the least, aims for, 'new maps of getting on together' (Thrift, 2006: 194).

This chapter has focused on the interactions of air passengers who are strangers. It would also be worth exploring relations between travel companions (family and friends) as they, too, contribute to the passenger's flight experience. The accounts reported here have highlighted conflict between passengers in terms of 'getting along'; further research could investigate the more favourable experiences of passenger–passenger contact. Another suggestion for future research would be the inclusion of voices other than English-speaking passengers/ commentators since air travel, especially international travel, is a 'mixed culture setting' (Nicholls, 2010: 93). In investigating the passenger– passenger experience, a critical approach has exposed discourses underlying the passenger experience of air travel and highlighted concepts related to rights and responsibilities, power and resistance, inclusion and exclusion which in turn raise questions of social justice. The circulating discourses (affirmed and contested), materiality of the aircraft, and embodied experiences of passengers affect not only *who* travels but also how the travel is experienced. The evidence suggests that passenger-to-passenger behaviour is fundamental to how air travel is experienced and that passengers expect the industry to play a role in managing this relationship.

Acknowledgement

My thanks go to Candice Harris for her contribution and co-authorship of publications on air passengers' relations with their fellow travellers.

References

air rage (n.d.a) *Cambridge Advanced Learner's Dictionary & Thesaurus*. See https:// dictionary.cambridge.org/dictionary/english/air-rage (accessed August 2019).
air rage (n.d.b) *English Oxford Dictionary*. See https://en.oxforddictionaries.com/ definition/air_rage (accessed November 2017).
Atanasova, D. and Koteyko, N. (2017) Obesity frames and counter-frames in British and German online newspapers. *Health* 21 (6), 650–669. https://doi.org/10.1177/ 1363459316649764.
Backer, E. and Schänzel, H. (2012) The stress of the family holiday. In H. Schanzel, I. Yeoman and E. Backer (eds) *Family Tourism: Multidisciplinary Perspectives* (pp. 105–124). Bristol: Channel View Publications.
BBC News (2020) US ends era of emotional support animals on planes, BBC News, 3 December. See https://www.bbc.com/news/world-us-canada-55177736 (accessed January 2021).
Bissell, D. (2010) Passenger mobilities: Affective atmospheres and the sociality of public transport. *Environment and Planning D: Society and Space* 28, 270–289. https://doi. org/10.1068/d3909.
Bradley, G. (2017) Fewer plane passengers behaving badly - but their antics getting worse, NZ Herald, 6 December. See https://www.nzherald.co.nz/business/fewer-plane-passengers-behaving-badly-but-their-antics-getting-worse/DOUCE6YNAYPZP6SVOMF72X52O4/ (accessed December 2017).
Brandt, S. (2018) Airlines crack down on emotional support animals in plane cabins, *ABC News*, 25 July. See https://abcnews.go.com/US/airlines-crack-emotional-support-animals-plane-cabins/story?id=56791124 (accessed March 2019).

Burrell, K. (2011) Going steerage on Ryanair: Cultures of migrant air travel between Poland and the UK. *Journal of Transport Geography* 19, 1023–1030. https://doi.org/10.1016/j.jtrangeo.2010.09.004.

Busch, S. (2017) 20 most rude and annoying things passengers do on planes, *CNN travel*, 4 May. See https://edition.cnn.com/travel/article/plane-annoying-things/index.html (accessed April 2019).

Calder, C. (2018) Flying with emotional support animals: The ups and downs of life in coach, *The Conversation*, 14 May. See https://theconversation.com/flying-with-emotional-support-animals-the-ups-and-downs-of-life-in-coach-102022 (accessed March 2019).

Carr, N. (2014) *Dogs in the Leisure Experience*. Wallingford, Oxfordshire: CABI.

Carr, N. (2017) Recognising the position of the pet dog in tourism. *Annals of Tourism Research* 62, 112–113. http://dx.doi.org/10.1016/j.annals.2016.10.011.

Cox, C. (2017) Gin-crazed mum punched stewardess and bit plane passenger who tried to stop her after downing bottle of Bombay Sapphire, *Mirror*, 19 December. See https://www.mirror.co.uk/news/uk-news/mum-kicked-plane-after-guzzled-11457177 (accessed November 2020).

Crede, M., Gelman, A. and Nickerson, C. (2016) Questionable association between front boarding and air rage. *Proceedings of the National Academy of Sciences* 113 (47), E7348. https://doi.org/10.1073/pnas.1611704113.

Cresswell, T. (2010) Towards a politics of mobility. *Environment and Planning D* 28, 17–31. https://doi.org/10.1068/d11407.

Cui, M., Graber, J., Metz, A. and Darling, C. (2019) Parental indulgence, self-regulation, and young adults' behavioral and emotional problems. *Journal of Family Studies* 25 (3), 233–249. https://doi.org/10.1080/13229400.2016.1237884.

Dahlberg, A. (2001) *Air Rage: The Underestimated Safety Risk*. Aldershot: Ashgate.

DeCelles, K., DeVoe, S., Rafaeli, A. and Agasi, S. (2019) Helping to reduce fights before flights: How environmental stressors in organizations shape customer emotions and customer–employee interactions. *Personnel Psychology* 72, 49–80. https://doi.org/10.1111/peps.12292.

DeCelles, K.A. and Norton, M.I. (2016) Physical and situational inequality on airplanes predicts air rage. *Proceedings of the National Academy of Sciences* 113 (20), 5588–5591. https://doi.org/10.1073/pnas.1521727113.

Expedia.com (2018) Expedia's airplane + hotel etiquette study reveals the latest in travel annoyances, *Expedia* website, 30 April. See https://newsroom.expedia.com/2018-04-30-Expedias-Airplane-Hotel-Etiquette-Study-Reveals-the-Latest-in-Travel-Annoyances (accessed April 2019).

Fairclough, N. (1993) *Discourse and Social Change*. Cambridge: Polity Press.

Giner-Sorolla, R. (2016) Linear controls are not enough to account for multiplicative confound effects on air rage. *Proceedings of the National Academy of Sciences* 113 (29), E4119. https://doi.org/10.1073/pnas.1607914113.

Goldsmid, S., Fuller, G., Coghian, S. and Brown, R. (2016) Responding to unruly airline passengers: The Australian context. *Trends & Issues in Crime and Criminal Justice* (510). Canberra: Australian Institute of Criminology. https://www.aic.gov.au/publications/tandi/tandi510.

Grove, S. and Fisk, R. (1997) The impact of other customers on service experiences: A critical incident examination of 'getting along'. *Journal of Retailing* 73 (1), 63–85.

Haldrup, M. and Larsen, J. (2010) *Tourism, Performance and the Everyday: Consuming the Orient*. London: Routledge.

Harris, S. (2017) Passenger shaming website highlights bad behaviour on planes, *CBC News*, 3 September. See https://www.cbc.ca/news/business/passengershaming-airlines-bad-behaviour-1.4270812 (accessed March 2019).

Harris, K. and Baron, S. (2004) Consumer-to-consumer conversations in service settings. *Journal of Service Research* 6 (3), 287–303. https://doi.org/10.1177/1094670503260132.

Hemmings, C. (2005) Invoking affect. *Cultural Studies* 19 (5), 548–567. https://doi.org/10.1080/09502380500365473.

Hu, H., Hu, H. and King, B. (2017) Impacts of misbehaving air passengers on frontline employees: Role stress and emotional labor. *International Journal of Contemporary Hospitality Management* 29 (7), 1793–1813. https://doi.org/10.1108/IJCHM-09-2015-0457.

Hunter, J.A. (2006) A correlational study of how airline customer service and consumer perception of airline customer service affect the air rage phenomenon. *Journal of Air Transportation* 11 (3), 78–109.

Hunter, J.A. (2016) *Anger in the Air: Combating the Air Rage Phenomenon.* Abingdon, Oxon: Routledge.

International Air Transport Association (IATA) (2019) *Unruly passengers.* See https://www.iata.org/contentassets/b7efd7f114b44a30b9cf1ade59a02f06/unruly_pax_infographic_2017.pdf (accessed October 2020).

Judge, A. (2011) Guidelines in response to degrees of anti-social behaviour: Airline passengers and children as a case study. See http://kairos.laetusinpraesens.org/restkids_m_h_7 (accessed July 2013).

Kellerman, A. (2008) International airports: Passengers in an environment of 'authorities'. *Mobilities* 3 (1) 161–178. https://doi.org/10.1080/17450100701797406.

Lewis, L., Patel, H., D'Cruz, M. and Cobb, S. (2017) What makes a space invader? Passenger perceptions of personal space invasion in aircraft travel. *Ergonomics* 60 (11), 1461–1470. https://doi.org/10.1080/00140139.2017.1313456.

Martin, C. (1995) The customer compatibility scale: Measuring service customers' perceptions of fellow customers. *Journal of Consumer Studies and Home Economics* 19, 299–311.

Martin, C. (1996) Consumer-to-consumer relationships: Satisfaction with other consumers' public behaviour. *The Journal of Consumer Affairs* 30 (1), 146–169.

Martin, C. and Pranter, C. (1989) Compatibility management: Customer-to-customer relationships in service environments. *The Journal of Services Marketing* 3 (3), 5–15.

Matousek, M. (2018) 'Child-free zones' on airplanes becomes growing movement, *Independent*, 19 February. See https://www.independent.co.uk/travel/news-and-advice/air-travel-child-free-zones-planes-movement-cabin-crew-noise-crying-a8217191.html (accessed March 2019).

McLinton, S., Drury, D., Masocha, S., Savelsberg, H., Martin, L. and Lushington, K. (2020) 'Air Rage': A systematic review of research on Disruptive Airline Passenger Behaviour 1985-2020. *Journal of Airline and Airport Management* 10 (1), 31–49. http://dx.doi.org/10.3926/jairm.156.

Nicholls, R. (2005) *Interactions between Service Customers: Managing On-site Customer-to-customer Interactions for Service Advantage.* Poznam: The Poznan University of Economics.

Nicholls, R. (2010) New directions for customer-to-customer interaction research. *Journal of Services Marketing* 24, 1, 87–97. https://doi.org/10.1108/08876041011017916.

Nicholls, R. (2019) Customer-to-customer interaction (CCI) in tourism – A customer diversity perspective. In Travel and Tourism Research Association, *Tourism in the Era of Connectivity*, 8th–10th April 2019, Bournemouth University. (Unpublished).

Passenger Shaming (2018) Facebook. See https://www.facebook.com/PassengerShaming/ (accessed December 2018).

passengershaming (2018) Instagram. See https://www.instagram.com/passengershaming/?hl=en (accessed December 2018).

Patel, H. and D'Cruz, M. (2018) Passenger-centric factors influencing the experience of aircraft comfort. *Transport Reviews* 38 (2), 252–269. https://doi.org/10.1080/01441647.2017.1307877.

Pearce, P. (2005) *Tourist Behaviour: Themes and Conceptual Schemes.* Clevedon: Channel View Publications.

Poria, Y. and Beal, J. (2017) An exploratory study about obese people's flight experience. *Journal of Travel Research* 56 (3), 370–380. https://doi.org/10.1177/0047287516643416.

Pranter, C. and Martin, C. (1991) Compatibility management: Roles in service performers. *Journal of Services Marketing* 5 (2), 43–53.

Puhl, R. and Brownell, K.D. (2001) Bias, discrimination, and obesity. *Obesity Research* 9, 788–805. https://doi.org/10.1038/oby.2001.108.

Schaberg, C. (2017) *Airportness: The Nature of Flight*. New York: Bloomsbury.

Sedgley, D., Pritchard, A., Morgan, N. and Hanna, P. (2017) Tourism and autism: Journeys of mixed emotions. *Annals of Tourism Research* 66, 14–25. https://doi.org/10.1016/j.annals.2017.05.009.

Simmel, G. (1950) *The Sociology of Georg Simmel*. (H. Woolf, trans.). New York: Free Press of Glencoe.

Small, J. (2005) Women's holidays: The disruption of the motherhood myth. *Tourism Review International* 9, 139–154. https://doi.org/10.3727/154427205774791645.

Small, J. and Harris, C. (2012) Obesity and tourism: Rights and responsibilities. *Annals of Tourism Research* 39 (2), 686–707. https://doi.org/10.1016/j.annals.2011.09.002.

Small, J. and Harris, C. (2014) Crying babies on planes: Aeromobility and parenting. *Annals of Tourism Research* 48, 27–41. https://doi.org/10.1016/j.annals.2014.04.009.

Small, J. and Harris, C. (2018) Air rage: Who is responsible for unruly behaviour? Paper presented to 28th Annual CAUTHE Conference, *Get Smart: Paradoxes and Possibilities in Tourism, Hospitality and Events Education and Research*, 5–8 February, Newcastle: University of Newcastle.

Small, J. and Harris, C. (2019) 'THEY DID WHAT?' Air travel passenger-shaming representations on Facebook and Instagram. *Critical Tourism Studies Proceedings* Article 19. https://digitalcommons.library.tru.ca/cts-proceedings/vol2019/iss1/19.

Thrift, N. (2006) Donna Haraway's dreams. *Theory, Culture & Society* 23 (7–8), 189–195. https://doi.org/10.1177/0263276406069231.

Thrift, N. (2008) *Non-representational Theory: Space, Politics, Affect*. London: Routledge.

Timmis, A., Ison, S.G. and Budd, L. (2018) *International comparison of disruptive passenger prevalence,* Briefing note prepared for the Department for Transport. DOI: 10.13140/RG.2.2.29532.64645.

Traveller.com.au (2011) Travellers hate children – even their own, *Traveller*, 8 August. See https://www.traveller.com.au/travellers-hate-children-even-their-own-survey-1iids (accessed July 2013).

Tsang, S., Masiero, L. and Schuckert, M. (2018) Investigating air passengers' acceptance level of unruly in-flight behavior. *Tourism Analysis* 23, 31–43. https://doi-org.ezproxy.lib.uts.edu.au/10.3727/108354218X15143857349477.

Vartanian, L. (2010) Disgust and perceived control in attitudes toward obese people. *International Journal of Obesity* 34, 1302–1307. https://doi.org/10.1038/ijo.2010.45.

Vredenburgh, A., Zackowitz, I. and Vredenburgh, A. (2015) Air rage: What factors influence airline passenger anger? *Proceedings of the Human Factors and Ergonomics Society 59th Annual Meeting* 59 (1), 400–404. https://doi.org/10.1177/1541931215591084.

Wetherell, M., Taylor, S. and Yates, S. (2001) *Discourse Theory and Practice: A Reader*. London: Sage.

Whitley, A. and Gross, S. (2019) *Legroom on planes has been shrinking for years. It's about to get much, much worse.* See https://time.com/5636154/airplane-legroom-shrinking-asia/ (accessed October 2020).

World Health Organization (2020) Obesity and overweight, *WHO Newsroom*, 1 April. See https://www.who.int/news-room/fact-sheets/detail/obesity-and-overweight (accessed January 2021).

4 Flying and Appearance

Jennie Small

Introduction

A welcome development in tourism studies has been the incorporation of the tourist *body* into the academic discourse, acknowledging the body's centrality 'in how we encounter, interact and communicate with the social and physical world' (Pritchard & Morgan, 2005: 285). Yet, while the sensual and mobile experience of the tourist body has been studied, there has been little focus on the appearance, the *look* of that body. It is worth considering how the presentation of one's body, and others' reaction to it, can affect our mobility. We construct meanings and make judgements about bodies according to how they look: their colour, age, gender, size, impairment, dress, hairstyle, makeup, cleanliness and so on. When we discriminate or are prejudiced against people on the grounds of their appearance, we are said to exhibit 'lookism' (Tietje & Cresap, 2005). Although there is limited focus on appearance in travel and tourism research, we can certainly find evidence of 'lookism'. In Chapters 5 and 6, the authors provide examples of appearance discrimination by airline crew against passengers with disabilities. These include (wrong and offensive) assumptions about the person's disability/ disabilities. Passengers, too, may discriminate against other passengers based on their appearance. As discussed in Chapter 3, passengers with larger bodies were criticised not only because they intruded on another's space but also because of the way they looked. Certainly, a passenger's appearance can affect their experience of airport surveillance and their passage through security (see Chapter 2).

While passengers gaze on each other, they also gaze on airline staff. As we board a plane, a quick glance into the cockpit (where possible) at the *look of* the pilots can confirm whether or not we feel we are in safe hands. We might make judgements based on perceived age, gender, race, attractiveness or size of body. Certainly, the uniforms and bodily presentation of pilots, flight attendants and ground staff have been carefully designed and orchestrated by the airlines to say 'professional' and to reassure. The first section of this chapter continues the discussion on passenger-to-passenger interaction but with the focus here on passenger clothing and how passengers react to the dress of other passengers. It follows with an examination of the appearance of airline staff, in particular, female flight attendants, and how passengers experience their appearance.

Passenger Appearance – How Passengers Experience Other Passengers' Dress

How we ourselves are clothed and how we view other passengers' clothing contribute to our air travel experience. Clothing is part of our embodied experience, both the physical corporeal experience of clothing on the body and the socially constructed meaning of that clothing. Adam and Galinsky (2012: 918) propose the term 'enclothed cognition' to refer to the co-occurrence of 'the symbolic meaning of the clothes *and* the physical experience of wearing them'. Despite the contribution of clothing to our embodied experience, clothing has been a neglected area of tourism research as Pritchard and Morgan (2005) explain:

> The study of fashion and dress has been doubly disadvantaged since the long academic silence over the body marginalized the study of dress and clothing, both areas which in turn have also been long dismissed by 'serious' research fields as a frivolous feminine indulgence (Neissen and Bryden, 1998). (Pritchard & Morgan, 2005: 286)

At the same time, mobility researchers have also ignored the issue of clothing – *what we wear* when we are mobile – despite recognising that mobility entails embodiment.

We need to turn to other social science fields to appreciate that the subject of clothing is not trivial. How we dress is part of our 'body project' (Shilling, 2003). Through dress we communicate who we are; our feelings, beliefs and desires (Johnson & Hokanson, 2015: 1). Dress is a means of producing and reproducing values (Fandy, 1998; O'Neil, 2010), of expressing or asserting our position in social space (Bourdieu, 1984). Following Goffman (1961), Bovone (2003) explains that dress signifies the interaction when the actor defines who they wish to be, choosing one of 'multiple self-identifications' and deciding which self-identification to present in a particular situation (Bovone, 2003: 208). Johnson and Hokanson (2015: 1) explain: 'we use fashion to express our gender, aesthetics, power, wealth, status, and desirability'. With certain styles of dress deemed suitable or unsuitable as we age, clothes are also part of the long-established phenomenon of age ordering (Twigg, 2012). We can turn to Judith Butler's (1990) theories of performativity to understand the importance of dress as a means through which the self is constituted (Butler, 1990; Peters, 2014). To comprehend the meaning of clothes we need to examine their embeddedness in social relations and contexts. As Aspers and Godart (2013) remind us, clothes have no meaning in themselves. Studying dress allows us to explore 'the interface between the body and social meanings attached to it' (Twigg & Majima, 2014: 25).

Dress not only affects the behaviour of self but also the behaviour of others toward the self (see Johnson & Lennon, 2014). While playing a vital role in the on-going negotiation of self (Twigg & Buse, 2013), clothing is a means for the expression of social differentiation and can serve as a means of legitimating and contesting authority. Although mobility or tourism scholars may have shown little interest in clothing, there has been debate in the media triggered by the removal, or threat of removal, of airline passengers for wearing what was considered dress that was offensive to others. High profile incidents have related to the wearing of low-hanging pants, low-cut dresses, too short skirts, t-shirt slogans with expletives or reference to terrorism and a cross-dressing man in women's underwear (the latter of interest because he was not considered inappropriately attired) (Associated Press, 2012; Costello, 2012; Denham, 2019). Such incidents and the media discussion surrounding them were the impetus for Harris and Small (2014) to investigate passenger attitudes to 'appropriate' passenger dress and airline enforcement of a dress code. The data were 340 online reader comments in response to a published online article on the topic from six newspaper and two travel websites (published November 2011 to March 2015). To provide a critical lens on the issue of passenger clothing on planes, Fairclough's Critical Discourse Analysis (1993) was employed to unpack the texts produced and posted on this topic.

Analysis of the online public comments confirmed the changing nature of passenger dress with today's clothing less formal than in the past and focused on comfort, especially on long-haul flights. For some, comfort was the prime consideration: shorts, pants, t-shirt. Comfortable clothing was also considered safer in an emergency (flat shoes and natural fibres). Some also questioned the logic of dressing up for air travel considering the cramped conditions and declining service of today's airlines. However, while comfortable clothing was considered acceptable, it was clear that there was appropriate and inappropriate 'comfortable' clothing; some passengers could take 'comfort' too far, beyond the standards of common decency – *'dressed as if they're going to the beach or a bordello'*. Comments reflected passenger disgust at sloppy and slovenly dress with the suggestion that no one had told the masses (who now had access to air travel) that the standard of dress required on a plane *'is not the same as on a bus, train or covered wagon!'* The substance of much of the discourse was the request for passengers to be thoughtful and considerate to avoid offending and inconveniencing others. Included in these comments was concern for children exposed to the offensive dress of others. The message was: as a paying customer, one should expect to share the space with 'suitably' attired others. An aeroplane is different from other leisure spaces. The passenger cannot move away from an offending person and, if long haul, may have to spend a long time in close proximity. Whether dressing well resulted in better treatment from staff and the possibility of an upgrade was also debated.

A theme that emerged in many comments related to questions over the public versus private nature of airlines and the airline's right (or not) to enforce a dress code. Some also queried whether the United States ban on clothing with political slogans went against the (US) First Amendment. Others highlighted the definitional subjectivity of 'offensive' clothing: a curse word to some is *'standard vocabulary to others'*. The enforcement of a dress code by an airline was clearly unacceptable to some. However, many comments were supportive of the airlines taking a stance 'to restore civility and decency' in passenger dress. Solutions for airline action included: publishing dress codes on their website, making available t-shirts or overalls for the passenger to cover up or asking the passenger to turn their t-shirt inside out (if bearing an offensive slogan). The solution for the passenger was to bring a spare set of clothes.

The discourse above highlights that what we wear on a plane is part of our embodied experience. There is the corporeal experience: clothes affect our physical comfort, warmth/coolness, ease of movement and health. There is also the social meaning of clothes, especially diverse in the public space of a plane as passengers diverge by class, age, culture, gender and so on. As the plane is both a business and leisure space, conflicts over dress style among the different users, and in different spaces (First Class, Business, Economy), are not unexpected. From a practical stance, what is worn on the plane may be influenced by packing choices for the destination (Small & Harris, 2012a) and/or airline regulations governing weight and size of our luggage.

To understand the discourse and tensions surrounding appropriate passenger dress, Social Identity Theory (Tajfel & Turner, 1979) goes some way to explain how individuals derive identity from the groups to which they belong. Dress can be seen as one characteristic that defines groups. Dress communicates a personal identity (something unique to the individual as well as a social identity (signalling the group to which the individual belongs) (Kang *et al.*, 2011). Through social comparison between group memberships, we understand who we are and who we are not. Puhl and Brownell (2003: 219) explain the connection between identity and prejudice. 'The desire to maintain a positive social identity is at the core of prejudice. This is achieved by stereotyping other groups as inferior on attributes that are valued by the in-group'. In the present study, negative comments about the dress style of others can be viewed as prejudice where the identity and self-esteem of 'better, appropriately dressed' passengers are partly determined by the ability of this social group to see their group as superior to the 'inappropriately dressed' passenger group. With the 'democratisation' of travel, some of these comments hint at social class prejudice. While it is clear that the clothing one wears can affect the experience of other passengers, one can only assume passenger clothing also affects the experience of airline staff. Certainly, Vilnai-Yavetz and Gilboa (2014) found in their study in fashion and sportswear stores that customer appearance can play an important role in the service process, and that salespeople and service employees are highly influenced by customer dress.

Taking a critical approach to the discourse on passenger dress on planes requires extending the analysis to an examination of the ideologies supporting the discursive practice, that is, the sociocultural practice (Fairclough, 1993): 'the context around the content: the interests, power bases and motivations of the various players behind the discourse' (Small & Harris, 2012b: 693). Fashion can only be understood within the sociocultural, historical context. To comprehend the focus on comfort initially requires consideration of the broader meaning of clothes in the 21st century. At least in the West, the formality of dress has declined in many social situations with a greater preference for comfort, health and low maintenance. The nature of travel has also changed the amount (and weight) of luggage we take when we need to carry it ourselves (porters rarely to be seen) and when airlines charge extra for luggage. Today, for the purposes of travelling, we have special 'Travel clothing', with manufacturers and retailers stressing comfort, weight, low maintenance, quick drying, sun-safe and 'wicking' features. Schaberg (2017) alerts us to a modified version of the travel shirt, the fishing shirt (with its vents, mesh linings, key loops, sun protection collars etc.), and asks: 'What are these things that would seem dissonant with airport life and yet have come to define it in their own small way' (Schaberg, 2017: 41). He explains what is so attractive about this shirt at the airport – and so galling. 'It pledges to spirit us through the world with foresight, durability, and protection; but it also nestles blandly into the consumerscape numbly taking place all around' (Schaberg, 2017: 43). Certainly, online travel sites, in their 'what to wear/what not to wear' in-flight advice, reinforce comfort: natural, breathable fabrics, loose clothes, comfortable shoes and layers. Airline websites which advise on passenger dress, similarly emphasise comfort and health.

To contextualise the passenger discourse on clothing we need to appreciate the part played by the airlines with their changing product and service provision, the result of a neoliberal agenda based on the notion of unregulated competitive markets. The deregulation of air transport with the introduction of low-cost airlines and cheaper fares has affected the *corporeal* experience of air travel. Economic decisions to reduce passenger space (seat size and legroom) have impacted the passenger physically. The resulting discomfort (and potential health risks) have meant comfort (and health) of dress have become a priority.

The conditions that have led to cheaper fares, reduced space and diminished service, have also changed the *meaning* of travel. The event no longer warrants 'dressing up' as it previously did, especially in the 'golden age' of travel of the 1950s and 1960s, when air travel was considered luxurious, glamorous and elegant. Then, air travel, an infrequent experience, was exciting – an occasion for which it was worth dressing more formally: a dress for women and suit and tie for men (Kokonis in Harris, 2017). Today, the journey, rather than viewed as 'an occasion', is more commonly perceived by passengers as 'holiday time wasted', an endurance, in order 'to reach the location that they really want to visit' (Weaver & Lawton, 2014: 35). While industry representations of air travel as glamorous and luxurious have continued, the reality today is often far from thus.

The 'democratisation' of travel, enabled by low-cost travel, has meant a more heterogenous travel group with a less clear and agreed-upon meaning of air travel including its rules of dress. When Tulloch (2013) writes: 'There they go - lining up for immigration in flannelette pyjama pants with pink pigs on them, wearing thongs, a hoodie and clutching a pillow', we can see how far dress rules have relaxed. Whether a deliberate retro 1950s fashion statement or a casual dressing down, wearing hair in curlers on a flight would not have happened in the past; see Figure 4.1.

Muther (2014) refers to 'the slobification of travel' while airline analyst, Robert Kokonis (Harris, 2017), adds, 'It's a bit of the Wild West now'. Much of the debate on online sites focuses on the rights and responsibilities of passengers in regards to how they dress. On the one hand, is the argument that passengers have a responsibility not to offend others through inappropriate exposure of body flesh or clothing slogans. On the other, is the discourse which resists dress codes arguing for the right to dress how one chooses, supported by a neoliberal ideology with its focus on individuality at the expense of the collective. Passenger understanding is not assisted by the airlines' virtual silence on the matter of dress rules. As stated earlier, tension between passengers can be exacerbated by the material conditions of the plane – passenger proximity in an enclosed space often for an extended period of time. When one introduces bodies whose appearance and clothing are very different from one's own, tensions can be exacerbated.

If passengers associate clothing with behaviour, slogans on t-shirts, whether they be political or lewd messages, can be perceived as threatening and add to already existing anxieties and security fears associated with air travel. There are further implications of passenger dress that need to be considered if what is worn on the plane is also worn on arrival. As travel writer, Tulloch (2013), writes in *The Sydney Morning Herald*: 'I can't help feeling that arriving at your destination wearing flannelette pyjamas isn't the best psychological approach to take

Figure 4.1 Passenger on transit bus from international flight to terminal (2015 © Jennie Small)

to travel. Maybe I'm old-fashioned, but I like to arrive how I intend to continue – with a certain amount of dignity'. The sensibilities of the destination host also need to be taken into account.

Dress, while serving as a mechanism for expressing self-identity, can also be used as a form of control. In many environments, written dress codes and regulations stipulate customer dress (Entwistle, 2000). While there may be few written rules for dress on the aeroplane, a number of airlines make reference (however vague) to suitable attire for club lounges. Qantas, for example enforced more vigorously its club dress code in its major Australian lounges in 2015 'to create an environment everyone can enjoy'. Items of clothing not permitted are: thongs and bare feet, head-to-toe gym wear, beachwear (including boardshorts), sleepwear (including Ugg boots and slippers), clothing featuring offensive images or slogans, revealing, unclean or torn clothing (Qantas, 2020; Tulloch, 2015). Nonetheless, the enforcement of a dress code can result in conflict, as it does in other environments such as the workplace (Ainsworth, 2014). Enforcement can be less welcome by some where the space is for leisure since leisure is perceived as a time and space for freedom: 'A state in which the person feels that what she or he is doing is done by choice and because one wants to do it' (Neulinger, 1981: 15), where one can leave behind the rules and regulations that govern day-to-day home and work lives.

Pritchard and Morgan (2006) explain that, although 'liminality is bound up with freedom of expression and action', tourists in different spaces 'are increasingly subject to the disciplinary gaze (Foucault, 1982)' (Pritchard & Morgan, 2006: 770). This gaze is particularly evident in air travel. On boarding an aeroplane, passenger clothing is under the surveillance of gate attendants and flight attendants. In addition, passengers are both the subject and object of other passengers' gaze (Gottdiener, 2001). As has been found in previous studies (Small & Harris, 2012b, 2014), it is difficult to avoid the scrutiny of others in the close quarters of a plane and over an extended period of time, especially when the flight is long haul. It was clear from the present findings that power was not only the province of the airlines but also resided with the passengers as they conformed to or resisted social norms of dress. Passengers had the power to 'make or break' another's experience of air travel. While the wearing of a t-shirt with the F-word on it might represent a passenger's right to express themselves through their 'fashion' choice, for others, the same t-shirt represents an offensive word from which they want to distance themselves. For the wearer, the t-shirt can represent 'their individualism'; for fellow passengers it brings offensive fashion into their space, causes discomfort and brings the decency of the wearer into question. While some passengers might intentionally resist a dress code, others cited in the media have appeared genuinely mystified that their dress could be deemed offensive. Ignorance of social (airline) norms is a better explanation for their clothing choice than resistance.

When the dress rules are not publicised or understood, staff enforcement of a dress code can appear arbitrary and an abuse of power. Anolik, a San Francisco-based attorney who specialises in travel law, claims that the wide latitude given to airline staff can be 'problematic, as inherent biases and hang-ups can come into play when the employees make the determination' (Sampson, 2019). Accusations of racist and sexist discrimination (Sampson, 2019) in the determination of appropriate dress are damaging for all concerned, including the airlines, and have led to demands by passengers for clarification on what constitutes offensive clothing (Sampson, 2019). Some issues have arisen in the United States in relation to differing dress codes for 'pass riders' (employees or their family and friends who are travelling with heavily discounted fares) as they are considered representatives of the company compared with 'revenue customers' (regular paying customers) (Deb, 2017). The consequences of denied boarding can have greater consequences than denied entry to many other types of spaces in that a missed flight can have financial and time consequences, precluding opportunities at the destination. That a person's identity is bound up in how they dress, can make the enforcement of rules even more objectionable.

Passenger Experience of Female Flight Attendants' Appearance

While there has been a decline in the formality of passenger dress over the years and increased ambiguity over what is acceptable clothing for air travel, high fashion and precise tailoring are still required for the airline crew and clearly stipulated in dress codes. Referring to the uniform of flight attendants, Conde Nast Traveler Editors and Kwak (2018) recognise 'there's still a tiny sliver of elegance when airborne' in the not-very-glamorous environment of Economy Class. Traditionally, the release of new cabin crew uniforms, often designed by high-end designers, has been met with pomp and ceremony. The uniform, representing the public face of the airline, is most distinguishable in the female flight attendant's dress. While the dress of pilots and male cabin crew over time and across airlines remains much the same, there are cultural variations in the dress of flight attendants. It is her uniform which is judged and ranked with that of other airlines in terms of style and fashion by the online media. At the same time, the uniform and appearance requirements for female flight attendants have caused controversy with airlines accused of sexism in their required dress codes (makeup, hair, skirts, high heels etc.). Arguments of functionality and safety over sex appeal have been at the core of the argument but as Hill (as cited in Lagrave, 2019) says, 'the shift to functionality over sex appeal has been slow'.

Traditionally, appearance has been a strictly enforced criterion of employment in the airline industry. In recent years, some airlines (including most US airlines) have responded to demands from female crew for a similar dress code for men and women. Other aspects of appearance have also been relaxed by some airlines. Barry (2007) explains the overall appearance requirements for US flight attendants up to the 1970s. During this time, height, weight and age (under 32 or 35 to ensure 'youthful appeal') were conditions of employment (as was marital status – single). In the United States, by the late 1960s, civil rights/antidiscrimination legislation led to a waning in discriminatory activity against flight attendants. The age restriction was lifted. Despite societal changes in some countries which have led to greater inclusion, age still remains under scrutiny in the airline sector as some airlines continue to employ only younger attendants. The chief executive of Qatar Airways made headlines in 2017 when he said that US airline passengers are 'always being served by grandmothers' while boasting that 'the average age of my cabin crew is only 26' (BBC News, 2017). It is not only dress that contributes to the sexual appeal of female flight attendants but also a body that is youthful. The relaxation of age requirements disrupts the traditional 'trolley dolly' image of flight attendants, a circumstance which has caught the attention of the online media.

As passengers gaze on the crew in the shared space of the aircraft, the appearance of the crew becomes part of the passenger experience. To explore passenger experience and response to older flight attendants, Small and Harris (2015) used Fairclough's (1993) Critical Discourse Analysis to study public comments on six websites that were directly focused on flight attendant age or indirectly mentioned age in discussion about the *look* of flight attendants. Due to the source of the websites, most participants contributing to the discussion appeared to be from the United States, thus the focus of the discussion on ageing related, primarily, to US female flight attendants. While some supported the older workers, many of the comments exuded regret for the declining sexual appeal of flight attendants, suggesting that the introduction of anti-discrimination legislation was not welcome.

> *Sometime during the late 70s and I was still a young man, the stewardesses stopp[ed] looking like potential date candidates and more like my mother. Ick.* (as cited in Small & Harris, 2015: 714)

American flight attendants were compared unfavourably with those from other nations/regions/airlines, particularly Asian or Middle-Eastern, who were considered to be younger and 'hotter'.

> *... I would much rather fly Singapore or China Air because they [sic] attendants do look good.* (as cited in Small & Harris, 2015: 714)

Older flight attendants, especially on US airlines, were also portrayed as having bad attitude: grumpy, surly, less enthusiastic about their job and providing poor service.

> *I can assure you that most, but not all U.S. carriers are filled with rude, old, unattractive bitches who act like I should be thankful to be in their presence. Now contrast that with Qatar, Emirates or even Lufthansa or KLM. Stunning beauties cheerfully cater to my every request.* (as cited in Small & Harris, 2015: 714)

Comments supporting older workers emphasised their right to work, their greater work experience, professionalism and safety experience as more important than looks. They were preferred to younger flight attendants who were considered too self-involved, focused more on themselves than the passengers. Comments sympathetic to older attendants (in the United States) explained the attendants' need to work for health care benefits and sometimes a retirement pension; if there were poor service, government deregulation of airlines was considered partly to blame. As Bergman and Gillberg (2015) found in their study of Scandinavian Airlines' (SAS) cabin attendants, the deregulated competitive market has had a dramatic impact on the working conditions of cabin attendants, especially the older (middle-aged) female attendants.

> The combination of work intensification, vulnerability, and aging boosted pressure on them and fueled both health problems and negative emotions toward work. Consequently, cabin attendants' attitudes of satisfaction and commitment gradually changed to frustration. Job satisfaction and trust in management and the union both diminished drastically and loyalty waned. (Bergman & Gillberg, 2015: 35)

While the authors do not suggest that the frustration of the SAS cabin attendants affected their interactions with passengers, it would not be surprising if it did!

To understand the online public discourse about older flight attendants as portrayed above (Small & Harris, 2015), we need to look at the context around the content – the sociocultural practice (Fairclough, 1993) which has sexualised female flight attendants and which supports the discourse. Reflected in many of the comments are the importance of appearance and the negative association of female beauty/sexual attractiveness with older age (at least in Western society). The airline industry, in particular, is renowned for its preoccupation with employee appearance; the young female 'air hostess' is the traditional embodiment of societal values of beauty and sexuality/masculine imagination. Baum (2012) describes how this representation has been further reinforced in the broad genre of airline-related employment literature. However, as Baum notes, the representation of flight attendants has not been static: 'women in the context of airline work moved beyond the discrete and demure glamour of the early era of flight, building towards the increasingly liberal sexual "revolution" of the 1960s' (Baum, 2012: 1190) when they became 'a flying sex symbol' (Escolme-Schmidt, 2009: 19), helped by their mini-skirt uniforms. Referring to the women as 'centerfold creatures', Stadiem (2014) claims, 'no women of the era were considered more covetable sex objects than jet airline stewardesses' (Chapter 12, para 4).

Hochschild (1983), referring to the service work of flight attendants as 'emotional labour', described their requirement to portray both motherliness and sexual allure (often simultaneously). However, Spiess and Waring (2005) argue that this concept conflates the visual with the emotional. They suggest 'aesthetic labour' as a more satisfactory construct to describe the work of flight attendants who are selected for their embodied capacities and attributes which employers then mobilise, develop and commodify to appeal to customers (Nickson et al., 2001).

Yet, Spiess and Waring (2005) suggest that we need to go further, beyond 'aesthetic labour' as an explanatory device if we are to capture the sexualised aspects of the flight attendant. They explain, 'Aesthetic labour's purpose is to appeal to the senses, but this is not necessarily a sexualised appeal' (2005: 198). They suggest that the concept of sexualised labour complements aesthetic labour 'in explaining how the mobilisation of employees' physical dispositions can move beyond mere aesthetic appeal to appealing to the sexual desires of some customers' (2005: 198).

Through marketing slogans and images (from the blatant to the subtle) and organisational practices (recruitment, training and management), the beauty and sexuality of female flight attendants has been appropriated to 'sell' the airline. Ayuttacorn (2016: 464), in her study of the body politics of Thai female flight attendants, says 'Through media representation, the flight attendant's body, as an icon, frames consumer expectation that passengers will see young, beautiful Asian women in the cabin'. Lin's (2015: 292) study of Singapore Airlines describes how the Singapore Girl's alluring body has been constructed (along with her demeanour and service) to contribute to the airline's onboard atmosphere:

> In contrast to Western flight attendants who wore formal jackets and skirts, the Singapore Girl was thus to perfume the air with a different kind of quality through her accoutrement. By first appearance at least, she was to (re)enchant the cabin not with the crass glamour of mini-skirts or hot pants, but a graceful indigeneity that suited a Western(er's) imagination of 'Asian' hospitality.

Evident to this day, and as noted by Baum (2012: 1190), 'The lasting legacy of the female flight attendant as a sexualised marketing icon… is "Singapore Girl"'. As the airline's website states, 'She was born in the '70s… Yet she remains timeless across generations. Her beauty, unfading. Her elegance always in style' (Singapore Airlines, 2020).

Flight attendants become part of the attraction and the passenger invited through gaze to come and experience the body as part of their passenger experience. In that gaze, the passenger may also experience national cultural values related to the body. Ayuttacorn (2016) describes how Thai flight attendants' bodies are disciplined not only by the rules of the organisation but also by Thai nationalist ideology of Thai female beauty. Escolme-Schmidt (2009), in her book, *Glamour in the skies: The golden age of the air stewardess*, describes the allure of the air hostess in which appearance and beauty feature strongly, with BOAC even using 'their girls' in beauty competitions. She quotes Charles Reid in a 1952 article from *World Digest*: 'The charm of an air hostess, like the complimentary cocktails and glossy magazines that are handed out at the beginning of a flight, is up to a point an official treat which comes to us by courtesy of the management' (Escolme-Schmidt, 2009: 19). The stewardess was viewed as 'an anodyne for the tired businessman in flight, every man's dream'; 'the tired businessman's entitlement' (Escolme-Schmidt, 2009: 23). The airlines reflected and shaped this expectation, as seen in the tagline for one of Braniff's popular commercials: 'Does your wife know you're flying with us?'

While the provocative advertising campaigns (such as National Airlines *'I'm Margie* [or Nancy, or Cheryl, or Barbara] *Fly Me'*) were 'a thing' of the 1970s, sexual imagery in airline advertising has not disappeared. In 2009, Virgin Atlantic's 25th anniversary retro campaign, *Still Red Hot*, prompted a series of complaints to the Advertising Standards Authority. It is only recently, in 2015, that Ryanair ceased producing its annual calendar of bikini-clad female crew despite complaints to authorities over the years; see Figure 4.2.

Figure 4.2 Michael O'Leary CEO of Ryanair launching the 2011 Ryanair Cabin Crew charity calendar, London, Britain (Ray Tang/Shutterstock)

With a particular focus on Virgin Atlantic's 2009 campaign, Duffy *et al.* (2017: 269) explain:

> Because of adverts such as these, and the wider corporate landscape they instantiate, male customers have strong expectations about the kind of service to which they are entitled, female customers... are positioned within the same hyper-heteronormative service scape, and men and women more generally celebrate a postfeminist choice narrative that re-engages gender and sexual essentialism, precluding critique in the name of (self) irony and (self) objectification.

Spiess and Waring (2005) point out that it is the customer's interpretation that largely defines the boundary between aesthetic and sexualised labour. The construction of the female flight attendant as a sexual being, in the service of the passenger, can invite male passengers to expect more than just a visual gaze. Discussing the feminised labour of the female flight attendant, Veijola and Valtonen (2007: 26) claim that, with a few exceptions, 'There are no societally significant meanings or codes of desire attached to women serving other women'.

Research indicates that sexual harassment is not an uncommon experience for female flight attendants. A study of Italian female flight attendants by Ballard *et al.* (2006) found that 22% had experienced sexual harassment by a passenger. More recently, the Association of Flight Attendants – CWA (2018a) conducted a survey of more than 3500 flight attendants (80% women) – from 29 US airlines, finding that 68% had experienced sexual harassment during their flying career. In the previous year, 35% had experienced verbal sexual harassment and 18% had experienced physical sexual harassment from passengers; many had experienced harassment many times in the previous year. Similarly, a survey by the Transport Workers Union (2019) of more than 400 Australian airline cabin crew, (of whom 71% of those reporting their gender were women), found that 65% had experienced sexual harassment at work. Once again, many had experienced harassment multiple times. Four in five crew had experienced sexual harassment from co-workers and three in five from passengers. Gale *et al.* (2019), from their sample of 4459 US- and Canada-based participants (almost 80% women) from the Harvard Flight Attendant Health Study, confirmed that 'exposures to verbal abuse, sexual harassment, and sexual assault are common among cabin crew, with 63, 26 and 2% of respondents, respectively, reporting harassment in the past year alone'. The primary perpetrators of abuse were found to be passengers. While the above studies deepen our knowledge of sexual harassment of flight attendants, it would be useful to have a better understanding of the instances of harassment disaggregated by gender of perpetrator and cabin crew. McLinton *et al.* (2020: 35) draw attention to the 'paucity of research regarding the nature of sexual harassment from passengers'.

There are a number of factors thought to exacerbate harassment for female cabin crew, one of which is the dress code which governs their appearance. According to business psychologist, Binna Kandola (as cited in Bullock, 2018), 'Dress codes that require women to wear more feminine clothes send a clear message about men and women's perceived roles in the workplace and often have little to do with the actual requirements of the job'. Based on the belief that highly feminine uniforms can provoke derogatory behaviour from some customers, Kandola says 'we should no longer accept the excuse (from management) that this type of female employee image is "what the customers expect"; it is no longer relevant' (Bullock, 2018). As Sara Nelson, President of the Association of Flight Attendants (Association of Flight Attendants-CWA, 2018) insists: 'The time when flight attendants were objectified in airline marketing and people joked about "coffee, tea, or me" needs to be permanently grounded. #TimesUp for the industry to put an end to its sexist past'.

Certainly, there have been advances in advertising, recruitment and management practices related to flight attendant appearance due to legislation or voluntary action by the airline. Complaints about gendered dress have led some airlines to permit their female flight attendants to wear more functional clothing, such as pants or flat shoes. Some have decided that female flight attendants are no longer required to wear makeup during flights. However, airlines differ in their loosening of regulations. While Ayuttacorn (2016) provides examples of Thai flight attendant resistance to airline policy on their bodily appearance (for example, the body mass index policy that attendants maintain a specified weight), she provides ample evidence that these bodies remain highly disciplined. While Virgin Atlantic's decision to allow flight attendants to go makeup free was seen as a welcome development, firmly encoded in the public consciousness is the sexualisation of female cabin crew (Hancock & Tyler, 2019). Hancock and Tyler (2019) interpret the message from Virgin: 'you don't have to look like this [wearing makeup] but we'd really like you to. And more to the point, we'd like it to be not because it is what we want, but what you want'. Inherent in this message is the airline's desire for flight attendants who embody the corporate brand 'and its reified versions of feminine sexuality' (Hancock & Tyler, 2019).[1] While Schaberg (2017: 142) argues that we no longer care whether flight attendants present as male or female ('gender in flight is not a problem'), the above, sadly, suggests many do care.

Conclusion

With limited distraction in the close confines of the aeroplane, we become very aware of the bodies of others. As passengers gaze on others, they register others' appearance: body size and shape, hair, eyes, skin, makeup, clothing and accessories and, based on what they see, make assumptions on a person's age, gender, sexuality, ethnicity, physical ability, social class and value. Judgements are made on whether the look of the person meets their expectations for that role. In some cases, expectations involve an aesthetic and sexual being. On an aeroplane, those in the passenger's gaze are other passengers and flight attendants. This chapter has focused on two issues that have gained media attention in recent years. The first concerns social discourse on passenger clothing with a focus on passenger perception of others' dress performance, its appropriateness/inappropriateness for air travel. Although not discussed in the travel and mobility literature, our clothing (and that of others) should be recognised as important in the travel experience. Clothing reflects our identity. What we wear affects how we move, how we practice/perform mobility. The discourse on wellbeing, comfort, health and safety affirms that our clothes contribute to our corporeal experience of air travel. It is not just the materiality of our clothing that shapes our experience but our clothing in conjunction with the other materialities of air travel such as the passenger seat – its size and location. If movement in our seat is restricted or we have to climb over others to exit our seat, comfort may depend on the clothing we wear. The temperature of the plane and duration of flight also affect how we experience our clothing in air travel. At the same time, our clothing choices can affect our relations with others. Passenger clothing may be deemed offensive and, in extreme cases, eventuate in 'social sorting' by the airline in order to ensure its image.

Understanding the 'clothes on planes' discourse requires an appreciation of change in Western views on dress in general as well as change in the nature of air travel from comfortable, 'luxury' transport to uncomfortable 'mass' transport. With air travel now open to a broader range of passenger, consensus on a dress standard is not always achievable. On many counts, 'clothes on planes' is a moral issue – we judge the wearer for violating the (usually) unwritten rules for air travel dress. Inherent in the debate on appropriateness or inappropriateness of clothing is the issue of social responsibility: care for the collective versus neoliberal individuality. In the constrained temporal and physical space of a plane, sensibilities of others become more important. Although it may be difficult for airlines to publicise a precise dress code, guidance from the industry may go some way to defuse tensions between passengers and ensure passenger satisfaction. Clearer guidelines might prevent what some have seen as the abuse of power and authority by air crew when passengers have been denied boarding based on a judgement of inappropriate clothing.

The second issue discussed in this chapter relates to the passenger gaze on female flight attendants, in particular, older flight attendants, whose age disrupts the constructed imagined embodiment (the romantic, sexualised ideal) of the flight attendant/hostess/stewardess/'trolley dolly'. Despite some posts supporting the employment of older flight attendants, others saw this development as just one more example of the declining service of airlines. Along with a reduction in seat size and free luggage allowance was the loss of the female flight attendant as 'eye candy', an object to please the (male) passenger. The discourse equating ageing with a loss of beauty and sexual appeal (and thus social value) reflects a common ageist and sexist attitude to older women/workers in appearance- and youth-obsessed societies.

A critical analysis of passengers' experience of female flight attendants requires an appreciation of the interests and motivation of the airlines in the production of this body. While airlines, for the most part, are silent on the required appearance of passengers (until they break the airline's [unwritten] rules of acceptability), the airlines have been heavily involved in prescribing the appearance of their flight attendants, especially the female crew. Strict recruitment policies and management of employees' bodies (including firing of obese flight attendants) has sustained an image of beauty and sexual allure, reinforced through the marketing of the flight attendant body. Through all these practices, the flight attendant has become the brand, with 'great service' guaranteed when her emotional, aesthetic and sexualised labour coalesce (Duffy *et al.*, 2017: 269). With reinforcement of this message over the decades from airlines and other sources, it is perhaps no surprise that ageist and sexist attitudes persist. Hopefully, feminist action which has allowed women in many airlines to work beyond their youth and which has relaxed the restrictions on the appearance of female flight attendants will continue to liberate women from the traditional stereotype of their role. Nonetheless, some are less optimistic of industry's intent, seeing the appropriation of post-feminism as perpetuating discrimination and, in turn, the passenger experience.

As demonstrated above, it is not just what others do but also how they 'look', that can affect the passenger experience. From the above discussion, it is apparent that an aeroplane is not a non-place, but a space imbued with complex meanings and sociality. How we look, including what we wear, is a moral and political issue as airline management, crew and passengers pass judgement on the appearance of others in flight. While there may be class issues in the discourse on the appearance of other passengers, sexism and ageism can be seen to underly the discourse on flight attendants. One could say that the 'democratisation' of air travel (for the passenger) and anti-discrimination legislation (for the flight attendant) have not been welcomed by all.

Note

(1) The sexualisation of flight attendants also extends to the stereotypical male gay attendant. Tiemeyer (2013) in his history of male flight notes that male flight attendants were beginning to stand out as '*plainly queer*' even in the 1930s. He explains:

'Their status as white men doing servile "women's work" or "colored work" compromised them as failed men and suspected homosexuals' (2013: 238). In the 1930s both Pan Am and Eastern saw the marketing potential of the gay steward: 'Pan Am developed promotional materials like "Rodney the Smiling Steward", while Eastern adorned its stewards in sharp outfits that highlighted their sexual appeal in an effort to court new customers – both male and female' (2013: 239). However, he notes that this trend did not continue in the 1950s, referring to this decade and the 1980s as being particularly antagonistic to gay men working as flight attendants. It is difficult to dissociate appearance, sexuality, sexism and homophobia, especially in particular historical times.

References

Adam, H. and Galinsky, A. (2012) Enclothed cognition. *Journal of Experimental Social Psychology* 48 (4), 918–925. https://doi.org/10.1016/j.jesp.2012.02.008.

Ainsworth, J. (2014) What's wrong with pink pearls and cornrow braids? Employee dress codes and the semiotic performance of race and gender in the workplace. In A. Wagner and R. Sherwin (eds) *Law, Culture and Visual Studies* (pp. 241–260). Netherlands: Springer.

Aspers, P. and Godart, F. (2013) Sociology of fashion: Order and change. *Annual Review of Sociology* 39, 171–192. https://doi.org/10.1146/annurev-soc-071811-145526.

Associated Press (2012) Your in-flight dress code: Fliers who have been banned from the skies for too much cleavage or too-high hemlines. *Daily Mail*, 26 August. See http://www.dailymail.co.uk/news/article-2193523/Airline-dress-codes-Fliers-try-navigate-unclear-rules-wear-flight.html (accessed February 2015).

Association of Flight Attendants-CWA (2018) Survey reveals widespread harassment of flight attendants, *AFA News Release*, 10 May. See https://www.afacwa.org/survey_reveals_widespread_harassment_of_flight_attendants (accessed March 2019).

Ayuttacorn, A. (2016) Air crafting: Corporate mandate and Thai female flight attendants' negotiation of body politics. *South East Asia Research* 24 (4), 462–476. https://doi.org/10.1177/0967828X16673941.

Ballard, T.J., Romito, P., Lauria, L., Vigiliano, V., Caldora, M., Mazzanti, C. and Verdecchia, A. (2006) Self perceived health and mental health among women flight attendants. *Occupational and Environmental Medicine* 63 (1), 33–38. https://doi.org/10.1136/oem.2004.018812.

Barry, K. (2007) *Femininity in Flight: A History of Flight Attendants*, North Carolina: Duke University Press.

Baum, T. (2012) Working the skies: Changing representations of gendered work in the airline industry, 1930-2011. *Tourism Management* 33 (5), 1185–1194. https://doi.org/10.1016/j.tourman.2011.11.012.

BBC News (2017) Qatar Airways CEO sorry for calling US air hostesses 'grandmothers', *BBC News*, 13 July. See https://www.bbc.com/news/world-middle-east-40593396 (accessed May 2020).

Bergman, A. and Gillberg, G. (2015) The cabin crew blues: Middle-aged cabin attendants and their working conditions. *Nordic Journal of Working Life Studies* 5 (4), 23–39. https://doi.org/10.19154/njwls.v5i4.4842.

Bourdieu, P. (1984) *Distinction: A Social Critique of the Judgment of Taste*. Cambridge, MA: Harvard University Press.

Bovone, L. (2003) Clothing: The authentic image? The point of view of young people. *International Journal of Contemporary Sociology* 40 (2), 205–218.

Bullock, C. (2018) What dress codes really mean for cabin crew, *BBC*, 20 February. See https://www.bbc.com/worklife/article/20180219-what-dress-codes-really-mean-for-cabin-crew (accessed September 2019).

Butler, J. (1990) *Gender Trouble: Feminism and the Subversion of Identity*. New York: Routledge.
Conde Nast Traveler Editors and Kwak, C. (2018) The most stylish flight attendant uniforms, 15 October. See https://www.cntraveler.com/galleries/2015-11-06/the-chicest-new-airline-uniforms-from-prabal-gurung-to-christian-lacroix (accessed May 2020).
Costello, C. (2012) Are airline dress codes too extreme? *Smarter Travel,* 28 August. See http://www.smartertravel.com/blogs/today-in-travel/are-airline-dress-codes-too-extreme.html?id=12412344 (accessed May 2020).
Deb, S. (2017) What can you wear on a plane? It depends who's paying. *The New York Times,* 27 March. See https://www.nytimes.com/2017/03/27/business/united-leggings-passes-dress-code.html (accessed May 2020).
Denham, H. (2019) Woman confronted by American Airlines for her clothing says she hasn't received refund, *The Washington Post,* 10 July. See https://www.washingtonpost.com/business/2019/07/09/woman-barred-american-airlines-flight-unless-she-covered-up-denies-receiving-refund/ (accessed May 2020).
Duffy, K., Hancock, P. and Tyler, M. (2017) Still Red Hot? Postfeminism and gender subjectivity in the airline industry. *Gender, Work and Organization* 24 (3), 260–273. https://doi.org/10.1111/gwao.12147.
Entwistle, J. (2000) *The Fashioned Body: Fashion, Dress and Modern Social Theory*. Cambridge: Polity Press.
Escolme-Schmidt, L. (2009) *Glamour in the Skies: The Golden Age of the Air Stewardess*. Cheltenham: The History Press.
Fairclough, N. (1993) *Discourse and Social Change*. Cambridge: Polity Press.
Fandy, M. (1998) Political science without clothes: The politics of dress or contesting the spatiality of Egypt. *Arab Studies Quarterly* 29 (2), 87–101.
Gale, S., Mordukhovich, I., Newlan, S. and McNeely, E. (2019) The impact of workplace harassment on health in a working cohort. *Frontiers in Psychology,* 24 May. https://doi.org/10.3389/fpsyg.2019.01181.
Goffman, E. (1961) *Encounters*. Indianapolis: Bobbs-Merril.
Gottdiener, M. (ed.) (2001) *Life in the Air: Surviving the New Culture of Air Travel*. Lanham Maryland: Rowman and Littlefield Publishers.
Hancock, P. and Tyler, M. (2019) Why Virgin Atlantic's new makeup policy is mostly concealer and gloss, *The Conversation,* 9 March. See https://theconversation.com/why-virgin-atlantics-new-makeup-policy-is-mostly-concealer-and-gloss-113211 (accessed May 2020).
Harris, C. and Small, J. (2014) Changing airline fashion: An improvement in passenger wellbeing? In *Council for Australasian University Tourism and Hospitality Education, Proceedings of the 24th Annual Conference, 2014* (pp. 1–5). Queensland: School of Tourism, The University of Queensland.
Harris, S. (2017) Passenger shaming website highlights bad behaviour on planes. *CBC News,* 3 September. See https://www.cbc.ca/news/business/passengershaming-airlines-bad-behaviour-1.4270812 (accessed May 2020).
Hochschild, A. (1983) *The Managed Heart*. Berkeley, CA: University of California Press.
Johnson, K. and Hokanson, B. (2015) Introduction to the focused issue on fashion and communication. *International Journal of Fashion Design, Technology and Education* 8 (1), 1–2. https://doi.org/10.1080/17543266.2014.1000476.
Johnson, K. and Lennon, S. (2014) The social psychology of dress. In J. Eicher (ed.) *Encyclopedia of World Dress and Fashion*. New York, NY: Berg.
Kang, M., Sklar, M. and Johnson, K. (2011) Men at work: Using dress to communicate identities. *Journal of Fashion Marketing and Management: An International Journal* 15 (4), 412–427. https://doi.org/10.1108/13612021111169924.
Lagrave, K. (2019) Why airline beauty standards are still stuck in the past. *Conde Nast Traveler,* 10 April. See https://www.cntraveler.com/story/why-flight-attendant-uniforms-and-airline-beauty-standards-are-still-stuck-in-the-past (accessed May 2020).

Lin, W. (2015) 'Cabin pressure': Designing affective atmospheres in airline travel. *Transactions of the Institute of British Geographers* 40, 287–299. https://doi.org/10.1111/tran.12079.

McLinton, S., Drury, D., Masocha, S., Savelsberg, H., Martin, L. and Lushington, K. (2020) 'Air rage': A systematic review of research on Disruptive Airline Passenger Behaviour 1985-2020. *Journal of Airline and Airport Management* 10 (1), 31–49. https://doi.org/10.3926/jairm.156.

Muther, C. (2014) What happened to the glamour of air travel? *Boston Globe*. 6 September. See http://www.bostonglobe.com/lifestyle/travel/2014/09/06/what-happened-glamour-air-travel/D2tH33b60WzmIkKPmUQMBP/story.html (accessed February 2015).

Neulinger, J. (1981) *The Psychology of Leisure* (2nd edn). Springfield, IL: Charles C. Thomas, Publisher.

Nickson, D., Warhurst, C., Witz, A. and Cullen, A. (2001) The importance of being aesthetic: Work, employment and service organization. In A. Sturdy, I. Grugulis and H. Wilmott (eds) *Customer Service: Empowerment and Entrapment* (pp. 170–90). Basingstoke: Palgrave.

O'Neil, M.L. (2010) You are what you wear: Clothing/appearance laws and the construction of the public citizen in Turkey. *Fashion Theory: The Journal of Dress, Body & Culture* 14 (1), 65–82. https://doi.org/10.2752/175174110X12544983515231.

Peters, L.D. (2014) You are what you wear: How plus-size fashion figures in fat identity formation. *Fashion Theory: The Journal of Dress, Body & Culture* 18 (1), 45–72. https://doi.org/10.2752/175174114X13788163471668.

Pritchard, A. and Morgan, N. (2005) 'On location': Re(viewing) bodies of fashion and places of desire. *Tourist Studies* 5 (3), 283–302. https://doi.org/10.1177/1468797605070338.

Pritchard, A. and Morgan, N. (2006) Hotel Babylon? Exploring hotels as liminal sites of transition and transgression. *Tourism Management* 27 (5), 762–772. https://doi.org/10.1016/j.tourman.2005.05.015.

Puhl, R. and Brownell, K. (2003) Psychosocial origins of obesity stigma: Toward changing a powerful and pervasive bias. *Obesity Reviews* 4, 213–227. https://doi.org/10.1046/j.1467-789X.2003.00122.x.

Qantas (2020) Dress guidelines, Qantas website. See https://www.qantas.com/au/en/frequent-flyer/the-qantas-club/dress-guidelines.html (accessed May 2020).

Sampson, H. (2019) Recent incident over attire highlights the ambiguity in airline dress codes, *The Washington Post*, 11 July. See https://www.washingtonpost.com/travel/2019/07/11/recent-incident-over-attire-highlights-ambiguity-airline-dress-codes/?noredirect=on (accessed September 2019).

Schaberg, C. (2017) *Airportness: The Nature of Flight*. New York: Bloomsbury.

Shilling, C. (2003) *The Body and Social Theory* (2nd edn). London: Sage.

Singapore Airlines (2020) The Singapore Girl, Singapore Airlines website. See https://www.singaporeair.com/en_UK/us/flying-withus/our-story/singapore-girl/ (accessed May 2020).

Small, J. and Harris, C. (2012a) Packing through the ages: Gender and age related behaviour around packing for conference travel. In *CAUTHE 2012: The New Golden Age of Tourism and Hospitality; Book 2; Proceedings of the 22nd Annual Conference* (p. 567). Melbourne: La Trobe University.

Small, J. and Harris, C. (2012b) Obesity and tourism: Rights and responsibilities. *Annals of Tourism Research* 39 (2), 686–707. https://doi.org/10.1016/j.annals.2011.09.002.

Small, J. and Harris, C. (2014) Crying babies on planes: Aeromobility and parenting. *Annals of Tourism Research* 48, 27–41. https://doi.org/10.1016/j.annals.2014.04.009.

Small, J. and Harris, C. (2015) The older flight attendant: Treasured or dreaded? In E. Wilson and M. Witsel (eds) *Rising Tides and Sea Changes: Adaptation and Innovation in Tourism and Hospitality: Proceedings of the 25th Annual CAUTHE Conference*, Gold Coast, Queensland, 2–5 February 2015 (pp. 713–716). Gold Coast, Qld: Southern Cross University.

Spiess, L. and Waring, P. (2005) Aesthetic labour, cost minimisation and the labour process in the Asia Pacific airline industry. *Employee Relations* 27 (1/2), 193–207. https://doi.org/10.1108/01425450510572702.

Stadiem, W. (2014) *Jet Set: The People, the Planes, the Glamor, and the Romance in Aviation's Glory Years* [e-book]. New York: Ballantine Books.
Tajfel, H. and Turner, J. (1979) An integrative theory of intergroup conflict. In W. Austin and S. Worchel (eds) *The Social Psychology of Intergroup Relations* (pp. 33–48). Monterey, CA: Brooks/Cole.
Tiemeyer, P. (2013) *Plane Queer: Labor, Sexuality, and AIDS in the History of Male Flight Attendants*. Berkeley: University of California Press.
Tietje, L. and Cresap, S. (2005) Is lookism unjust?: The ethics of aesthetics and public policy implications. *Journal of Libertarian Studies* 19 (2), 31–50.
Transport Workers Union (2019) #CabinCrewToo, TWU website, 2 May. See https://www.twu.com.au/aviation/cabincrewtoo/ (accessed May 2020).
Tulloch, L. (2013) Keep yourself nice in the air. *The Sydney Morning Herald, Traveller*, 10 August. See http://www.traveller.com.au/keep-yourself-nice-in-the-air-2rg49 (accessed May 2020).
Tulloch, L. (2015) Passenger shaming on planes: Bad behaviour exposed on the web, *The Sydney Morning Herald, Traveller*, 2 March. See http://www.traveller.com.au/passenger-shaming-on-planes-bad-behaviour-exposed-on-the-web-13j2sz (accessed May 2020).
Twigg, J. (2012) Adjusting the cut: Fashion, the body and age on the UK high street. *Ageing and Society* 32 (6), 1030–1054. https://doi.org/10.1017/S0144686X11000754.
Twigg, J. and Buse, C. (2013) Dress, dementia and the embodiment of identity. *Dementia* 12 (3), 326–336. https://doi.org/10.1177/1471301213476504.
Twigg, J. and Majima, S. (2014) Consumption and the constitution of age: Expenditure patterns on clothing, hair and cosmetics among post-war 'Baby Boomers'. *Journal of Aging Studies* 30, 23–32. https://doi.org/10.1016/j.jaging.2014.03.003.
Veijola, S. and Valtonen, A. (2007) The body in tourism industry. In A. Pritchard, N. Morgan, I. Ateljevic and C. Harris (eds) *Tourism and Gender: Embodiment, Sensuality and Experience* (pp. 13–31). Wallingford, Oxfordshire: CABI.
Vilnai-Yavetz, I. and Gilboa, S. (2014) The cost (and the value) of customer attire: Linking high-and low-end dress styles to service quality and prices offered by service employees. *Service Business* 8 (2), 355–373. DOI: 10.1007/s11628-013-0199-5.
Weaver, D. and Lawton, L. (2014) *Tourism Management* (5th edn). Milton, Qld: Wiley.

5 Flying into Uncertainty: Part 1 – Flying with Mobility Disability[1]

Simon Darcy, Jennie Small and Barbara Almond

One of the most valuable aspects of this focus on mobility has been to show that mobility is a resource distributed unequally among social groups (Frith, 2012: 134).

Introduction

The 'new mobilities' paradigm proposes that, in today's world, we are on the move. At the same time, there are writers within mobility studies (such as Gale, 2008; Hall, 2010; Hannam *et al.*, 2006; Sheller, 2016) who have taken a critical perspective, acknowledging the concept of *im*mobilities and 'the unequal power relations which unevenly distribute motility, the potential for mobility' (Hannam *et al.*, 2006: 15). However, a consideration of immobilities/mobilities requires caution as Hall warns that the dichotomy 'is extremely artificial' (Hall, 2010: 37). Some may never leave home to travel while others may travel but, along the way, experience constraints to their mobility. We may question whether any of us have 'complete' mobility or immobility. Adey (2006) refers to 'relative immobilities'– mobility and immobility are experienced in relation to each other. One must also remember that mobility is not always empowering or immobility disempowering. As Frith (2012: 134) reminds us, 'a blind equation of mobility with freedom will not do'. He explains: 'Maybe as important as actual movement (mobility), or the potential for movement (motility), is *how* people move through space'. In other words, the qualitative nature of mobility needs to consider the way that movement is experienced and how much choice or control we have over our movement. Sawchuck (2014) speaks of 'differential mobility' while Sheller (2016) refers to the *unevenness* of mobility. Drawing on Adey *et al.* (2014), Sheller (2016: 17) explains that unevenness 'may take the form of uneven qualities of experience, uneven access to infrastructure, uneven materialities, uneven subjects of mobility, and uneven events of stopping, going, passing, pausing, and waiting'. When we consider the mobility of those with disabilities (mobility, sensory, cognitive and mental health), the unevenness of the air travel experience is evident.

Defining mobility as 'the entanglement of movement, representation, and practice', Cresswell (2010: 19) highlights a 'politics of mobility': the production and distribution of power in each of these aspects of mobility. A politics of mobility stresses the social differentiation, inequalities and inequities of mobilities since mobilities are co-constituted with the hierarchies of social class, age, gender, sexuality, race, nationality, ethnicity, stage of life cycle, generation and/or dis/ability. Yet, none of these subjectivities exist on their own. They all (age, gender, social class etc.) intersect in mobile spaces and places. Underlying critical mobility studies are the notions of fairness and justice. While literature on transport justice goes back to the 1960s, more recently, writers (such as Cook & Butz, 2019; Sheller, 2018, 2019) have taken a broader, more holistic approach preferring the concept, *mobility justice* – the intersection of the '"mobilities paradigm" scholarship and social justice theorizing' (Cook & Butz, 2019: 3). Sheller (2019) explains: 'Mobility justice is an overarching concept for thinking about how power and inequality inform the governance and control of movement, shaping the patterns of unequal mobility and immobility in the circulation of people, resources and information' (Sheller, 2019: 21). To understand mobility injustice requires an examination of past social and political struggles. As Sheller (2019: 21) says, 'mobility injustices do not occur after entities "enter" a space [in our case, an airport or plane] but *are the process through which unequal spatial conditions and differential subjects are made*'.

This, and the following two chapters look at one group of passengers who experience uneven mobility and injustice across all areas of intersectionality – those with a disability/disabilities. At the same time, the right to travel and tourism, as outlined in Article 30 of the *Convention on the Rights of People with Disabilities* (CRPWD) (United Nations, 2006), stresses that people with disabilities should expect the same rights to citizenship and quality of life as those who are nondisabled (Darcy & Taylor, 2009). While mobility is a frequent concept within critical disability studies, Parent argues that, despite discussions of the politics of embodiment and power relations being central to mobilities research, 'this interdisciplinary field has so far failed to seriously engage with critical disability studies' (Parent, 2016: 522) – a problem if we are to understand the experience of air passengers with disability. Critical disability studies start with a social model of disability which sees the cause of 'the problem' as located within the structures of society rather than the individual and their 'tragedy' (Oliver, 1990). Such a model 'considers that disabling social practices, which include physical barriers, social attitudes and material relations of power, are responsible for transforming the individual's *impairment* (embodiment) into a disability' (Small, 2014: 5). Yet, there are criticisms of the social model, for focusing on the social environment while neglecting the physical reality of the person's impairment in their life experience, thus leading to the concept of 'embodied ontology' (Shakespeare & Watson, 2001). This approach is useful in advancing our understanding of the experiences of those with disability as it incorporates both the social and the physical, embodied explanations for life/travel experience. 'In effect, the embodied ontology challenges the dichotomies of impairment/disability and illness/health and offers a model that intertwines structure and agency' (Small & Darcy, 2011: 75).

In any discussion of disability, it is important to consider the type of disability, the degree of disability and the other intersecting subjectivities. Since impairment is strongly related to the ageing process, it is relevant to consider age in the passenger experience of air travel. We also need to recognise that disability may be permanent or temporary and due to injury or illness. When one considers the number of passengers who are (temporarily) ill (with the flu, gastric upset, allergies etc.) or who have young children and travel with prams, then the number with travel or mobility support needs rises considerably. As Darcy and Dickson (2009) identified, at any time, some 31% of travellers may require assisted travel arrangements. Indeed, as Oostveen and Lehtonen (2018: 60) say, 'in reality the whole population risks becoming chronically ill or disabled at some point in their lives'. Yet, these embodied experiences have largely been ignored within tourism or, when they are considered, it is through a monolithic or homogenous construct of disability rather than its embodied or impaired constituent parts.

As studies of tourism and disability have evolved, we have seen the development of accessible tourism as a subfield of study within tourism (Darcy & Burke, 2018). Buhalis and Darcy (2011: 10–11) explain accessible tourism:

> Accessible tourism is a form of tourism that involves collaborative processes between stakeholders that enables people with access requirements, including mobility, vision, hearing and cognitive dimensions of access, to function independently and with equity and dignity through the delivery of universally designed tourism products, services and environments. This definition adopts a whole of life approach where people through their lifespan benefit from accessible tourism provision. These include people with permanent and temporary disabilities, seniors, obese, families with young children and those working in safer and more socially sustainable designed environments. (adapted from Darcy & Dickson, 2009: 34)

Accessible tourism brings together critical tourism and critical disability studies in recognising the complexity of travel in local, regional, national and international destinations. The complexity of travel increases the further afield we go and requires understanding of the embodied experience within the whole travel planning process. As studies have shown, there are many factors which constrain travel for those with disabilities across private and public modes of transport (Darcy & Burke, 2018). However, as stated by Small *et al.* (2012):

> These studies identified that the majority of people did not cite their impairment (intrapersonal constraint) or their interpersonal relationships as a reason for nonparticipation. Instead they identified a series of structural constraints (environment and attitudes encountered) to explain their nonparticipation. (Small *et al.*, 2012: 942)

Travelling independently can be exceptionally challenging for a passenger with disability. Since many will choose to travel with other/s, we find that what constrains the person with disability may also constrain the travel companions. This chapter examines the general field of air travel and disability and then focuses on one group of air travellers who encounter constraints and unevenness in travel, those with *mobility* disability. (In the following chapter we will explore the experiences of those with other impairments – vision, hearing, cognitive and mental health conditions and, in Chapter 7, those who experience fear of flying.)

While this chapter concerns air travel, it is important to recognise that for a person with mobility impairment to travel, there needs to be a continuous travel chain beginning with accessible private or public modes of transport from home to connect to a local, regional, or international airport (Darcy, 2012; Darcy & Burke, 2018). Airports and aircraft must be accessible as must accommodation, transport, attractions and leisure/workspaces at the destination (if the trip is to achieve its purpose). While many of the constraints are general across the travel experience, some are sector specific (see McKercher & Darcy, 2018).

Airlines and Disability

With the growth of tourism in recent decades, the travel industry, and airlines especially, have been required to service an increasing number of people with disability (and with different types of disability). In particular, the number of travellers with reduced mobility is rapidly growing (World Health Organization, 2018). The World Health Organization (2018) explains that much of this increase is the result of an ageing population as well as increasing obesity rates, but it can also be linked to an increased confidence amongst travellers with disability due to the application of disability legislation and policies in many major travel destinations. Despite this newfound confidence, Graham and Metz (2017) note that having a disability is still an influential factor that may inhibit air travel. This idea is supported by data from the UK Civil Aviation Authority (2015) which reports that 42% of travellers with restricted mobility named access issues as a reason for not flying in the previous 12 months. The research further indicates that while many potential travellers with disability would like to travel more frequently, most are unsure or unaware of how they can access air travel. A lack of easily accessible information and a lack of consistency in the information that is available are often cited (Civil Aviation Authority, 2015; Graham & Metz, 2017).

While issues with air travel and service provision for those with disabilities will make media headlines, a review of the academic literature indicates limited scholarly research around access to air travel and disabilities. What research has been done often focuses on *mobility* disabilities rather than the range of disabilities that are present (such as vision, hearing, cognition etc.). From their study of Israeli passengers with disability, Poria *et al.* (2010) remind us that, in practice, there are problems generalising about passengers with disabilities. Experience of air travel varies significantly according to the type of disability of a passenger; the difficulties encountered by passengers using wheelchairs are different from those with crutches or those with vision or hearing impairment.

With a growing market of older travellers (see Graham *et al.*, 2019), the intersection of disability and ageing cannot be ignored as the likelihood of mobility, vision, hearing and/or cognitive impairment will increase with age. Bosch and Gharaveis (2017) stress the decline in spatial cognition which affects our navigation and wayfinding as we age. Changes in vision can exacerbate our ability to wayfind and contribute to air travel difficulties, especially in large, crowded and busy airports. Chang and Chen (2012a), in their study of the needs of air passengers over the age of 65 at Taiwan Taoyuan International Airport, found that there was a gap in importance and satisfaction in transport information to and from the airport, directional information in the airport, announcements of cancelled flights and information on emergency escape. For those aged over 75 there were additional required services. In Brazil, da Silva *et al.* (2015) examined the air transport experiences of older passengers. Their findings were similar to those of earlier researchers: older people encountered difficulties moving around an airport. Using stairs, escalators, ramps and elevators was challenging as was walking long distances. Lack of seating along the route and issues with wayfinding added to the difficulties. Waiting in long lines, lack of accurate information and lack of trained customer service staff were barriers to a comfortable experience. Boarding and disembarkation could prove difficult if there were no air or boarding bridges as passengers had to go up and down stairs carrying luggage. Lack of a boarding bridge also meant boarding and disembarking from shuttle buses which have high steps, few seats and are crowded. Within the aircraft cabin, limited space, inadequate seats, overhead lockers that are too small and too high, and limited accessibility and space to, and within, lavatories were all cited as difficult for the passengers.

Overall, the research in the field is predominantly around customer satisfaction and the cost to the airlines of providing support for travellers with disabilities. Not surprisingly, customer service in the airline industry is a major pain point. As Major and Hubbard (2019) explain, individual airlines often market their competitive advantage around their 'superior' service provision rather than compete solely based on price. The rapid growth in budget airlines has meant that competition in the industry has increased significantly in recent years but while price is important for some companies, many more airlines are now using the experience of 'flying with them' to differentiate their service from the competition. However, when considering passengers with disability, many airlines often fail in their service offerings. Findings from research undertaken in the United States indicate that while there has been a general increase in customer satisfaction shown through a reduction in complaints made to the Department of Transport (DOT) and the airlines themselves, complaints made by people with disability significantly outstrip those of the general population (Major & Hubbard, 2019). Indeed, 'the 2.5% of airline passengers that are disabled generate twice as many complaints than the 97.5% of travellers without a disability' (Major & Hubbard, 2019: 43). Similarly, in the United Kingdom, there is less satisfaction with the overall flying experience for those with disabilities compared with the total market (Graham *et al.*, 2019).

Darcy's (2012) finding that air travel passengers across a range of disabilities would never fly again or would choose other modes of transport (where their independence and dignity were maintained) was related to customer dissatisfaction with air travel. The negative experiences of service quality reported in Darcy's research highlight airlines' negative practices, procedures and attitudes that 'disrespect the independence, dignity and equitable citizenship rights' of passengers with disability (Darcy, 2012: 4). Darcy (2012) further explains that the constraints experienced by these passengers are not a direct result of their disability, but rather a product of economic and cultural practices and procedures imposed on people with impairments by airlines and airports.

As the passenger moves through the air transport spaces, they engage with, or are excluded from, certain materialities. One airport example identified by Oostveen and Lehtonen (2018) is the inaccessibility of most electronic border control gates, or e-gates, for passengers with disability in the European Union Member States, preventing these passengers from experiencing the airport in the same manner as able-bodied passengers.

As they say, 'We reflect this questionable situation against the notion of the good society and consider airports as normatively laden sociophysical zones contributing to experiences of exclusion' (Oostveen & Lehtonen, 2018: 60). Industry lack of knowledge about disabilities can mean incorrect assumptions. Poria *et al.* (2010: 221) found that those with mobility or vision impairment were often assumed by crew members to have cognitive impairment and thus were spoken to 'slowly, loudly, using very basic words' as if they were children. They also found that crew members, when asked for information would address the companion, not the person with disability. Graeme Innes (2016), Australia's Disability Discrimination Commissioner from 2005 to 2014 (and blind himself), reports the invisibility of those with disability. He cites his own experience when his wife (rather than he) was scolded by a flight attendant for his use of the business class (rather than the economy class) toilet.

As stated, the level of servicing offered by airlines to enhance customer satisfaction has always been a crucial issue in the highly competitive airline industry. Nonetheless, there has been an unspoken difference between full service and low-cost airlines in their provision for people with disability. However, with a growing number of travellers with disability wanting or needing to travel on budget airlines, it is becoming a contentious issue. It is also important for the airlines to recognise that customer satisfaction is a function of pre-purchase expectations as well as the actual airport and onboard experience, meaning that service must begin not just upon arrival at the airport but at the point of travel planning and the booking of flights.

Mobility Disability

The study of air travel and disability most often focuses on those with mobility impairment specifically those using wheelchairs. Davies and Christie (2017) explain that accessibility to air travel is an issue for those with mobility disabilities but that, as a broader concept, improved access to the service both throughout the airport and on the plane benefits all passengers. They also note that while some people have permanent mobility limitations, many of us will have temporary conditions that will limit mobility (due to injury, illness and simply changed circumstances) and so any improvements in access may, at some time, benefit all passengers.

Air travel can prove difficult for passengers with mobility disability as the different phases of the air travel service procedure: pre-travel (travel planning, reservation); pre-flight (check-in, passport control, boarding); during flight; and post flight (deplaning, passport control, baggage collection, leaving the airport) (Chang & Chen, 2012b) are often the responsibility of different organisations. As a result, there can be issues with communication between agencies and consistency in service throughout the different stages (Chang & Chen, 2011, 2012a). In many locations, transit through the airport is the responsibility of airport management while boarding of the plane and in-flight service are the responsibility of the airline. Exceptions to this are the EU 27 countries where airports with over 100,000 passengers per year have a central accessibility group responsible for all assisted passenger movements on all airlines (EU REGULATION (EC) No 1107/2006). As Ivor Ambrose of the European Network for Accessible Tourism states:

> Gradually the implementation of this Regulation is working and improving... although the way it is carried out varies from country to country, as you might expect, according to training practices etc. But the good thing is that all airlines are covered by it – for all incoming and outgoing flights in the European Union. (as cited in Darcy, 2013)

It is not only a diversity of responsibilities which may cause issues for travellers with disabilities but also local legislation. Figure 5.1 illustrates a customer service blueprint process for the customer in the United States, from arrival at the airport to departure, identifying the four separate regulators with whom people with mobility disabilities will negotiate on any single trip.

In the United States, airports, surrounding parking lots and transportation around the airport fall under the Americans with Disabilities Act (ADA), the Rehabilitation Act of 1973 and a range of state and local laws and statutes. Airlines and planes themselves fall under a different set of rules through the Air Carrier Access Act (ACAA) 1986 (four years before the ADA). The ACAA regulates facilities, such as bathroom size, seat size and aisle width, with the size of these areas very different to those defined in the ADA. Additionally, the ACAA standards

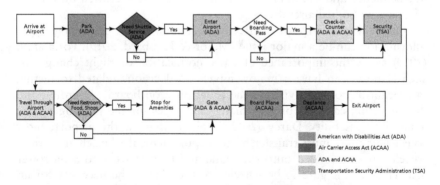

Figure 5.1 Travel processes for people with disabilities and US policies responsible for accessibility standards (Source: Major & Hubbard, 2019)

are enforced through the Department of Transportation and generally do not apply to planes under 60 seats or without two aisles (Major & Hubbard, 2019). Increased security at airports around the world can cause significant issues for people with mobility disability. In many airports, security is the responsibility of yet another government agency. As highlighted above, security measures at airports in the United States 'are the responsibility of the Transportation Security Administration (TSA) and are not covered in either the ACAA or ADA' (Major & Hubbard, 2019: 44). However, TSA officers only receive one to two hours of training on disability screening procedures, limiting their knowledge and understanding significantly (Morris, 2018). Regulations in the ACAA also lack clarification around training for staff. The ACAA outlines airlines' responsibilities to provide training but the section is vague and only refers to 'training to proficiency' without clearly defining what 'proficiency' might mean. It does not include objective measures which might ensure consistency in training and certification of staff (McCarthy, 2011). Processes and polices around access to air travel for those with disabilities should respond to the relevant local legislation, however, legislation across the globe – while similar in intent – may vary in application. Consistency in service for passengers is, thus, not assured. As Darcy (2012: 91) found, 'air travel practices routinely contravened disability discrimination legislation'. At the same time, as Major and Hubbard (2019) explain, there is often a very large disconnect between what people with mobility disability believe the law is and what it really is with many indicating that they did not know that there were different laws and forms of enforcement.

Examining the 'essence' of the air travel experience of passengers with mobility disability, Darcy (2012) highlights some of the difficulties at the pre-travel planning stage, for example, the need to phone the airline to doublecheck that the airline will honour the ticket in respect to the airline's access considerations. Airline staff can still refuse the right to board based on their perception of the passenger's level of independence and the number of power wheelchairs allowed on a flight of a narrow-bodied aircraft.

Once at the airport, ineffective communication regarding flight information can be a major issue (Major & Hubbard, 2019). Poria *et al.* (2010) stress the importance of early notification of flight changes as such changes can have a major impact on decisions related to fasting (a precaution to avoid visiting the toilet once on board). Boarding and disembarking can also present many challenges for the passenger with a mobility disability. Darcy (2012) explains that, at the airport, most wheelchair users must transfer to an airport manual wheelchair as their wheelchair gets loaded onto the plane and then transfer to a narrower aisle chair at the gate to be wheeled to the plane. The necessity for an aisle chair is explained by the inconsistencies between regulations: standard manual wheelchairs do not fit aeroplane aisles or doorways of onboard toilets under the ACAA. On other public transport in the United States, such as buses and trains, wheelchairs are able to be secured to the floor so the user does not have to transfer, eliminating potential accidents and being able to board and depart the transport more quickly while maintaining the seating ergonomics and comfort of the wheelchair user. These same supports are not made available on aircraft. However, a study by the National Academies of Sciences Engineering and Medicine (2020) is currently examining the possibility of motorised and non-motorised wheelchairs being directly boarded onto the aircraft and locked down with restraint systems thus alleviating the need for people with mobility disability to be separated from their mobility device during air travel. Figure 5.2 shows one of the authors preparing to be manually transferred from a power wheelchair to the much smaller aisle chair prior to boarding. For airports without air bridges, there are other challenges. As Figure 5.3 shows, a forklift equipped with an air cargo cage can be used to board the wheelchair user, otherwise, the person with disability needs to be physically carried up and down aircraft stairs in an aisle chair.

On entering the plane, airline personnel wheel the passenger in their aisle chair to their seat, where the user then transfers to the plane

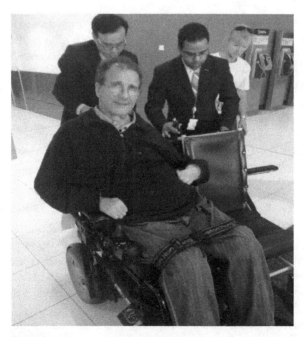

Figure 5.2 One of the authors, Simon Darcy, preparing to be manually transferred from a power wheelchair to the aisle chair (Singapore, 2015 © Fiona Darcy with permission)

Figure 5.3 Qantas forklift cage for airports without air bridges (Uluru Airport, 2004 © Fiona Darcy with permission)

seat. Usually, passengers with wheelchairs are boarded prior to other passengers but sometimes the procedures break down. Darcy (2012) found that 'This creates a spectacle that one interviewee likened to *"being a freak in a circus", where they felt that everyone was staring at them*' Darcy (2012: 6). The experience can be both humiliating and embarrassing as another passenger with mobility impairment reported:

> ... *there's been a nasty two or three experiences where I've been boarded last. That is embarrassing to be sort of transferred onto a chair and through the airplane, knocking everybody as you go, and then to have the embarrassment of being lifted into your seat in front of everybody ... I find it embarrassing.* (Davies & Christie, 2017: 91)

When one considers that the process to board the aeroplane involves up to three transfers, often requiring assistance from airline personnel, it becomes obvious that, in transfer, the wheelchair user is susceptible to injury from falling or other harm. There is anxiety for potential injury when being manhandled into one's seat, as one passenger explains:

> *They have to lift me into an aisle chair and then take me down the aisle in this chair then lift you across three seats so you're at the window seat, two people lifting, and it's caused me a lot of pain and problems. It's the worst part.* (Davies & Christie, 2017: 91)

Major and Hubbard (2019) cite inadequate boarding assistance as one of the four main areas of concern for passengers with mobility issues. As Darcy (2012) states, the expertise of staff in assisting passengers to board or disembark can vary enormously. Citing the Australian situation, he explains that while most major airports employ porters, assistance at regional airports may come from 'anyone who is available'. Delays in the provision of assistance (for example, for aisle chairs and trained staff) are stressful (Ancell & Graham, 2016; Poria *et al.*, 2010). Difficulties can arise if the passenger is left immobile for any period. Figure 5.4 shows the author left in the aisle chair (for an indeterminable period) before boarding. Depending on the type of disability, in this case spinal cord injury, sitting on an ill-fitting chair without a pressure cushion can lead to compromised health outcomes. Such a scenario (of waiting) is a reminder that discrimination not only indicates who can and cannot use public spaces but also '*whose* time is valued' (Sawchuk, 2014: 415). According to Major and Hubbard (2019), another major concern for passengers with mobility issues relates to the accessibility of their seat. The passenger hopes that the booking

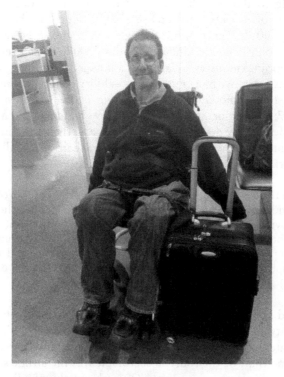

Figure 5.4 From mobility to immobility, one of the authors, Simon Darcy, immobile in an aisle chair (Singapore, 2015 © Fiona Darcy with permission)

details are correct and they have been allocated an appropriate seat with flip-up arm rests (Darcy, 2012).

Once in flight, there is anxiety around injury to oneself during turbulence and landing. The toilet experience on aeroplanes has been highlighted by writers (such as Darcy, 2012; Davies & Christie, 2017; Poria *et al.*, 2010; Yau *et al.*, 2004) as particularly problematic for users of wheelchairs. Due to the limited space, if a person had to use the facility they would need to be carried. To avoid this option, passengers often use a catheter or fast which raises health concerns if the person dehydrates. The humiliation and embarrassment if an accident occurs are reported by Poria *et al.* (2010):

> Every *disabled person is familiar with someone who's had an 'accident' during a flight; you'd guess correctly that this is very embarrassing. It's not only that you feel terrible because of your situation but also for the others near you, who cannot escape to another seat on board (Interviewee no. 24, Wheelchair user).* (Poria *et al.*, 2010: 221)

The placing of the user's chair in the cargo hold of the plane, making it vulnerable to damage due to poor or untrained staff handling, is further cause of anxiety and sense of helplessness for the user (Bailey, 2007; Darcy, 2012; Trailblazers Young Campaigners' Network, 2012). A common complaint identified by Bailey (2007) in her review of the Australian airline industry related to damaged and lost wheelchairs. As one passenger with a mobility disability said, *'airlines need to understand that removing our wheelchair is like breaking our legs'* (Bailey, 2007: ii). Major and Hubbard (2019) highlight the attitude and treatment of mobility devices by the airlines and their staff in the United States, accentuating the importance of a wheelchair or mobility device to a person with disability.

> Wheelchairs are a vital piece of medical equipment and are often custom made and tailored to the individual. An individual's wheelchair not only provides mobility but is also critical for good health, designed to assure correct propulsion techniques, seating and positioning and even change a person's orientation without moving hip, knee and ankle angles (Christopher and Dana Reeve Foundation, n.d.). (Major & Hubbard, 2019: 51)

Kim and Lehto (2012), in their study of complaints from customers with mobility disabilities, found that the most common airline service failures related to interaction with airline staff ('unsolicited employee conduct') and that, of the tourism sectors, it was the airline sector where this was most likely to occur. Innes (2016) highlights the 'bad deal' that people with disabilities get from airlines and sees much of the problem as one of attitude – 'a limiting and negative attitude by many airline staff towards people with disabilities'. Major and Hubbard (2019) and Poria et al. (2010) similarly emphasise the importance of the human dimension of services to the passenger experience. Innes (2016) highlights the invisibility of people with mobility disability as evident in the language used by airline staff. He explains: 'People who use wheelchairs often find themselves being discussed – in their presence – as if they were a package or simply not there. Many is the time I have heard airline passengers who use mobility aids referred to, in their presence, as "a wheelchair"' (Innes, 2016: 43). Darcy (2012) reports a case where a staff member, referring to a couple with mobility disability, yelled down the corridor 'I've got a couple of carry-ons here' (Darcy, 2012: 7).

Communication and training are key components of effective service provision. Bailey (2007) found that the failure of airlines to pass information between staff was a common cause of complaints. She explains that problems experienced by travellers included: a lack of knowledge by service staff about the airline's access policies; incorrect or conflicting information provided to travellers at different stages of the travel experience; and messages about passengers' needs not conveyed to airline flight crew. There were inconsistencies across the flight travel network and service provision between different airports and airlines, as previously stated. Significant differences were also noted in the quality, depth and detail provided in any training that staff did receive depending on whether they were employed by air carriers, airport contractors or security staff. The experience of air transport throughout the European Union for people with mobility disabilities has been reported by The Trailblazers Young Campaigners' Network (2012) after receiving numerous complaints from members about 'second-rate' service from European airlines. Complaints regarding different stages of the travel process included: inability to obtain cheapest fares (budget airlines had restrictions on wheelchair weight); damaged wheelchairs; personal injuries or humiliation during transfers to airline seats by poorly trained staff; and a generally low expectation of airlines to take care of mobility and medical equipment. Consequently, travellers with disability indicated that they often avoided flying.

For children with a disability (and their parents), travelling by air can be challenging. Davies and Christie (2018), studying the experiences of parents flying with a child with severe disabilities and complex care needs, noted similarities with adults with a disability. There were also differences. As the caregiver for a child with a disability, the role could be physically exerting for the parent, especially as they and the child age. Amongst caregiving duties was toileting. While adults with disabilities might avoid using the toilet, children often require the toilet which involves the parent carrying the child to the cubicle and supporting while in there or finding a private space where the child can be laid down for a change of pad or use of portable toilet. One mother explains the complicated procedure:

> *Really hideous. The airline crew were very kind I have to say, they let us take his portable toilet chair on the plane and we would signal for them when he needed it. They curtained off an area of the plane, a very small area near the galley, and my husband and I would lift him down, carry him down to that little area, I would lie him down in this curtained area, sort clothes, lift him up and then my husband would poke the toilet chair into... so that my son could use the toilet and then again it would be same afterwards, I would be trying to clean him up, lift him off, my husband would then have to deal with the contents whilst I laid him back down in this relatively small space, sorted him out, got his clothes back on and then we'd have to carry him back up the plane [Participant G, Female, 43].* (Davies & Christie, 2018: 126)

For a child with disability, seating on the plane can also be problematic when the seat is too big to support the child.

Unfortunately, rather than embracing the opportunity to provide a better service for those with disability, the supply-side organisations of airports and airlines have focused on the cost and logistics associated with 'passengers with reduced mobility' (PRM), defined by the European Commission as 'any person whose mobility when using transport is reduced due to any physical disability (sensory or locomotor, permanent or temporary), intellectual disability or impairment, or any other cause of disability' (Graham *et al.*, 2019: 2). As Ancell and Graham (2016) note in Table 5.1, they discuss disability and embodiment in terms of the 'cost' to airlines of passengers with reduced mobility, across nine areas. In doing so, they note how these costs are likely to increase with the increased number of travellers with mobility limitations. Yet, these arguments in the cost discourse are absent when discussing other passengers, such as family groups and sport tourists with equipment.

While much of the academic literature on the service needs of passengers with mobility disabilities is from the customers' standpoint, Wang and Cole (2014) investigated these needs from the perspective of the service provider – the flight attendants. The research identified four areas of in-flight service needs: the need for help with the use of amenities; the need to be treated the same as passengers without disability; the need for individualised services based on the passenger's disability; and the need for effective and accurate communication. The study participants indicated that greater training is necessary to improve service provision. In sum, the understanding by these cabin crew of the service needs of those with mobility disability reflects those cited by their customers.

It is clear from the above that air travel is an embodied and often a highly emotional experience for those with mobility disability. One might wonder why people take the risk to fly at all (Davies & Christie, 2017;

Table 5.1 Functional Key Factors (FKF) for measuring the airline costs of PRMs

FKF	Examples of measurements
PRM transfers	Number and type of PRMs carried each flight Level of service required by each PRM Excess weight over 100 kg standard Frequency of dismantling mobility scooters/wheelchairs, detachment and reattachment of batteries Number of hours of airport pre-notification required for PRMs Frequency of pre-notification of PRMs
Mobility aids	Number, weight and dimensions of PRM mobility aids per PRM per flight Additional fuel needed to carry heavier mobility aids
Aircraft delays/diversions costs	Cause of diversions Number of diversions Delays caused to aircraft turnround by loading and unloading heavy mobility aids Aircraft delay owing to late notified or late-delivered PRMs
Staff training costs	Cost of training staff to dismantle and reassemble mobility aids (at departure and destination) Crew training for assisting PRMs on board Airline ground staff training for PRMs
Staff health, safety and welfare	Injuries to PRM helpers Compensation payments to PRM helpers
Aircraft fixtures and fittings costs	Capital and operating costs for additional aircraft fixtures and fittings to enable PRM travel (e.g. lifting armrests, on board wheelchairs, additional toilet fixtures, fittings and possibly space) Additional fuel costs due to extra weight for additional aircraft fixtures and fittings
Airport costs	PRM passenger charge (levied by airport operator to cover their costs)
Transaction costs	Compensation to PRMs for mishandling them and/or their mobility equipment Compensation to other passengers who may have been delayed by PRM events
Opportunity costs	Loss of seating if required to enable accessible toilet compartment Weight penalty for aircraft fixtures and fittings (e.g. onboard wheelchairs, lifting armrests) Loss of freight space/weight if displaced by PRM equipment

Source: Ancell and Graham (2016: 43).

Poria *et al.*, 2010). Yet, despite the complaints and spaces for improvement in airport and airline facilities and service, there are many positive experiences for those with mobility disability. Trailblazers (2012) identified problems with the EU experiences of travellers with disabilities, however, when the industry gets the service experience correct, it is memorable for those on the receiving end, as Darcy recalls:

> ...I had nothing but an extraordinary level of service at both Milan and Rome International airports facilitated by a dedicated service support group provided across all airlines for people with (mobility) disabilities. ... my service team ... provided me a continuous service experience from arriving at the check-in counter to being seated on the plane.

Figure 5.5 Rome 2012, Simon Darcy, one of the authors, with the ADR Assistance team on the light rail transferring to the boarding gate (2012 © Fiona Darcy with permission)

> *This service should be provided no matter what airline I would have been travelling on. I liken the experience to being serviced by a Formula 1 pit crew, totally professional, courteous and the highest levels of service provision. Fantastico!* (adapted from Darcy, 2013)

See Figure 5.5.

Conclusion

As Saltes (2018: 84) states, 'Navigating space is more than just embodied motion or mobility; it involves interaction with material artifacts and others in the spaces where we find ourselves'. For those with a disability there are many structural barriers and negative attitudes. This chapter has identified the significant challenges, constraints, and issues in air travel for people with mobility disability or, as they are referred to by the industry, 'people with reduced mobility'. The paradox of the immobility/mobility dichotomy that Hall (2010) warns against for being over simplistic is nowhere more apparent than with respect to people with mobility disability. While the mobility studies literature recognises that access to local, regional, national and international mobilities is not always equitable, ironically, very little work on mobility theory has considered those with mobility disability and the embodied nature of their experiences. Regardless of whether the individual was born with their mobility disability (congenital) or acquired their mobility disability through some form of accident or longer-term onset through a medical condition (e.g. multiple sclerosis), the literature suggests that it is not the impairment that affects their motivation for air travel, but rather other interpersonal, attitudinal or predominantly structural factors (Darcy, 2012; Shi *et al.*, 2012). To service the group and support their embodied experiences, a series of attitudinal, communication and structural supports are required (Chang & Chen, 2011, 2012c) throughout the travel planning and journey. Understanding the process from pre-travel to post flight (Chang & Chen, 2012b) offers travel agents, airport and air travel providers and regulators an opportunity to streamline procedures for individuals to improve their air travel experience. While policies and procedures are in place on the supply side, they tend to concentrate on the logistics and cost of engaging with people with mobility disability rather than on improving customer service and, hence, their embodied experience. As Goggin (2016: 539) suggests:

> ... if we do not comprehend the 'becoming' of disability and mobilities in situ now, and the embodied sensory, social, cultural, collective and personal practices in place and space presently – how can we imagine, design and enact expansive, enabling, and just societies in the future?

People with mobility disability must be represented within international standards for aircraft design if their needs are to be met and their service experiences improved. While the US Access Board (National Academies of Sciences Engineering and Medicine, 2020) is currently investigating the possibility of boarding wheelchairs directly onto the aircraft allowing the individual to stay in their wheelchair during flight, it will take years to gain regulatory approval and then decades for the replacement of aircraft flying stock. In the interim, customer-centred approaches for people with mobility disability should be a focus of the airport and airline industry. Mobility disability is the most obvious group of travellers with disability. The next chapter examines those with vision, hearing, intellectual, cognitive and mental health disabilities who, while sharing some of the experiences of those with mobility disability, have their own unique experiences and responses.

Note

(1) While acknowledging the many factors which may affect the potential for mobility (social class, ethnicity, nationality, gender, impairment etc.), and thus the range of individuals who could be said to have a 'mobility disability', we use the term according to the Disability Studies literature to refer specifically to those whose gross or fine motor skills are impaired. This will include users of wheelchairs (manual or power), mobility scooters or other aids/equipment (walking sticks, crutches, walking frames).

References

Adey, P. (2006) If mobility is everything then it is nothing: Towards a relational politics of (im)mobilities. *Mobilities* 1 (1), 75–94. https://doi.org/10.1080/17450100500489080.

Adey, P., Bissell, D., Hannam, K., Merriman, P. and Sheller, M. (eds) (2014) *The Routledge Handbook of Mobilities*. London: Routledge.

Ancell, D. and Graham, A. (2016) A framework for evaluating the European airline costs of disabled persons and persons with reduced mobility. *Journal of Air Transport Management* 50, 41–44. https://doi.org/10.1016/j.jairtraman.2015.10.001.

Bailey, B. (2007) Flight closed: Report on the experiences of People with Disabilities in domestic airline travel in Australia. See https://www.infrastructure.gov.au/transport/disabilities/review/files/submissions/63_PIAC.pdf (accessed February 2020).

Bosch, S. and Gharaveis, A. (2017) Flying solo: A review of the literature on wayfinding for older adults experiencing visual or cognitive decline. *Applied Ergonomics* 58, 327–333. https://doi.org/10.1016/j.apergo.2016.07.010.

Buhalis, D. and Darcy, S. (2011) *Accessible Tourism: Concepts and Issues*. Bristol: Channel View Publications.

Chang, Y. and Chen, C. (2011) Identifying mobility service needs for disabled air passengers. *Tourism Management* 32 (5), 1214–1217. https://doi.org/10.1016/j.tourman.2010.11.001.

Chang, Y. and Chen, C. (2012a) Service needs of elderly air passengers. *Journal of Air Transport Management* 18, 26–29. https://doi.org/10.1016/j.jairtraman.2011.07.002.

Chang, Y. and Chen, C. (2012b) Overseas travel choice for persons with reduced mobility. *Journal of Air Transport Management* 20, 43–45. https://doi.org/10.1016/j.jairtraman.2011.11.005.

Chang, Y. and Chen, C. (2012c) Meeting the needs of disabled air passengers: Factors that facilitate help from airlines and airports. *Tourism Management* 33 (3), 529–536. https://doi.org/10.1016/j.tourman.2011.06.002.

Civil Aviation Authority (2015) Consumer research for the UK aviation sector – final report CAP 1303. See https://publicapps.caa.co.uk/docs/33/CAP1303ConsumerresearchfortheUKaviationsectorfinalreport.pdf (accessed February 2020).

Cook, N. and Butz, D. (2019) Moving toward mobility justice. In N. Cook and D.E. Butz (eds) *Mobilities, Mobility Justice and Social Justice* (pp. 3–21). London: Routledge.

Cresswell, T. (2010) Towards a politics of mobility. *Environment and Planning D: Society and Space* 28, 17–31. DOI: 10.1068/d11407.

Darcy, S. (2012) (Dis)Embodied air travel experiences: Disability, discrimination and the affect of a discontinuous air travel chain. *Journal of Hospitality and Tourism Management* 19 (1), 91–101. https://doi.org/10.1017/jht.2012.8.

Darcy, S. (2013) Air travel and disability – Ongoing dilemmas, discrimination and loss of dignity in national and international mobility. See http://accessibletourismresearch.blogspot.com/2013/02/air-travel-and-disability-ongoing.html (accessed February 2020).

Darcy, S. and Burke, P.F. (2018) On the road again: The barriers and benefits of automobility for people with disability. *Transportation Research Part A: Policy and Practice* 107, 229–245. https://doi.org/10.1016/j.tra.2017.11.002.

Darcy, S. and Dickson, T.J. (2009) A whole-of-life approach to tourism: The case for accessible tourism experiences. *Journal of Hospitality and Tourism Management* 16, 32–34. https://doi.org/10.1375/jhtm.16.1.32.

Darcy, S. and Taylor, T. (2009) Disability citizenship: An Australian human rights analysis of the cultural industries. *Leisure Studies* 28 (4), 419–441. https://doi.org/10.1080/02614360903071753.

da Silva, T., de Souza, J., da Silva, L., Figueiredo, J. and Menegon, N. (2015) Brazilain air transport: Experiences of elderly passengers. *Proceedings of 19th Triennial Congress of IEA*, Melbourne 9–14 August 2015.

Davies, A. and Christie, N. (2017) An exploratory study of the experiences of wheelchair users as aircraft passengers – implications for policy and practice. *IATSS Research* 41, 89–93. https://doi.org/10.1016/j.iatssr.2017.05.003.

Davies, A. and Christie, N. (2018) The experiences of parents with children with disabilities travelling on planes: An exploratory study. *Journal of Transport and Health* 11, 122–129. https://doi.org/10.1016/j.jth.2018.10.002.

Frith, J. (2012) Splintered space: Hybrid spaces and differential mobility. *Mobilities* 7 (1), 131–149. https://doi.org/10.1080/17450101.2012.631815.

Gale, T. (2008) The end of tourism, or endings in tourism. In P. Burns and M. Novelli (eds) *Tourism and Mobilities: Local-global Connections* (pp. 1–14). Wallingford: CABI.

Goggin, G. (2016) Disability and mobilities: Evening up social futures. *Mobilities* 11 (4), 533–541. https://doi.org/10.1080/17450101.2016.1211821.

Graham, A. and Metz, D. (2017) Limits to air travel growth: The case of infrequent flyers. *Journal of Air Transport Management* 62, 109–120. https://doi.org/10.1016/j.jairtraman.2017.03.011.

Graham, A., Budd, L., Ison, S. and Timmis, A. (2019) Airports and ageing passengers: A study of the UK. *Research in Transportation Business & Management* 30, 1–8. https://doi.org/10.1016/j.rtbm.2019.100380.

Hall, C.M. (2010) Equal access for all? Regulative mechanisms, inequality and tourism mobility. In S. Cole and N.M. (eds) *Tourism and Inequality* (pp. 34–48). Wallingford: CABI.

Hannam, K., Sheller, M. and Urry, J. (2006) Editorial: Mobilities, immobilities and moorings. *Mobilities* 1, 1–22. https://doi.org/10.1080/17450100500489189.

Innes, G. (2016) *Finding a Way*. St Lucia, Queensland: University of Queensland Press.

Kim, S. and Lehto, X. (2012) The voice of tourists with mobility disabilities: Insights from online customer complaint websites. *International Journal of Contemporary Hospitality Management* 24, 451–476. https://doi.org/10.1108/09596111211217905.

Major, W.L. and Hubbard, S.M. (2019) An examination of disability-related complaints in the United States commercial aviation sector. *Journal of Air Transport Management* 78, 43–53. https://doi.org/10.1016/j.jairtraman.2019.04.006.

McCarthy, M.J. (2011) Improving the United States airline industry's capacity to provide safe and dignified services to travelers with disabilities: Focus group findings. *Disability and Rehabilitation* 33, 25–26, 2612-2619. https://doi.org/10.3109/09638281003729540.

McKercher, B. and Darcy, S. (2018) Re-conceptualizing barriers to travel by people with disabilities. *Tourism Management Perspectives* 26, 59–66. https://doi.org/10.1016/j.tmp.2018.01.003.

Morris, J. (2018) What we learned at the 2018 TSA Disability Meeting. See https://wheelchairtravel.org/takeaways-2018-tsa-disability-conference/ (accessed February 2020).

National Academies of Sciences Engineering and Medicine (2020) Project information: Committee for a Study on the Feasibility of Wheelchair Restraint Systems in Passenger Aircraft. See https://www8.nationalacademies.org/pa/projectview.aspx?key=51840 (accessed May 2020).

Oliver, M. (1990) *The Politics of Disablement*. Basingstoke: Macmillan.

Oostveen, A. and Lehtonen, P. (2018) The requirement of accessibility: European automated border control systems for persons with disabilities. *Technology in Society* 52, 60–69. https://doi.org/10.1016/j.techsoc.2017.07.009.

Parent, L. (2016) The wheeling interview: Mobile methods and disability. *Mobilities* 11 (4), 521–532. https://doi.org/10.1080/17450101.2016.1211820.

Poria, Y., Reichel, A. and Brandt, Y. (2010) The flight experiences of people with disabilities: An exploratory study. *Journal of Travel Research* 49 (2), 216–227. https://doi.org/10.1177/0047287509336477.

Saltes, N. (2018) Navigating disabling spaces: Challenging ontological norms and the spatialization of difference through 'Embodied Practices of Mobility'. *Mobilities* 13 (1), 81–95. https://doi.org/10.1080/17450101.2017.1333279.

Sawchuck, K. (2014) Impaired. In P. Adey, D. Bissell, K. Hannam, P. Merriman and M. Sheller (eds) *Routledge Handbook of Mobilities* (pp. 409–420). New York: Routledge.

Shakespeare, T. and Watson, N. (2001) The social model of disability: An outdated ideology. *Research in Social Science and Disability* 2 (1), 9–28. https://doi.org/10.1016/S1479-3547(01)80018-X.

Sheller, M. (2016) Uneven mobility futures: A Foucauldian approach. *Mobilities* 11 (1), 15–31. https://doi.org/10.1080/17450101.2015.1097038.

Sheller, M. (2018) *Mobility Justice: The Politics of Movement in an Age of Extremes*. London: Verso.

Sheller, M. (2019) Theorizing mobility justice. In N. Cook and D. Butz (eds) *Mobilities, Mobility Justice and Social Justice* (pp. 22–36). London: Routledge.

Shi, L., Cole, S. and Chancellor, H.C. (2012) Understanding leisure travel motivations of travelers with acquired mobility impairments. *Tourism Management* 33, 228–231. https://doi.org/10.1016/j.tourman.2011.02.007.

Small, J. (2014) Interconnecting mobilities on tour: Tourists with vision impairment partnered with sighted tourists. *Tourism Geographies* (1), 76–90. https://doi.org/10.1080/14616688.2014.938690.

Small, J. and Darcy, S. (2011) Understanding tourist experience through embodiment: The contribution of Critical Tourism and Disability Studies. In D. Buhalis and S. Darcy (eds) *Accessible Tourism: Concepts and Issues* (pp. 73–97). Bristol: Channel View Publications.

Small, J., Darcy, S. and Packer, T. (2012) The embodied tourist experiences of people with vision impairment: Management implications beyond the visual gaze. *Tourism Management* 33 (4), 941–950. https://doi.org/10.1016/j.tourman.2011.09.015.

Trailblazers Young Campaigners' Network (2012) Up in the air – The Trailblazers' report on air travel. See http://www.musculardystrophyuk.org/wp-content/uploads/2015/04/Trailblazers_AirlineReport_WEB.pdf (accessed November 2019).

United Nations (2006) *Convention on the Rights of Persons with Disabilities* (A/61/611-6 December 2006). New York, NY: United Nations General Assembly.

Wang, W. and Cole, S. (2014) Perceived onboard service needs of passengers with mobility limitations: An investigation among flight attendants. *Asia Pacific Journal of Tourism Research* 19 (11), 1239–1259. https://doi.org/10.1080/10941665.2013.852116.

World Health Organization (2018) Disability and health. *WHO Newsroom*, 1 December. See https://www.who.int/en/news-room/fact-sheets/detail/disability-and-health (accessed January 2020).

Yau, M., McKercher, B. and Packer, T. (2004) Traveling with a disability: More than an access issue. *Annals of Tourism Research* 31 (4), 946–960. https://doi.org/10.1016/j.annals.2004.03.007.

6 Flying into Uncertainty: Part 2 – Flying with Non-Mobility Disabilities

Jennie Small, Alison McIntosh,
Barbara Almond and Simon Darcy

> ... the research agenda has moved on from accessibility and disability as 'hidden conditions' become important due to legislative requirements on making tourism accessible for all, that transcends physical and visible conditions. (Connell & Page, 2019: 39)

Introduction

While the academic literature on the air travel experience of those with disability has tended to focus on mobility disability, and the required service delivery associated with this group, a growing number of researchers are examining the experiences of passengers with non-mobility disabilities, many of which are considered 'hidden' disabilities. Much of what has been written in Chapter 5 about mobility, mobility disability and the air travel experience, is relevant to those with other types of impairment, however, there will be differences unique to the specific impairment. Non-mobility disabilities considered in this chapter include vision and hearing impairments, cognitive impairments, such as dementia, autism and epilepsy and mental health conditions. It must be remembered that some passengers with non-mobility impairment may have additional non-mobility and/or mobility impairments. As in Chapter 5, a discussion of the passenger experience of air travel by people with impairments other than mobility is based on the premise that they have the same rights to citizenship as non-disabled passengers. This includes the right to safe and comfortable travel and the feeling of inclusion as a flying passenger, from first booking a flight, to the airport and onboard experience. Nevertheless, commissioned research by the UK's Civil Aviation Authority (CAA) suggests that '7 per cent of UK citizens avoid travelling by air because of a hidden disability – such as dementia, autism or because they use a colostomy bag' (Berry, 2018). Indeed, those people with non-mobility impairments are among the least likely to travel by air. Despite having the same rights to travel, it is clear that the passenger's travel experience will vary according to their type and degree of impairment. As highlighted in Chapter 5, there are multiple forms of difference. The study of those with physical impairments highlights the multi-sensory nature of travel. For air passengers with sensory and cognitive impairments, other senses come to the fore such as the importance of touch for the blind. As many of the non-mobility disabilities are 'hidden disabilities', air passengers with these disabilities may face increased stress during flying. One of the important dilemmas faced by air passengers with hidden disabilities is the question of whether to disclose or conceal their disability – whether that will mean inclusion or exclusion.

In the United Kingdom, the Civil Aviation Authority (2016) has set out guidelines on how airports can support people with hidden disabilities, such as autism, dementia, mental health conditions and sensory impairment. These guidelines include: awareness and communication training for staff, information for the passenger regarding airport methods of identification (such as passenger lanyards or bracelets), the provision of a quiet waiting area and quiet route through the airport and clear images and messages to assist in the location of toilets etc. The CAA recommends that the person with disability is not separated from their companion when going through security and receives explanations by security staff about the security procedure. To facilitate familiarisation of the airport, detailed information and visits/open days are encouraged. Following guidance to assist people with hidden disabilities at airports, the Civil Aviation Authority (2018) has published guidance for airlines 'applicable to all flights from the UK and for flights to the UK on an EU registered airline' (Civil Aviation Authority, 2018: 4). The recommendations include: provision of information in an accessible format (prior to travel, at the airport and onboard the aircraft), assistance at the airport in areas for which the airline is responsible, assistance onboard the aircraft (such as accommodating seating requests) and assistance during flight disruptions. Training of airline staff to understand the needs of those with a hidden disability is essential. While a number of airports throughout the world have adopted procedures addressing the needs of those with hidden disabilities, these advances are not universal. In this chapter, we consider particular challenges for passengers with non-mobility impairments in their booking and information search, navigation of airports, boarding and in-flight experience, highlighting the particular embodied experience of those with non-mobility disabilities and the need for airports and airlines to explicitly cater for this group.

Non-Mobility Disabilities

Vision impairment

The logistics of travelling for those who are blind or with vision impairment are challenging. Small and Darcy (2010) report that this group is less likely to travel, especially internationally, than those with other disabilities (with the exception of those with mental illness). For those with vision impairment, senses other than vision come to the fore: touch, sound, smell, taste and kinaesthetic skills. Those with vision impairment are not a homogenous group, yet the sighted world treats them as such (Richards et al., 2010). To understand the needs of a passenger with vision impairment one needs to consider the particular type of vision impairment (for example, macular degeneration, glaucoma etc.) and the degree of visual acuity and visual field. In a study of the tourist experiences of people with vision impairment (PwVI), Small et al. (2012: 949) conclude:

> Vision impairment in itself is not a barrier to becoming a tourist and enjoying the benefits of tourism, yet PwVI are faced with a disabling environment specific to their embodiment. In particular, they are constrained by: access to information, wayfinding, knowledge or attitude of others and travelling with a guide dog.

Where there is no outward sign of disability (no cane or guide dog), there is the dilemma for the person whether to disclose their vision impairment to the travel staff. They have to make a judgement as to how the staff will respond. Will disclosure mean inclusion or exclusion? While much of the academic literature on disability has focused on mobility impairment, there have been several studies that have examined the air travel experiences of those with vision impairment.

One such study by Small in 2016 (unpublished) involved in-depth interviews with 21 (mostly Australian) participants who were blind or vision impaired, investigating their domestic and international air travel experiences: pre-departure when planning and booking, at the airport (departure, in transit and arrival at the destination) and on board the aeroplane. It was found that those with vision impairment share common experiences with those with other disabilities but there are also experiences which are specific to them. Of those who participated in the study, most travelled by air at least once or twice a year for work or pleasure, with business travellers flying more often than others. Most business travellers flew unaccompanied while others travelled mainly with a family member or friend. In terms of aids, most participants travelled with a cane. However, it must be remembered that not all people with vision impairment use a cane or guide dog especially if they have low vision. For some, a sighted companion will be their aid.

At the pre-departure planning and booking phase, difficulties were reported with both the airline and airport websites: they were too complicated, multi-layered, with formats that regularly changed and not easily navigable using screen reading software (to convert on-screen text to speech output) (see Domínguez *et al.*, 2018; W3C, 2019). Due to the inaccessibility of the websites, most bookings were done by family, friends, executive assistants, travel agents or the person with vision impairment phoning the airline. Very few of the participants knew about the support services on the airport websites. They preferred to phone the airlines for information and to request support. Further problems awaited the person on arrival at the airport. Limited wait time for cars at the drop-off zone meant they could not be escorted to the check-in counter and could be left 'stranded' on the pavement. Inside the terminal, there were issues with wayfinding and checking in. The electronic check-in kiosks were not accessible for PwVI and, at times, there were few staff to assist (especially when using a low-cost airline). Most check-in staff at the desk were reported to be helpful and would arrange meet-and-assist support to the departure gate, but as one participant said, PwVI are often concerned about being dropped off at the departure gate by the meet-and-assist service and then forgotten. Some have missed flights.

The airport is difficult for those with vision impairment. By nature, airports are large, noisy and busy. Unstructured spaces with few direct paths can make navigation difficult especially when there are few wayfinding cues. Further, as illustrated in Figure 6.1, the positioning of objects can be hazardous for PwVI if preventing a clear pathway. The design of modern airports, especially large international airports with their reflective surfaces, can also be challenging for some PwVI; see Figure 6.2.

The participants in Small's study cited gate changes as problematic as the change was often publicised via a visual screen rather than an announcement. Foreign airports with language and cultural barriers could add to the difficulties. Some participants who travelled for business had joined the airport lounge facilities (at own expense) to have certainty with assistance. And yet, as one participant said, '*I also know that people who have opted for this solution.... have also been "forgotten" and missed their flight (... no announcements in these lounges)*'. The process of going through security could be problematic especially when security staff removed the cane from the traveller's possession. As participants explained, security staff need to recognise that the person's cane is their eyes.

> *Staff... need to explain what they are doing, why they are doing it, and what might be expected to happen next. For people travelling with guide dogs, separation of the person from their dog should be minimised and good communication practiced. It's unfortunate that dogs' harnesses always trigger security alarms, resulting in the dog's handler being patted down.*

Figure 6.1 Display stands in a duty-free retail area at Doha Airport obstruct clear passage through the space (2019 © Jennie Small)

Figure 6.2 Lighting, glass and light-coloured floor tiles create reflection at Dubai Airport (2019 © Jennie Small)

Having valuable possessions removed from their immediate proximity during security screening could also be stressful for PwVI, as one participant explained,

> … *everyone has to part with their possessions during the security screening, however…, [usually] sighted passengers can see their possessions as*

they go through the screening. Blind passengers, on the other hand, hand over their most precious and necessary possessions without being able to track what happens to them. Especially on international flights, this is a significant issue, losing contact with personal identity papers, tickets, foreign currency, credit cards, and having the possibility of things being added to one's luggage.

Graham Innes (2016), Australia's Disability Discrimination Commissioner from 2005 to 2014, similarly describes his experience, as a person who is blind, of having his bags opened without his knowledge or permission, and his cane put in a place where he could not find it. The participants in Small's study explained that moving through the security scanner can be cumbersome and the process degrading, for example, when pushed and pulled through the scanner.

Small found that, once on board, there were other challenges for those with vision impairment. Toilets were reported as problematic due to variable layout and difficulty working the buttons and levers. Touch screen in-flight entertainment was not accessible, so most PwVI need to take their personal electronic devices and their own entertainment. Other in-flight controls (such as the overhead light and flight attendant call button), if operated by a touch screen, were, thus, also inaccessible, taking away from the independence of the traveller. It was reported that meals could be difficult with lots of little packages, small trays and restricted space. Menus need to be screen readable but never are. Disembarking the plane was an easier process. However, if required to disembark last (as is often the case), the delay, for the business traveller, could mean arriving late for a meeting. In disembarkation, there could also be the indignity of being offered a wheelchair. This experience has been confirmed by others (Innes, 2016; Richards *et al.*, 2010). Innes (2016) offered his solution: 'When my requested guide turns up with a wheelchair for me, I usually thank them and place my carry-on luggage on it, as the thing I most want to do when I get off a plane is walk' (Innes, 2016: 81). The participants expressed the need for a better whole-journey experience from the point of drop-off to end of journey and for an airport-based assistance service rather than an airline-by-airline service. Participants felt that there was more assistance available in countries where disability standards and compliance are regulated.

Findings from other studies have similarly exposed the anxiety and stress of air travel for passengers with vision impairment (da Silva *et al.*, 2019; Poria *et al.*, 2010; Small *et al.*, 2012). In a study of Brazilian air transport, da Silva *et al.* (2017) highlight the difficulties experienced by passengers with vision impairment at airports. Of note was the lack of guidance and information on arrival at the airport with most information in visual format. Information boards were difficult to read with low colour contrast, small font size, excessive information and high positioning. Throughout the airport, hazard and directional signage was inadequate for the safety of those with vision impairment, leading to the risk of passenger injury. There were also issues with the service provided to PwVI due to the lack of knowledge of staff at check-in and boarding. Ensuring the person was allocated their preferred seat was often problematic. In sum, the study identified non-compliance with the required regulations. Poria *et al.* (2010), studying the experiences of Israeli passengers who were blind, also identified the inaccessibility of flight information when in visual format. Passengers were fearful that they would miss information about a flight or gate change, especially when connecting to another flight. Regarding on-board experiences, Poria *et al.* (2010), while identifying some challenges for those with vision impairment (finding the earphone outlet, differentiating between salt and pepper, understanding the safety information), concluded, 'Blind people reported almost no difficulties, noting that they usually travel with a companion and that attendants approach them appropriately' (Poria *et al.*, 2010: 221). However, at the same time, Poria *et al.* (2010) found problems in communication with staff. As reported in Chapter 5, there was often the assumption by the crew that the passenger with vision impairment also had a cognitive impairment. In addition, the crew often preferred to address the companion rather than the person with vision impairment (Innes, 2016; Poria *et al.*, 2010). Another identified barrier to travel concerns travelling with a guide dog. Individual service providers may lack knowledge regarding the rules for such travel (Small *et al.*, 2012). There may also be issues regarding space for the animal to be accommodated with the passenger on the aircraft (da Silva *et al.*, 2017). The absence of toileting facilities for guide dogs at airports has also been reported (Innes, 2016).

Amar Latif, director of Traveleyes (a travel company for blind and sighted travellers), and blind himself, confirmed in an interview (personal communication, 25 July 2016) the findings from the above academic studies that there are many travel difficulties for passengers with vision impairment, from booking flights, navigating the airport and using the facilities onboard the plane. However, as he reports, it may depend on the airport and/or airline whether one feels supported and enabled or 'herded like cattle'. On a positive note, he explains,

> *I guess the advantages of being VI [Vision Impaired] and travelling across the world is... you land in, let's say, Paris... interconnecting. You'll have this intimate relationship with assistance staff ... suddenly you touch base with a local and as they're guiding you, you ask them... 'oh what's it like living here'? 'How's your life'? And then, suddenly, you're on your plane and... you've landed in Singapore and again you've got that ability. Whereas, sighted folk probably don't speak to anybody. So there are advantages.*

To allow a person with vision impairment to travel independently and free from anxiety, Latif recommends better education and training for staff. Here, Latif cites an example where better training might avert an uncomfortable situation.

> [Going through Security] you're supposed to fold your cane and put it in the box but once you do that nobody knows that you're a VI so quite often... they'll eye you suspiciously 'cause you're... walking, you're feeling around a bit. And then your sighted guide needs to... just signal to the person on the other side 'look, this person's blind that's coming through the security'... I don't know how to resolve that except more training for those guys.

Latif explains that while there are assistance programs at many airports, they are not seamless, for example, there is a gap in assistance between entering the airport and checking in, which he refers to as 'no-man's land'. Latif stresses the benefits of a technological solution, an app on the passenger's device, to improve the accessibility of air travel at all stages of the journey: from navigating the airport, managing the onboard facilities (for example, in-flight entertainment system and menu options) to locating one's luggage on the carousel at the destination. This would expand the experience of the passenger, giving them more control and independence, for example, they could access the airport shops rather than spending long periods waiting at the Gate. If travelling with a companion, such technology would also take pressure from the sighted guide and go some way to a true partnership between the blind and sighted traveller.

That new technologies can assist passengers with vision impairment to access their environment has been recognised by The Royal Society for the Blind (2020). It describes an app that, for the first time, allows wayfinding inside multilevel buildings. It is achieved through a combination of new positioning beacons that through algorithms are able to process location via smart phone-based apps. The app, which has already been deployed in universities and retail environments, could be suitable for airports. The Royal Society for the Blind (2020) explains: 'The program uses a simple audio system to describe where users are and what's around them, finding the best way to get to their chosen destination'.

Hearing impairment

There has been little in the academic travel and tourism literature concerning those whose impairment is solely hearing although there have been some studies on the travel experiences of deafblind travellers (Dann & Dann, 2012; Hersh, 2016). More specifically, there is scant information on the experiences of *air* travellers with a hearing impairment. Nonetheless, we can take the information from the more general travel experience studies as a starting point to understand their air travel experience. Darcy (2012) explains that the requirements for alternative information provision for people with hearing impairment are consistently ignored throughout the travel chain. Travellers with hearing impairment often rely on attendants to explain important information and interact with staff. Since travellers may have varying degrees of hearing impairment, there is a need for quiet travel environments in which announcements can be heard. This is relevant when considering noisy, busy airports where announcements may be in a foreign voice. Both Hersh (2016) and Dann and Dann (2012) highlight the importance of the sense of touch for those who are deafblind. Indeed, Elizabeth Dann, in her qualitative analysis of her own sensory experiences as a deafblind person, calculated 'that the sense of touch accounts for 42.9% of all my sensory experiences of tourism' (Dann & Dann, 2012: 135). From studying the experiences of deafblind travellers, Hersh (2016), too, highlights the importance of tactile information. She also cites the variability of her participants' ability to represent space and form mental maps, important in navigation. When we consider air travel and navigation of airports, such cognitive skills may prove particularly difficult where a terminal is unfamiliar due to it being foreign or constantly remodelled (see Chapter 2).

One study which has reported the air travel experiences of a traveller with hearing impairment is the autoethnographic study of Jain (Jain *et al.*, 2019). This study highlights the importance of visual communication strategies (facial expressions, body language signing and gestures) for someone with a hearing impairment. Due to Jain's particular hearing disability, he cites difficulties when experiencing insufficient visual cues, high frequency sounds and background noise:

> *[when I was seated in a window seat on a plane] it was terribly difficult to communicate drinks or food choice. I couldn't hear the attendant very well. [...] And since I can't hear my own voice well, I did not know how loud I was speaking. Thus, the crew also had a hard time understanding me. Somehow, through gestures and repetitions, we made it work but I skipped one meal and compromised with cold water instead of the hot water (which I wanted).* (Flight from Milan to Sharm el sheikh, Mar'17) (Jain *et al.*, 2019)

As with travellers with other hidden disabilities, there is the dilemma of disclosing or concealing hearing disability. In this autoethnographic account, Jain explains how he used a speech-to-text translator for in-flight announcements, communicating with the flight crew and immigration staff (situations with high background noise).

> *I found that I could access a range of information that was previously inaccessible (e.g., flight safety briefings, information about [the] destination such as weather and sightseeing details, information about in-flight service such as food and drinks).* (Jain et al., 2019)

Nonetheless, there were difficulties associated with this method such as the unnaturalness of two-way conversation due to the transcription delay.

Eghtesadi *et al.* (2012) describe the development of an accessible in-flight entertainment system specifically for people with sensory disabilities. For passengers who are deaf or have hearing limitations the system provides access to content through user selection caption display. The system also provides options for those who are blind or have low vision to access content through talking menus and descriptions of key visual content. Under the Air Carrier Access Act of 1986, the U.S. Department of Transport (DOT) has established the accessibility requirements of people with disability as they relate to air travel. However, this legislation has limitations. Beyond the aircraft safety information, there is currently no requirement to make other information or entertainment services accessible to those with vision or hearing impairments (Eghtesadi *et al.*, 2012). However, from the perspective of service provision, this is an area where significant improvement can be made using currently available technologies.

Cognitive impairment

Cognitive impairment has also not received the travel and tourism research attention that more visible types of impairment have attracted. Although researchers' definitions of disability may recognise intellectual disability, there has, for the most part, been little or no analysis of this impairment (for example, Ancell & Graham, 2016). The airline industry, too, has tended to ignore those with cognitive impairment. While it has disability access policies for physical disabilities, 'most do not explicitly cater for people with cognitive impairments such as dementia' (O'Reilly & Shepherd, 2016). Rosenkvist *et al.* (2010: 132) explain that cognitive functional limitations 'can mean difficulties to remember, to orientate in time and space, to solve co-ordination problems, to express oneself verbally etc.'. Those with cognitive functional limitations may also have other impairments, such as mobility or vision. In a study of experts' perspectives on the mobility of those with cognitive impairment, Rosenkvist *et al.* (2010: 138) made the point that moving around in the world can be exhausting as 'this group of people requires tranquillity to cope with decision-making on the basis of a lot of information'. Familiarity with the environment can provide confidence and lessen stress, anxiety, and fear. Qualitative research undertaken in the United Kingdom by the Civil Aviation Authority (2015) noted that those with cognitive disabilities and mental health conditions required help and support to access air travel due to numerous issues and stressors when travelling by air. 'These include anxiety, strong personal preferences, difficulty interacting with people, difficulty processing and retaining information, difficulty navigating spaces etc.' (Civil Aviation Authority, 2015). For those with such limitations, strength and stamina can vary day by day. Rosenkvist et al. (2010) also highlight that, amongst this group, individuals vary in awareness of their cognitive capacity – what they can or cannot manage. While their study was focused on mobility in public environments, the findings are no doubt also relevant for air travel.

Dementia

An increase in the number of those with dementia, associated with ageing populations, should attract the attention of the travel and tourism industries. Among researchers, a slowly emerging interest in dementia and tourism is based on the belief that 'helping people to live well with dementia through tourism can have positive benefits' (Connell & Page, 2019: 39). To date, there has been some focus on the dementia 'friendliness' of tourism destinations (Connell & Page, 2019; Page et al., 2014), tourism attractions and venues (Connell et al., 2017) and the broad tourism product (Klímová, 2018). What we know is that there are many common problems faced by people with dementia in the visitor economy. According to Klug et al. (as cited in Connell & Page, 2019: 29), these include:

> ...mobility issues (e.g. getting to the venue, moving around the venue, disorientation caused by background noise, patterned décor and shiny surfaces, fear of getting lost or not knowing where to go); memory-related problems (e.g. ... finding the right words to communicate with people); problems of visual perception or spatial awareness (e.g. bumping into things, responding to visual interpretation in unexpected ways and the effect of low light levels on perception); and, impaired ability to interact with the environment and problems with paying for goods and services (e.g. counting money or remembering chip and pin numbers).

We know that much of the above is likely to be common to the air transport experience. As for those with sensory or other cognitive impairments, 'Airports and aircrafts can be noisy and confusing environments for people with dementia' (Dementia Australia, 2018). Nonetheless, there have been few studies whose focus is the air travel experience of those with dementia. From medical research, we are informed of the potential medical problems for those with dementia: passengers with dementia face a possible danger of delirium in long-haul travel (Kelly & Kaplan, 2009; McCabe, 2017) with McCabe reporting that length of flight or descent from high altitude can increase the possibility of deterioration. Writers (such as Kelly & Kaplan, 2009; McCabe, 2017) have made the point that airline screening for fitness to fly is concentrated on a physical check, rather than cognitive check. In one of the few studies of air travel that has included the perspective of those with dementia and their carers, Australian researchers, O'Reilly and Shepherd (2016) found that the most challenging aspect of the air travel experience was navigating the airport, 'such as finding restrooms and the correct boarding gate, hearing announcements, checking in, reading information on signboards and bag screening'. Once on the aircraft, the small size of the lavatory was problematic with no room to accommodate a second person. The researchers cited instances of passengers with dementia becoming agitated during the flight. However, they noted that: 'Most companions said that once they were on the plane they were able to relax... flight crew had been very polite and able to accommodate their needs'. Similarly, a UK group of researchers at Plymouth University (Warren *et al.*, 2019) identified the issues that can be problematic for those with dementia: the security checkpoint (lack of communication, being separated from carer, pressure of queuing), assistance (lack of clarity in entitlement to assistance or the level of assistance offered), staff awareness (inconsistent approaches by staff even when the passenger had disclosed their dementia) and information (range of practical information difficult to find).

O'Reilly *et al.* (2017) likewise stressed the challenges of security and immigration procedures for those with dementia. Planning is considered the key to a positive flying experience. See below the air travel tips, as outlined by O'Reilly and Shepherd (2016) for people with dementia.

Box 1: Air Travel Tips for People with Dementia

- Talk to the airline about the assistance they can offer people with disabilities. Some airlines will escort you through the security and immigration checkpoints and on to your boarding gate. Find an airline you like and stick with them. Familiarity with the airline may help reduce anxiety.
- Book a flight that leaves at a quiet time of day. For example, some airports are very busy between 6am and 10am and 4pm and 7pm. It will be a lot easier for you to find your way and access assistance if you are traveling outside of the busy period.

- Plan to arrive at the airport an hour and a half early to allow unforeseen delays. Go through the security checkpoints straight away and then find somewhere to relax.
- You can often find information about the seating configuration of the airplane online. Find the best seats for you, for example, many people choose aisle seats close to the toilets.
- Find out about the airport prior to the day of your trip. You can visit the airport beforehand to get your bearings and look for information on the airport website. For example, there may be special parking zones for people with a disability that you can use.
- Don't be afraid to ask for help and explain your medical condition.
- Keep hand luggage to a minimum.
- If you wear a lanyard with a pocket on it around your neck, you can safely tuck away your travel documents in a place that is easy to access when you already have your hands full.
- Long haul travel can be the most difficult, particularly during the stopover. Schedule flights which enable you to rest and give you plenty of time to meet your connecting flight. If possible, travel with two carers.
- Some people with dementia get agitated at particular times on the flight, such as when everyone is boarding, during the take-off or landing. The use of distraction techniques such as using noise cancelling headphones to listen to music, or eating a favourite snack can reduce anxiety.

Source: O'Reilly and Shepherd (2016)

Connell and Page (2019) highlight the poor publicity that the air transport sector has attracted in the past in relation to dementia but see progress in the United Kingdom, as evidenced in the House of Commons debate on issues raised by the Prime Minister's Dementia Challenge Group for Air Transport (UK Parliament, 2016). As explained by Warren *et al.* (2019), the Prime Minister's Group 'is changing how the aviation industry sees people living with dementia and is improving how airports and airlines support them, and those who travel with them, so they can remain engaged in air travel'. In 2016, London's Heathrow Airport announced it was the first 'dementia-friendly' airport in the world (Miles, 2016). In the same year Gatwick Airport received a dementia innovation award for introducing passenger lanyards for staff to recognise those with hidden disabilities who might need assistance (Gatwick Airport, 2016). Reviewing UK airports from 2016 to 2019, Napolitano (2020) found that, by 2019, 90% of airports were offering some form of support to passengers with dementia. In Australia, Brisbane Airport was the first dementia-friendly airport with a guide developed for users of the airport (Dementia Centre for Research Collaboration, 2017).

Autism

For those with autism and their attendants, travel, including air travel, can be a challenging experience. Sedgley *et al.* (2017), in their study of the tourism experiences of mothers caring for a child diagnosed with Autism Spectrum Disorders (ASDs), reported that much groundwork had to be done by the mothers prior to travel by air as the airline websites lacked information for passengers with cognitive impairments. 'The need for tranquillity make airports and aeroplanes highly challenging environments for these children, not only as noisy and frenetic places but also as sites of surveillance, which require well-ordered behaviour (Morgan & Pritchard, 2005)' (Sedgley *et al.*, 2017: 20). They also reported the anxiety experienced by mothers due to the heightened security and the stress experienced by delays and long flights.

To limit the overwhelming sensory impact of air travel and, in particular, the airport environment, a growing number of airports are now providing 'multi-sensory' rooms or quiet rooms around the departure lounge (Poling, 2017). Following the release of guidelines in 2016 by the CAA which encouraged airports in the United Kingdom to provide greater support to passengers with 'hidden disabilities', such as autism and Alzheimers (Civil Aviation Authority, 2018), Ireland's Shannon Airport became the first airport in Europe to provide a multi-sensory room. The room includes 'such calming features as an aquatic bubble tube, an undulated wavy wall, color changing LED's and a wheel projector' (Poling, 2017). Similar spaces have also been established at a number of US airports in recent years. Harpaz (2017) reports that Delta airlines opened a multi-sensory room at Hartsfield-Jackson Atlanta International Airport in April 2016 in partnership with The Arc, an Autism advocacy group. Similarly, a quiet room opened at the Myrtle Beach Airport in South Carolina, USA, following a request from a local mother and founder of the Champion Autism Network for the airport to 'provide some sort of support for families' when flying with children with autism. To enable staff to identify and interact appropriately with passengers with autism and other hidden disabilities, a growing number of airports have introduced 'discreet' lanyards, wristbands, caps etc. to be worn by the passenger. At Vancouver International Airport in Canada, a special sticker on the passenger's boarding pass helps staff and crew identify passengers with autism and provide appropriate assistance and support when required (Poling, 2017).

For families with a member with autism, some airports and airlines also offer an opportunity to become familiar with the airport experience (including the often-stressful sights and sounds associated with air travel) – a 'rehearsal' – through a program called 'Wings for All'. This program has operated successfully at a number of airports in the United States and has recently been implemented at Perth Airport in Western Australia (Tetlow, 2017). The program allows children with autism and sensory processing disorders to experience a 'run through' of the process of air travel, from check-in, through security and boarding, to onboard service (Adams, 2018; Poling, 2017; Tetlow, 2017). The program also provides staff training, to develop staff empathy and understanding for such travellers.

Cerdan Chiscano (2021), in her study of families of children with autism spectrum disorder, found that (a) communication about the airport experience, (b) usage of the airport (such as, sensory rooms, priority check-in, easy wayfinding and boarding) and (c) service (staff awareness of autism, appropriate language and empathy) were all critical to ensure a successful inclusive airport experience design. She reinforced the importance of stakeholder involvement, the use of value co-creation, to design positive air travel experiences.

Epilepsy

The neurological condition of epilepsy can pose hazards for a person's use of transportation, especially air travel (Cummins & Schubach, 1989; Shand, 2000; Silverman & Gendreau, 2009; Skjenna *et al.*, 1991; Trevorrow, 2006). Indeed, air travel has been described by some as a potential 'safety threat' for people with epilepsy (Unsworth, 1999). Epilepsy is recognised as a complex spectrum of disorders with about 40 different seizure types. People living with epilepsy can experience differing frequencies and severity of seizures. Researchers have found that air travel may be linked to an increase in the occurrence of epileptic seizures in the first few days after a flight, especially among air passengers who have a prior history of flight-related seizures and experience a higher frequency of seizures generally (Trevorrow, 2006). In addition, epileptic seizures have been reported as one of the most frequent reasons for flight diversion (Drazkowski, 2007). Most seizures do not require immediate medical intervention, but prolonged convulsive status can lead to irreversible neuronal injury, and even death. It is thus important that attention be given to the medical management of air travel for passengers with epilepsy (Trevorrow, 2006).

While the probability of having a seizure during a flight is low (Devkota & Karki, 2010), passengers with poorly controlled epilepsy may be refused transport, or only permitted under certain conditions (Graf *et al.*, 2012). For example, if a person has experienced a tonic-clonic seizure less than 24 hours before flying, many airlines will require that person to provide medical clearance as set out by the guidelines of the International Air Travel Association (IATA). In general, flying with epilepsy requires health counselling and common-sense consideration of an individual's fitness to cope with the environmental and physiological demands of air travel on the human body (Drazkowski, 2007). The physiological challenges of flying are related to the exposure to reduced atmospheric pressure inside the cabin, oxygen desaturation, low humidity, high levels of cosmic radiation, postural immobility and jet lag from crossing time zones. In addition to disrupting sleep patterns, air travel also disturbs eating patterns. All of these variables can trigger epileptic seizures (Devkota & Karki, 2010).

While there appears no conclusive direct link between the occurrence of seizures and air travel in relation to flight distance, time zones and duration of the flight, air travel holds a theoretical risk for passengers, meaning that it is impossible to claim that a seizure will never be triggered by these variables (Shand, 2000). Air passengers with epilepsy worry about having a seizure during a flight with the potential for the occurrence of seizures reducing a person's sense of control. The unpredictable, uncontrollable and distressing nature of epileptic seizures can arouse fear in both the sufferer and those witnessing the seizure (Jacoby & Austin, 2007). Seizures are described as starting with 'feelings that "something is not quite right"; "an uneasy feeling"; "feeling a little bit confused"; "daydreaming"; "like a zombie"' (McIntosh, 2020: 5). Many people are unaware they have had a seizure until it is over (McIntosh, 2020). Devkota and Karki (2010: 60) report the medical account of a 29-year-old female who had a generalised tonic-clonic seizure during a long-haul flight:

> After 16 hours flight, one hour before landing in Paris she fell down in the corridor while she was trying to go to toilet. Her body was stiff lasted for about one minute; she had up rolling of eyes but no frothing, tongue bite or incontinence. She did not have any external injury or injury to head. After the episode she was confused for few minutes. Her vitals were stable and oxygen saturation was maintained. Oral diazepam 5 mg was given and she slept well. Remaining flight was uneventful.

Some air passengers manage complete seizure control through regular medication. That said, careful travel planning to stick to usual routines becomes important in maintaining control over seizures during air travel. A respondent in McIntosh's (2020) study explained:

> *If I can board a plane near to sleep time or the evening, I am in the same sleep pattern as what I would be at home. Going to England which we've done three times, we'd stop off, it would be in Asia, and you were in a plane, what, ten hours. We stop over there for three to four days and then we catch a flight again at night time. So I'm keeping the same pattern as I would do. I have had no repercussions from that.*

Planning for travel may include getting clearance from a doctor, wearing a medical identification bracelet, knowing the details of the travel itinerary, having emergency phone contacts, carrying plenty of snacks, water and medication, carrying a prescription and local hospital details and knowing a safe space to go in the event of the onset of a seizure, usually the closest restroom (McIntosh, 2020). The potential for personal physical harm, as well as the stigma and anxiety of having seizures in public, may mean that some people avoid air travel altogether (Jacoby, 2002). Alternatively, it may mean that some people will only travel accompanied with someone who can look after them, and/or their support service animal (McIntosh, 2020). Flying accompanied by a support person or 'carer' is required by some airlines if the person with disability is deemed not to meet 'independent travel criteria' or there is a legitimate safety risk (Darcy, 2012; Qantas Airways Limited, 2020). In her study of epilepsy and tourism, McIntosh (2020) found that, due to the often hidden and stigmatising condition of epilepsy, travellers concealed their condition, keeping it secret as a coping strategy, and/or avoided situations that might risk them experiencing a seizure in public. This was despite medical advice that it is better to inform airline crew as to how they can help in the event of a seizure during the flight than not to disclose (Shand, 2000). Given the series of constraints, there is a need for research to examine further the stigmatising nature (the fear and shame) of epilepsy and tourism. As an invisible and often uncontrollable condition, there is a greater need to examine the impact of the neurological condition on the air travel experience, the ways in which it may be managed in-flight and the ways to support travel planning.

Mental health conditions

When examining the propensity to travel amongst disability groups, it was found that those with mental illness were the least likely to travel (Small & Darcy, 2010). There is little documentation on the air travel experience for this group. However, there is evidence that air travel is stressful for those with mental health conditions. Seeman (2016: 79), in discussing the travel risks for those with a serious mental illness, claims: 'Travel, even when embarked on for the purpose of relaxation and enjoyment, can prove so stressful for individuals with pre-existing severe mental illness that it can result in psychotic relapse'. In particular, she cites reports, since at least the 1950s, 'of travelers with psychiatric illness suffering travel-related psychotic decompensation, during air travel especially' (Seeman, 2016: 76). Lack of sleep, disruption of circadian rhythms, dehydration, nausea and sharing a close space with unfamiliar people are some of the stressors of flying. It is thought that those with serious mental illness can be particularly anxious when events are perceived as out of their control. However, Seeman concludes that there are many ways to prepare the person for travel and obviate potential stressors.

A number of passengers with mental health conditions travel with emotional support animals. While limited academic research has been undertaken, some significant media reporting has occurred in the United

States around the carriage of emotional support animals on planes (Dombroff, 2018; McGonigle, 2018; Wood, 2018). Unfortunately, while the original intent of airlines in regard to such carriage was positive, the practical application of the regulations has often caused difficulties for both airline operations and other passengers. Media reports explain that airlines in the United States have been struggling to deal with the impacts of the rapidly increasing numbers and types of emotional support animals on flights. Delta Airlines reported 'a 150 percent increase in passengers bringing animals onto planes since 2015, with an attendant 84 percent jump in incidents such as people being bitten or attacked, or animals urinating or defecating during flights' (Dombroff, 2018). In response, the U.S. Department of Transport has undertaken a review of the rules around emotional support animals and limited the definition in its regulations to dogs, reversing the previous policy that permitted a wide range of other animals to fly (U.S. Department of Transport, 2020; Vann, 2020). See Chapter 3 for further discussion.

Other media reports relating to mental health and travel concern travel insurance. Recently, the Victorian Equal Opportunity and Human Rights Commission (VEOHRC) launched an investigation into the major travel insurance companies, concluding that the companies did not have the right to discriminate against people with mental health conditions by implementing blanket bans, as they have done in the past (Bainbridge & Florance, 2019). While insurance companies are able to discriminate on a variety of grounds involving previous health conditions, challenging their right to discriminate against people with episodic mental health conditions can lead to change. Other disability groups, including those with previous health conditions, may be able to leverage other travel insurance challenges from this case.

Conclusion

Consideration of the air travel experiences of those with disability requires extending the definition of disability to include those with non-mobility related disabilities that are often hidden. While passengers with any type of disability have the same rights to citizenship as non-disabled passengers, people with non-mobility impairments may be among the least likely to travel. This chapter highlights the significance of sensory, cognitive and mental health impairments in the embodied experience of those who do take to the air. There are particular challenges for passengers with non-mobility disabilities at airports when visual or audio cues are inappropriate, background noise is high, information is inaccessible due to lack of provision of alternative formats, and wayfinding is difficult, especially in multilevel buildings. Additional challenges may occur during customs checks (in international travel) and on board the plane. Here, the physiological effects of air travel can exacerbate certain conditions. In addition, the potential for unexpected experiences and uncontrollable triggers resulting from a 'hidden' condition may increase stress and anxiety during air travel. Certainly, the knowledge and attitudes of staff can 'make or break' the travel experience. A key to a positive flying experience is to plan ahead. While there will be some commonality in experience, there will also be differences depending on: the type and degree of impairment, the required communication supports and whether the person travels independently, in a group and/or with an assistant animal. Throughout the journey, we can see the corporeal interaction of the passenger with the materialities of the airport and the aircraft – the signage, check-in desks, baggage carousel, passenger seat, in-flight entertainment system, toilet cubicle, lighting and so on.

Highlighted in this chapter is the disabling environment of air travel, specific to the embodiment of a person's non-mobility disability. For passengers with a hidden disability, there is the added dilemma of whether to disclose their condition, and the likely consequence of doing so (or not). This is particularly so with people who may have a psychosocial or mental health-related condition. Judgements need to be made as to how others will respond: will disclosure pre-boarding lead to inclusion or exclusion? It is important to recognise that the difficulties faced by the passenger with a non-mobility disability are not limited to that person but shared by companions, for example, the sighted companion trying to navigate the blind partner (Small, 2015) through a busy terminal or the companion communicating to security staff on behalf of the passenger with hearing impairment. More attention is required to raise awareness of the needs of the companions, in addition to those with non-mobility disabilities, and the ways in which airline staff can be trained, and technologies employed (Bosch & Gharaveis, 2017) to provide greater support to both groups of passengers.

da Silva *et al.* (2019) conclude that transport accessibility is the responsibility of multiple organisations from airport operators, airline staff, aircraft manufacturers and regulatory agencies. Recommendations by the Civil Aviation Authority (2016) and initiatives by various airports to provide for passengers with hidden disabilities are positive steps in making the airport experience inclusive for all. It is hoped that similar guidelines and initiatives might be extended to airports in other parts of the world. Sensitivity to the needs of those with non-mobility disabilities are also required before arrival at the airport (at the information search/booking stage) and on the aircraft, as Civil Aviation Authority (2018) recommends, if the individual (and their companion/s) are to have a fully inclusive air travel experience. The following chapter introduces another group of individuals who may be excluded from the air travel experience or for whom air travel is an anxious experience – those with a fear of flying.

References

Adams, M. (2018) Opening up the world for kids with autism. *Hemispheres* April, 12.
Ancell, D. and Graham, A. (2016) A framework for evaluating the European airline costs of disabled persons and persons with reduced mobility. *Journal of Air Transport Management* 50, 41–44. https://doi.org/10.1016/j.jairtraman.2015.10.001.
Bainbridge, A. and Florance, L. (2019) Travel insurers refusing to cover mental illness 'widespread', investigation finds. *ABC News*. See https://www.abc.net.au/news/2019-06-12/travel-insurers-refusing-to-cover-mental-illness-widespread/11197028 (accessed June 2020).
Berry, S. (2018) Recognising the impact of hidden disabilities on passenger confidence. *International Airport Review*. See https://www.internationalairportreview.com/article/69277/omniserv-hidden-disabilities/ (accessed July 2020).
Bosch, S. and Gharaveis, A. (2017) Flying solo: A review of the literature on wayfinding for older adults experiencing visual or cognitive decline. *Applied Ergonomics* 58, 327–333. https://doi.org/10.1016/j.apergo.2016.07.010.
Cerdan Chiscano M. (2021) Autism Spectrum Disorder (ASD) and the family inclusive airport design experience. *International Journal of Environmental Research and Public Health* 18 (13), 7206. https://doi.org/10.3390/ijerph18137206.
Civil Aviation Authority (2015) Consumer research for the UK aviation sector – Final report, CAP 1303. See https://publicapps.caa.co.uk/docs/33/CAP1303ConsumerresearchfortheUKaviationsectorfinalreport.pdf (accessed February 2020).
Civil Aviation Authority (2016) CAA guidance for airports on providing assistance to people with hidden disabilities, CAP 1411. See https://publicapps.caa.co.uk/modalapplication.aspx?appid=11&mode=detail&id=7390 (accessed July 2022).
Civil Aviation Authority (2018) Guidance for airlines on assisting people with hidden disabilities, CAP 1603. See http://publicapps.caa.co.uk/docs/33/CAP1603Assistingpeoplewithhiddendisabilities.pdf (accessed July 2020).
Connell, J. and Page, S. (2019) Case study: Destination readiness for dementia-friendly visitor experiences: A scoping study. *Tourism Management* 70, 29–41. https://doi.org/10.1016/j.tourman.2018.05.013.
Connell, J., Page, S., Sheriff, I. and Hibbert, J. (2017) Business engagement in a civil society: Transitioning towards a dementia-friendly visitor economy. *Tourism Management* 61, 110–128. https://doi.org/10.1016/j.tourman.2016.12.018.
Cummins, R. and Schubach, J. (1989) Frequency and types of medical emergencies among commercial air travelers. *Journal of the American Medical Association* 261, 1295–1299.
Dann, E. and Dann, G. (2012) Sightseeing for the sightless and soundless: Tourism experiences of the deafblind. *Tourism Culture & Communication* 12 (2), 125–140. https://doi.org/10.3727/109830413X13575858951248.
Darcy, S. (2012) (Dis)embodied air travel experiences: Disability, discrimination and the affect of a discontinuous air travel chain. *Journal of Hospitality and Tourism Management* 19 (1), 91–101. https://doi.org/10.1017/jht.2012.9.
da Silva, T., de Souza, J., da Silva, L., Figueiredo, J. and Menegon, N. (2017) Passengers with disabilities in the Brazilian air transport: Different actors and similar perspectives. *Gestão & Produção* 24 (1), 136–147. https://doi.org/10.1590/0104-530x1681-15.
da Silva, T., Silva, A., Caetano, V., Silvestrini, G. and Menegon, N. (2019) Passengers with visual disability in air transport: Evaluation of airports' accessibility. *Brazilian Journal of Occupational Therapy* 27 (2), 372–383. https://doi.org/10.4322/2526-8910.ctoAO1677.
Dementia Australia (2018) *Travelling and Holidays with Dementia*. Australian Government, Canberra.
Dementia Centre for Research Collaboration (2017) Ensuring a smooth journey for people living with dementia and their travel companions. See https://dementiaresearch.org.au/resources/airport-user-guide/ (accessed July 2020).

Devkota, A.R. and Karki, A.R. (2010) Seizure precipitated during long haul flight. *Journal of the Institute of Medicine* 32 (3), 59–61. https://doi.org/10.3126/jiom.v32i3.4962.

Dombroff, M. (2018) Beyond Dexter the peacock. *AviationPros*. See https://www.aviationpros.com/airports/article/12403537/beyond-dexter-the-peacock-us-airlines-struggle-to-cope-with-a-surge-in-emotional-support-animals (accessed July 2020).

Domínguez, T., Alén, E. and Darcy, S. (2018) Website accessibility in the tourism industry: An analysis of official national tourism organisation websites around the world. *Disability and Rehabilitation* 40, 2895–2906. https://doi.org/10.1080/09638288.2017.1362709.

Drazkowski, J.F. (2007) Driving and flying with epilepsy. *Current Neurology and Neuroscience Reports* 7 (4), 329–334. https://doi.org/10.1007/s11910-007-0050-2.

Eghtesadi, C., Goldberg, L., Botkin, B. and O'Connell, T. (2012) Accessible in-flight entertainment systems for blind and deaf passengers. *Ergonomics in Design* 20 (3), 7–13. https://doi.org/10.1177/1064804612444786.

Gatwick Airport (2016) Gatwick wins Dementia Innovation Award for hidden disability lanyard [Press release]. See http://www.mediacentre.gatwickairport.com/press-releases/2016/16-12-02-gatwick-wins-dementia-innovation-award.aspx (accessed July 2020).

Graf, J., Stuben, U. and Pump, S. (2012) In-flight medical emergencies. *Deutsches Arzteblatt International* 109 (37), 591–602.

Harpaz, B. (2017) Quiet rooms for autistic children popping up at airports. *Chicago Tribune*. See https://www.chicagotribune.com/travel/ct-quiet-rooms-for-autistic-children-popping-up-at-airports-20170412-story.html (accessed July 2020).

Hersh, M.A. (2016) Improving deafblind travelers' experiences: An international survey. *Journal of Travel Research* 55 (3), 380–394. https://doi.org/10.1177/0047287514546225.

Innes, G. (2016) *Finding a Way*. St Lucia Queensland: University of Queensland Press.

Jacoby, A. (2002) Stigma, epilepsy and quality of life. *Epilepsy & Behavior* 3 (6) (Suppl.), S10–S20.

Jacoby, A. and Austin, J.K. (2007) Social stigma for adults and children with epilepsy. *Epilepsia* 48 (9), 6–9.

Jain, D., Desjardins, A., Findlater, L. and Froehlich, J. (2019) Autoethnography of a hard of hearing traveler. Paper presented at the ASSETS '19: The 21st International ACM SIGACCESS Conference on Computers and Accessibility, Pittsburgh, PA.

Kelly, L. and Kaplan, G. (2009) Delirium and long haul travel. *Age and Ageing* 38 (6), 262. https://doi.org/10.1093/ageing/afp171.

Klímová, B. (2018) Tourists with dementia – A unique challenge for the tourism industry. *Pertanika Journal of Social Sciences & Humanities* 26 (1), 583–588.

McCabe, T. (2017) 'Doc, can I fly to Australia?' A case report and review of delirium following long-haul flight. *BJPsych Bulletin* 41 (1), 30–32. https://doi.org/10.1192/pb.bp.115.052209.

McGonigle, P. (2018) Delta Airlines cracks down on fake service dogs (and snakes, turkeys and spiders, too). *Fox 4 News*. See https://fox4kc.com/news/delta-airlines-cracks-down-on-fake-service-dogs-and-snakes-turkeys-and-spiders-too/ (accessed July 2020).

McIntosh, A. (2020) The hidden side of travel: Epilepsy and tourism. *Annals of Tourism Research* 81, 102856. https://doi.org/10.1016/j.annals.2019.102856.

Miles, J. (2016) Heathrow announces it is world's first 'dementia-friendly' airport [Press release]. See https://www.firstresponsetraining.com/news/heathrow-announces-it-is-worlds-first-dementia-friendly-airport/ (accessed July 2020).

Napolitano, F. (2020) Flying with dementia: Why we need dementia friendly airports. See https://www.airport-parking-shop.co.uk/blog/dementia-friendly-airports/ (accessed July 2020).

O'Reilly, M. and Shepherd, N. (2016) Making air travel easier for people with dementia. *Australian Journal of Dementia Care* 5 (4), 24–25.

O'Reilly, M., Shepherd, N., Edwards, H., Franz, J., Wilmott, L. and Fielding, E. (2017) Aging in the era of air travel: Improving the accessibility of airports for travelers with dementia. *Innovation Aging* 1 (1), 607.

Page, S., Innes, A. and Cutler, C. (2014) Developing dementia-friendly tourism destinations: An exploratory analysis. *Journal of Travel Research* 54 (4), 467–481. https://doi.org/10.1177/0047287514522881.

Poling, M. (2017) Airports pave the way for passengers with autism. *Travel Pulse*. See https://www.travelpulse.com/news/airlines/airports-pave-the-way-for-passengers-with-autism.html (accessed July 2020).

Poria, Y., Reichel, A. and Brandt, Y. (2010) The flight experiences of people with disabilities: An exploratory study. *Journal of Travel Research* 49 (2), 216–227. https://doi.org/10.1177/0047287509336477.

Qantas Airways Limited (2020) *Travelling with a carer*. See https://www.qantas.com/au/en/travel-info/specific-needs/travelling-with-specific-needs/travelling-with-a-carer.html (accessed June 2020).

Richards, V., Pritchard, A. and Morgan, N. (2010) (Re)envisioning tourism and visual impairment. *Annals of Tourism Research* 37 (4), 1097–1116. https://doi.org/10.1016/j.annals.2010.04.011.

Rosenkvist, J., Risser, R., Iwarsson, S. and Ståhl, A. (2010) Exploring mobility in public environments among people with cognitive functional limitations – Challenges and implications for planning. *Mobilities* 5 (1), 131–145. https://doi.org/10.1080/17450100903435011.

Royal Society for the Blind (2020) Bindimaps Wayfiding App. See https://www.rsb.org.au/bindimaps-wayfinding-app (accessed July 2020).

Sedgley, D., Pritchard, A., Morgan, N. and Hanna, P. (2017) Tourism and autism: Journeys of mixed emotions. *Annals of Tourism Research* 66, 14–25. http://dx.doi.org/10.1016/j.annals.2017.05.009.

Seeman, M.V. (2016) Travel risks for those with serious mental illness. *International Journal of Travel Medicine and Global Health* 4 (3), 76–81. DOI: 10.21859/ijtmgh-040302.

Shand, D. (2000) The assessment of fitness to travel. *Occupational Medicine* 50 (8), 566–571.

Silverman, D. and Gendreau, M. (2009) Medical issues associated with commercial flights. *The Lancet* 373 (9680), 2067–2077. https://doi.org/10.1016/S0140-6736(09)60209-9.

Skjenna, O. W., Evans, J. F., Moore, M., Thibeault, C. and Tucker, G. (1991) Helping patients travel by air. *Canadian Medical Association Journal* 144 (3), 287–293.

Small, J. (2015) Interconnecting mobilities on tour: Tourists with vision impairment partnered with sighted tourists. *Tourism Geographies* 17 (1), 76–90. https://doi.org/10.1080/14616688.2014.938690.

Small, J. and Darcy, S. (2010) Tourism, disability and mobility. In S. Cole and N. Morgan (eds) *Tourism and Inequality: Problems and Prospects* (pp. 1–20). Wallingford: CABI.

Small, J., Darcy, S. and Packer, T. (2012) The embodied tourist experiences of people with vision impairment: Management implications beyond the visual gaze. *Tourism Management* 33 (4), 941–950. https://doi.org/10.1016/j.tourman.2011.09.015.

Tetlow, R. (2017) Wings for Autism: New program helps WA kids with autism find their wings. *PerthNow*. See https://www.perthnow.com.au/news/wa/wings-for-autism-new-program-helps-wa-kids-with-autism-find-their-wings-ng-b88671255z (accessed June 2020).

Trevorrow, T. (2006) Air travel and seizure frequency for individuals with epilepsy. *Seizure* 15, 320–327.

UK Parliament (2016) Hansard – Air passengers with dementia. See https://hansard.parliament.uk/commons/2016-06-14/debates/34E8601C-DFFF-4A7C-B2A8-5CE4C5FE712C/AirPassengersWithDementia (accessed July 2020).

Unsworth, C. (1999) Living with epilepsy: Safety during home, leisure and work activities. *Australian Occupational Therapy Journal* 46 (3), 89–98.

U.S. Department of Transport (2020) Notice of proposed rulemaking (NPRM) - Traveling by air with service animals. See https://www.transportation.gov/airconsumer/latest-news (accessed July 2020).

Vann, M. (2020) DOT proposes new rules for emotional support animals on planes. *ABC News USA*. See https://abcnews.go.com/Politics/dot-proposes-rules-emotional-support-animals-aboard-planes/story?id=68452828 (accessed June 2020).

WRC (World Wide Web Consortium) (2019) W3C Standards. See https://www.w3.org/standards/ (accessed July 2020).

Warren, A., Sherriff, I., Turner, K., Bourne, S., Roberts, C., Goodrick, J. and Fremantle, J. (2019) Air travel connections: Creating a hub of collaborators to enhance flight experiences for people with dementia and their companions. Paper presented at the 29th Alzheimer's Europe Conference, The Hague.

Wood, D. (2018) American announces changes to emotional support animal policy. *Travel Pulse*. See https://www.travelpulse.com/news/airlines/american-announces-changes-to-emotional-support-animal-policy.html (accessed June 2020).

7 Fear of Flying

Jennie Small and Cheryl Cockburn-Wootten

'Oh, why can't I control my body?', I wail internally to myself. People are looking at me, but my self-talk is not working. Words, information and talking have always worked for me at other times in my life. They make me understand, feel safe and in control. Not now. The feelings are taking over. My body is not listening.

It all starts with entering the aeroplane on my return trip home to New Zealand from a conference in Australia. My heartbeat starts to increase. I face the dilemma of whether to tell the flight attendants or try to be 'normal' and 'brave'? Would I jinx myself if I don't say anything? I'm not sure what to do or say, my mind is starting to unravel as it tries to control my breathing and body. So, I smile, say, 'Hi' and then tell the flight attendants, 'I've been on the Flying Without Fear course – twice' (oh the shame of failing!). I continue, 'I'm ok with take-off and landing. I just don't like turbulence'. They smile, look at me and take a note of my seat number and I am welcomed aboard. I squeeze down the aisle and find the number for my aisle seat. I put my hand luggage in the overhead locker, sort out the pillow, blanket, and seatbelt (so many extra things to organise and I'm not sure what to do with them all), then I can sit down and buckle in. Blanket and pillow end up on the floor in a heap in front of me. My friend who loves flying is not seated near me. If I look behind, I can just see her. She is giving me reassuring smiles. Looking out through the window, I can see we are over the wings. That's good. I recall the Flying Without Fear instructor saying that we feel less turbulence (Oops, sorry! 'Movement') over the wings. He said we should call it 'movement', not 'turbulence'. I tell myself: 'Ok, I can do this – this is normal. Lots of people do this every minute of every day. Remember to breathe, wiggle those toes on take-off, take a hard mint to suck and start the movie to distract you'. The advice has worked on my previous long-haul international flights. This is a short one from Perth to Auckland – 6 hours – 'I can do this'.

The flight attendant arrives and kneels beside me. She's smiling. She informs me that there will be an hour of very bumpy turbulence. She says that, since I don't like turbulence, I can leave the plane now while the door is open. 'Mmmmm', I am starting to zone out, my breathing and heart rate increases. I try to smile but a huge fat tear drops down my face, then another in quick succession. She gets me a tissue and I say 'I need to stay onboard. I have to go home, I have to go to work in the morning' (though I have visions of the trolley cart flying up to the ceiling of the plane and children screaming as the plane dives down and up in the night sky). I try to shake these images away. Despite my mind telling me that I shouldn't ask (It's a stupid question but I just need to confirm this to feel safe), I ask very tentatively: 'The other planes got through it and landed in Auckland, didn't they?'. 'Yes, they did', she says. 'So, we will get there and land ... won't we?', I ask. She replies, 'Yes, we will'.

After the plane takes off the turbulence starts. The dipping, twisting, lunging and swaying make two passengers near me vomit. I'm trying to use my mind to tell my body that it's ok, 'Breathe, hold on, you can do this, don't worry, the other planes made it through'. But then the panic takes over and I give in to my body's senses, fears, and reactions. Images flash in my mind of my family, as I try to cling to happy memories to get me through. The movie continues playing but it isn't doing a good job of distracting me. I recall the safety video instructions. This is it, my life could end now, too short (I always wanted to see the pyramids...). I can't hold back – the instructor on the course did say letting words out helps.... 'Wow!!!!' I yelp. I can hear the Captain's announcement apologising for the turbulence. I shout a few more 'wows' and look at the time. It has been 20 minutes. The dipping and twisting get worse... I look at my watch, it has only been 36 minutes. Why does time go so slowly? I can only see the space in front of my lap. But I hear people being sick again. More bumps and swaying and twisting. I become Catholic 'Jesus, Mary and Joseph!!'. I pray to my ancestors and then to God asking 'Can I be saved, perhaps ... please? I'm a good person and have got so much still to do in my life'. Eventually, that's it! I can't hold back - this big dip and twisting is too much to bear–I have to let it out, I have to swear. Any more of this and I will have to hold the hand of the strange man sitting next to me. After an hour, the pilot comes on to apologise again and to say the plane has been cleared to go higher to clearer air. But it will take half an hour. I think, 'Just get on with it!!'. I look at my watch as the promised 30 minutes deadline comes closer.

The bumping reduces to small bumps. The swaying is no more. They announce that meals will now be served. I breathe, the shoulders start to relax, and my heart starts to return to normal. Or at least I think so until I go to pause the movie. I notice my hand and finger are still trembling. After the meal, things settle down and I now feel a fool. The passenger sitting next to me is trying to ignore this emotional middle-aged woman – me. He must think I am bonkers. Eventually, the plane lands and we all get off. I see my colleague and she says, 'I tried to tell you it's ok and I could see you weren't breathing – you were hyper ventilating. But you didn't look up from your lap and you kept your earphones on'. After recounting my experience to her she says jokingly, 'So, are you thinking of going to the conference in Japan next year?'. My response: 'At this moment, **No!!**'.

A Fearful Flyer's Narrative

Introduction

Flying has become a commonplace activity for many in the developed world, yet, as the above memory recounts, it can still incite extreme emotions, bodily reactions and social consequences. While we usually consider mobility a favourable condition of modernity, for one group, travel by air can be an anxious experience with emotions ranging from severe anxiety to mild fear. Van Gerwen *et al*. (1997) explain the three groups of individuals affected by fear of flying:

> one that does not fly at all; one that restricts flying to an absolute minimum and experiences considerable discomfort prior to and /or during each flight; and one that shows continuous mild or moderate apprehension about flying but does not avoid it, even though it remains an unpleasant experience (Ekeberg *et al.*, 1989). (Van Gerwen *et al.*, 1997: 237)

While estimates vary, a number of studies have found that anywhere between 10 and 40% of the population are reluctant to fly (Foreman *et al.*, 2006). Perhaps surprising, is that passengers are not the only ones to experience fear of flying. Pilots, air crew and military aircraft members have also been identified as either having fearful brief episodes or a flying phobia (Medialdea & Tejada, 2005; Oakes & Bor, 2010a). Foreman & van Gerwen (2008) describe fear of flying (also called aviophobia or aerophobia) as 'characterized by a marked, persistent, excessive fear that is precipitated by the experience or immediate prospect of air travel'. They further explain: 'Exposure to this phobic stimulus almost invariably provokes an anxiety response – sometimes to the point of a panic attack – which the individual recognizes as unreasonable, and which produces significant interference or distress' (Foreman & van Gerwen 2008: 27). Whether the person's fear of flying is mild, moderate or severe, it can have implications for their personal, family, social and professional life. On a personal level, fear of flying is associated with anxiety and shame and unpleasant physiological experiences.

Avoiding or minimising flying can have an impact on social relationships if a person is unable to visit family or friends. It can restrict the travel of not only the fearful passenger but also family members and friends who might otherwise have enjoyed a holiday together. In an individual's work life, restricted flying can impact career prospects as, in many jobs, flying is a requirement. Maul (2016) gives the example of director, Stanley Kubrick, whose 'legendary fear of flying confined him to the U.K., where he constructed massive studio sets to replicate a snowbound Colorado hotel, battlefields in Vietnam, and finally upper-class Manhattan'. With the world becoming more mobile, the consequences of avoiding/restricting flying are likely to be greater today than in previous generations. For the airlines, there are financial implications in loss of revenue through disruption to flights when passengers fail to board or have to be put off a flight. There is also the issue of managing fearful flyers, especially if they resort to disruptive or violent behaviour (Oakes & Bor, 2010a; Tsang *et al.*, 2018).

Whereas in the early years of commercial flying fear was considered 'rational', today, mental health professionals label it a disorder and define it as an irrational fear, a phobia, with adverse personal, social, professional and financial consequences. Along with psychologists and psychiatrists, the airline industry is also involved in programmes to ensure happy, relaxed customers (and staff). Despite the prevalence of fear of flying, the research into causes, symptoms and treatment has been limited compared with other specific phobias (see Oakes & Bor, 2010a).

The first part of this chapter presents the conventional, mental health approach to the subject matter. It considers aircraft safety, the factors behind fear of flying, individuals' responses (cognitive, physiological and behavioural) and the solutions offered by mental health professionals to overcome the fear. The second part of the chapter moves beyond the medical, individualised, mental health perspective to take a critical mobilities approach to the subject. Viewing fear as socially constructed, it pays attention to the context, environment and organisational structures less evident in traditional approaches. It takes into account the discourse, practice and materialities of flying, and the power structures that underly this social activity. The chapter draws on the above narrative of 'a fearful flyer' to provide further insight to those living with this fear.

A Mental Health Perspective

In the early decades of flying, fear was considered a normal reaction to an activity which often led to injury or death (Oakes & Bor, 2010a). As commercial flying expanded and the need to recruit flyers increased, marketers worked to allay the public's fears even as airline safety improved (Popp, 2016). Today, air travel is undoubtedly safer than other forms of transport. Over the years, there has been a significant decline in the number of accidents and fatalities despite the increase in the number of flights (see Table 7.1). From 2014 to 2019 (prior to the COVID-19 pandemic), there was a 28% increase in the number of flights but a 31%

Table 7.1 Airline safety performance (2014–2019)

	2014	2015	2016	2017	2018	2019
Yearly flights (millions)	36.5	36.9	39.0	41.3	46.1	46.8
Total Accidents	77	67	64	46	62	53
Fatal Accidents	12	4	8	6	11	8
Fatalities	641	136	198	19	523	240

Source: International Air Transport Association (IATA) (2019, 2020b).

decrease in the number of Total Accidents, with 1.13 or 1 accident for every 884,000 flights in 2019 compared with the 5-year average (2014–2019) of 1.56 or 1 accident every 640,000 flights (IATA, 2020a). The safest year on record with no passenger fatalities on jet aircraft was 2017 (IATA, 2018).

Yet, while there is statistical evidence that flying is safe, fear of flying remains a common experience ranking 'among the top ten of all fears and phobias in the adult population' (van Gerwen & Koopmans, 2018: 184). As Smith (2015) says, '[t]hose of us with aviophobia know that flying is safe–it just doesn't *feel* safe'. Emotions can range from mild anxiety to a clinical diagnosis of psychological pathology that meets the *Diagnostic and Statistical Manual of Mental Disorders-5* (DSM-5) criteria (American Psychiatric Association, 2013). In the DSM-5, these fears are encompassed in the broad category, *Anxiety Disorders*. Some are classified as a *Specific Phobia*: fear of aeroplanes (Specific Phobia – Situational) and fear of heights (Specific Phobia – Natural environment).

Oakes and Bor (2010a: 332) highlight the diagnostic complexity of fear of flying as the fear can present as 'a psychological disorder in its own right or as a symptom or co-morbid factor of a primary psychological diagnosis'. In other words, fear of flying can be a specific fear related to flying such as the plane crashing or can encompass a variety of fears and phobias, such as claustrophobia, agoraphobia, acrophobia, social anxiety and panic attacks. Separation anxiety may also be involved. The fear of loss of control is seen as central to a fear of flying. This may be a loss of external control where the individual has no control or influence over what happens to the plane. As Foreman and van Gerwen (2008) note, an individual's fear can vary to 'include heights, turbulence, bad weather, take-off, landing, and "just being up there", plus all the factors particularly associated with crashing' (2008: 15). Or the fear might be one of losing internal control: 'the person fears some form of internal catastrophe, where in some way they will go "out of control"' (Foreman & van Gerwen, 2008: 15). Associated with loss of internal control is the public shame in displaying such fear to other passengers and crew. Some passengers experience both a loss of internal and external control (Foreman & van Gerwen, 2008).

In their model of the aetiology of fear of flying, Oakes and Bor (2010a) identify the many factors that might cause, or help maintain, the fear. They propose that reaction to air travel may be the consequence of an individual's experience of air travel which includes: social context (life stress, reasons for travel and cultural attitude to travel), learning history (trauma associated with flying, media exposure and modelled behaviour) and physiology (hypoxia, spatial disorientation and vestibular dysfunction). They see experience of air travel as mediated by characteristics of the individual: cognitive vulnerability (the perception of air travel as dangerous, unpredictable, uncontrollable) and psychological characteristics: personality traits (for example, anxiety sensitivity, comorbid psychiatric disorders, mood and coping strategies).

Responses to flying are considered to be cognitive, physiological and behavioural. *Cognitive* responses are interpreted as relating to images and thoughts of the behaviour of the plane and those onboard, including thoughts of crashing, mutilation and death. In the fearful flyer narrative, the passenger conveys her cognitions through her images and thoughts: *I have visions of the trolley cart flying up to the ceiling of the plane and children screaming as the plane dives down and up in the night sky. I try to shake these images away.* Thoughts may include memories of media reports of airline crashes. Kinderman (2014) explains that when people are making judgements about their situation, such as evaluating their air safety, high profile air tragedies can exacerbate fears. He draws on the 'availability heuristic' (Tversky & Kahneman, 1973) to explain that many of our judgements in life are based on 'rules of thumb'; we use short-hand methods, rather than detailed logical deductions. This means that if we have recently seen or heard about an air disaster, we tend to judge it as more common or likely than the statistical reality. The *physiological* responses to the emotion of fear highlight the embodied experience of the passenger. These may include increased heart rate and blood pressure, upset stomach, sweating palms, shaking, hyperventilation 'irrespective of the nature of the cognitive response' (Oakes & Bor 2010a: 332). Such responses are evident in the narrative: *I am starting to zone out, my breathing and heart rate increases … I notice my hand and finger are still trembling. Behavioural* responses may involve passengers acting out their fear. In the narrative, we see the passenger vocalising her emotions: *I can't hold back … I have to let it out, I have to swear.*

Passengers are said to use different cognitive, physiological and behavioural means to attempt to manage or control their fears. In the narrative we see the passenger commanding her thoughts, body and behaviour: '*Ok, I can do this – this is normal. Lots of people do this every minute of every day. Remember to breathe, wiggle those toes on take-off, take a hard mint to suck and start the movie to distract you. The advice has worked on my previous long-haul international flights*'. Oakes and Bor (2010a: 332) state that:

> Anxious flyers may exhibit a number of safety behaviours such as having a preference for a specific seat (aisle or exit seats for 'quick escapes' or window seats to minimise interaction with others). They may question airline staff about the weather, delays, technical problems or the pilot's qualifications.

In our narrative the passenger seeks reassurance from the flight attendant: '*The other planes got through it and landed in Auckland, didn't they?'*. A passenger with a fear of flying may grip the armrests tightly, may brace themselves during take-off and landing and may help to brake during landing by pushing back against the seat and bracing feet on the seat in front or on the floor. They may also try to make themselves as light as possible during turbulence by raising their feet from the floor or sitting lightly on the seat or on one buttock. They may lean left in a right turn, sit motionless or rigidly in their seat, talk incessantly (or not at all) or close their eyes. However, as Foreman and van Gerwen (2008) explain, many of these measures are counterproductive, exacerbating the fear for the individual and possibly infecting other passengers (if their behaviour is observable). Prescription medicines, herbal remedies and alcohol are other means by which individuals have tried to manage their fear (successfully or unsuccessfully).

It is apparent in the narrative that much of the anxiety for the passenger lies in her sense of individual responsibility for the management of the situation. There is a battle between her emotions, cognitions, body (physiology) and behavioural responses: *'Oh, why can't I control my body?', I wail internally to myself.* Having attended a Fear of Flying course (twice) she has been taught various measures – thoughts and behaviours to deal with her fear, yet the emotions break through. Her distress is exacerbated by the knowledge that she cannot align mind and body, leading to her sense of failure: *The feelings are taking over. My body is not listening I'm trying to use my mind to tell my body that it's ok, 'Breathe, hold on, you can do this, don't worry, the other planes made it through'. But then the panic takes over and I give in to my body's senses, fears, and reactions.* The experience is intensified by her loss of control in public and awareness of others' reactions. *People are looking at me, but my self-talk is not working ... I now feel a fool. The passenger sitting next to me is trying to ignore this emotional middle-aged woman – me. He must think I am bonkers.* She wants to present a public face of normality in what she considers a fearful environment.

Those experiencing fear of flying are advised to access an intervention programme, even if their fear is at a sub clinical level of anxiety. The most widely offered Fear of Flying programmes are group programmes, often run by the airlines. Treatment can also be available via an anxiety clinic or through individual therapy with a mental health professional. There are various treatments for fear of flying but, since the 1970s, most involve cognitive behavioural techniques with exposure *in vivo*. Cognitive techniques involve examination of maladaptive patterns of thought, and retraining thoughts about flying: 'cognitive restructuring, thought stopping, coaching in cognitive coping skills and identifying and "talking back to" negative thoughts' (Oakes & Bor, 2010b: 342). Exposure involves confronting the fear by exposing the individual to the situations that triggered the fear or which were being avoided (such as the aeroplane and airport). Exposure to the stimulus may be *in vivo* (real life), simulated or provided through technology. Many *in vivo* exposure programs will conclude with a real-life flight, visit to an airport and going behind the scenes to view the control tower.

Other exposure techniques are computer-assisted treatments which have helped overcome some of the limitations of *in vivo* exposure: the difficulty of access to the feared stimulus (the airport or the plane), the financial cost of treatment, the difficulty of applying the exposure technique in an appropriate way and controlling important variables, such as the duration of the exposure or the number of sessions (Campos *et al.*, 2016). Foreman and van Gerwen (2008) explain that computer-assisted programs 'use specific types of software that aims to confront people, in a hierarchically structured way, with real images and sounds related to the fear stimuli presented on the screen of a personal computer' (2008: 176). An alternative computer-based technique is Virtual Reality which, as Foreman and van Gerwen (2008) say, 'allows individuals to become active participants, interacting through sight, sound, and touch, in a computer-generated, three-dimensional world' (2008: 176). Campos *et al.* (2016) report the benefits of virtual reality methods in overcoming the limitations of *in vivo* therapy as well as ensuring client confidentiality. They found that there was a willingness amongst many clients to undergo virtual reality therapy where they would not undertake therapy in real, physical flight situations. However, for such methods to be successful, the client must be exposed to situations that activate fear. Limitations of virtual reality methods are reported by Oakes and Bor (2010b): the cost, the unpredictability of real-life situations and the unsuitability for those who experience a form of motion sickness from intolerance of the virtual environment.

Oakes and Bor (2010a: 327) explain that, to be effective, psychological interventions must be tailored to the individual as fear of flying is acquired 'under the influence of complex psychological, social and physiological factors unique to each affected individual'. They argue for Cognitive Behaviour Therapy which offers possibilities for individualised treatment, rather than the 'one size fits all' which is the basis of multi-component group programmes (Oakes & Bor, 2010b).

A Critical Approach to Fear of Flying

The literature and professional response to fear of flying has emerged predominantly from the disciplines of psychiatry and psychology with the concomitant issues regarding labelling (an irrational phobia) and classification which designates boundaries. Even within psychology there is the concern that in creating disorder boundaries, 'The natural overlap of dimensions across the syndromal boundaries is artificially constrained by eliminating "comorbid disorders"' (Bilder, 2015: 182). The traditional mental health perspective, focusing on psychopathology and the medical model, is framed within a positivist paradigm, situating the problem, the impairment, with the person and thus individual-directed treatment (Oakes & Bor, 2010a). In the personal narrative above, we see the flyer's account reflecting individual ownership of the problem. Yet, as we argue, such an approach ignores the wider societal and organisational framing constructing the activity (Cockburn-Wootten et al., 2008; Popp, 2016).

A critical approach to fear of flying would argue for a 'sociology of psychiatric critique' (Pickersgill, 2014: 521). To understand the complexity of fear of flying requires a move beyond the individual focus to consider a social model. Taking a social constructionist approach, emotions, such as fear (of flying), are understood as a social process, that is, they are 'appropriated from the social and cultural realm in interaction' (Crawford et al., 1992: 123). As Crawford et al. (1992) would explain, it is through the passenger's appraisal or evaluation of flying in the light of others' evaluation of flying that emotions are constructed. Perceptions of safety and danger (inherent in fear) are thus seen as '"intersubjective" – products of social construction, collective agreement, and socialization (Zerubavel, 1991)' (Simpson, 1996: 550). Simpson explains that, since 'the objective environment provides only inconsistent and ambiguous clues about danger ... beliefs about danger, and particularly safety, can arise with little or no reference to the objective world they describe' (1996: 550). The appropriate framework for a specific situation is arrived at through collective agreement. What is viewed as 'appropriate' has variable meanings. Simpson prefers to think of phobias (which would include fear of flying) as violations of these frameworks, rather than 'irrational' behaviour.

Explaining the gendered nature of emotions, Crawford et al. (1992: 112) state, 'social meanings are appropriated according to the power relations in which our actions are situated'. From a broad, Western-thinking perspective, the traditional association of men with rationality and women with emotion has privileged reason over emotion. If we look further to the emotion of fear associated with cowardice (or lack of fear associated with bravery), we see gendered constructions. An interesting analysis of the marketing and representation of air travel in the mid-20th century highlights the gendering of fear of flying by the advertising industry (Popp, 2016). Plagued by accidents in the early days of air travel, security, safety and comfort were emphasised in marketing campaigns from the 1930s onwards to counteract passenger fear impeding industry growth (Mills, 1996). In order to gain consumer trust and thus encourage more people to fly, the role of airline marketing communications was to 'encourage consumers to make sense of the emotions elicited by flight' (Popp, 2016: 74). Advertisers did this by drawing on gendered and pathological themes to stigmatise fear of flying 'as an irrational, neurotic, and thus shameful stance toward technological risk' (Popp, 2016: 62). Fear of flying was represented as feminine in nature with overly-cautious women holding sway over the flying behaviour of the men in their lives. The theory went:

> Wives, mothers, daughters, and sweethearts, petrified by the thought of boarding a plane, forbid their husbands, sons, fathers, and partners from doing the same ...; more interested in keeping household harmony than shaving time off their itineraries, men who might otherwise fly took the train. (Popp, 2016: 68)

Women were considered selfish in placing their own psychological wellbeing above that of their menfolk – the primary targeted air traveller. To placate women, advertising agencies took a different pitch of persuasion focusing on 'family togetherness'. They argued: if men travelled by plane, they would spend less time in travel and more at home with the family. Popp (2016: 70) explains, 'In the figure of the worried wife ... audiences were urged to understand timidity as not only the product of distinctly feminine irrationality, but also as emasculating'.

Fear of flying was not only represented as gendered but also as 'symptomatic of an underdeveloped psyche' (Popp, 2016: 61), as understood in psychoanalysis which was current at the time. Central to the discourse was the unacceptability of fear of flying once one had reached adulthood. Popp (2016: 75) concludes: 'gender and mental health provided mediums through which advertisers could stigmatize cautiousness as outside the bounds of acceptable, and normatively manly, stances toward risk-laden technological systems'. Popp (2016) makes the point that the presence of women as airline attendants 'subtly suggested that no self-respecting man should fear air travel' (Popp, 2016: 67). If men were fearful, their individual circumstances and family history were to blame – not the mode of transport. In other words, the campaigns individualised the fear (Popp, 2016). As Gillovic et al. (2018: 615) explain, organisational communications and 'choice of language employed ... construct an identity that has powerful institutional and social consequences for shaping ... attitudes, perceptions, responses and actions'.

In shifting the focus from the individual, the authors of this chapter question the role of the transport industry in relation to fear of flying. In many countries, the declining availability of alternative modes of public transport (trains, ships, buses) has reduced transport options for those who are fearful of flying. Even where other options are available, the value placed on speed in the modern world may necessitate the 90-minute flight as opposed to the nine-hour trip by land. In particular, the airline industry can be questioned for its processes and systems that may exacerbate fear. The industry's move to economies of scale has brought a range of stresses that can contribute to flying anxiety. At the airport, DIY check-ins and security checks may cause anxiety (Martinussen *et al.*, 2011). Boarding procedures that are rushed, unstructured and disorderly can also be stressful. Onboard the aircraft, reduced personal space, comfort and control may create the potential for passenger anxiety such as claustrophobia. Minimisation of service may also contribute to stress. Certainly, the cost-cutting measures have been associated with an increase in the number of passengers who misbehave (Tsang *et al.*, 2018) which can be a stressful experience for other passengers. Other aspects of the cabin environment can have an impact on passenger cognitive function: hypoxia (oxygen deficiency), spatial disorientation and vestibular dysfunction (a consequence of air pressure changes) (Oakes & Bor, 2010a).

Solutions range from reconstruction of the physical environment of the aircraft to providing choices for passengers in elements of their physical environment – seat type and position (and seat maps), arm rests, lighting etc. Providing choices in service such as meal plans, can also provide passengers with some degree (however minimal) of being in control. Since lack of knowledge about the flight creates feelings of loss of control, explanation as to what is happening (for example 'Movement is going to last 5 minutes') is important, as is the language used: 'movement' is less threatening than 'turbulence'. Trust is essential for fearful passengers to relinquish their need for control. Attention from the crew allows for relationships and trust in the service/flight to develop. Since behaviour of other passengers (as described in Chapters 3 and 4) can also be challenging, especially for a passenger prone to fear of flying, airline management of passenger behaviour is important in defusing a potentially stressful environment.

Preston (2014), who calls fear of flying, 'the spectre that haunts modern life', reports that, as we fly more, aviophobia seems to be growing. Looking beyond the individual, it is useful to consider how today's media constructs emotions related to flying. Preston argues that the manner in which news channels deal with accidents ('reported at length in rolling Technicolor') has changed the way many people view flying. As the mental health perspective has acknowledged, media portrayal of plane crashes, particularly that of 9/11, can feed into people's uncertainty about flying. We need to consider the media's responsibility in presenting accurate accounts of flying safety. After 9/11, significant differences were found in flying demand by gender, education and country of origin (Webber, 2009), suggesting that fear of flying is constructed differently amongst groups. In recent years, the rise of social media has increased access to the more dramatic examples of flying, for instance, a New Zealand newspaper, drawing on an online social media Reddit thread discussion, asked readers to share their worst ever airport and airline experiences (Stuff, 2016) while another online report from 'Insider' identifies '22 horrible things passengers have done while flying' (Lakritz, 2019). (See Chapters 3 and 4 for online reports of negative flying experiences.) Fears about air safety may also be related to developments in air transport technology. According to the findings from the National Geographic study (Open Access Government, 2018), 'More than half of Brits (51%) believe that cyber security, such as flight systems being hacked, will be one of the biggest future threats to our flights over the next ten years, whilst 52% think drone collisions will be an issue'. It would seem that the airline industry needs to counteract these media reports by disseminating information that normalises and familiarises people with air travel.

Finally, a critical approach to travel raises questions of equality and inequality; in the case of flying, who is included and, crucially, who is excluded from the flying experience? Social justice issues emerge when a passenger's fear of flying has a significant impact on their employment and career. While fear of flying can affect all types of travellers, here we consider the business traveller and question what workplaces are doing to adjust their demands for someone with fear of flying. For some professions flying is a crucial element of the job description. Academics, for example, are expected to maintain networks, enhance their (and their university's) reputation and share knowledge through attending meetings and conferences. However, while critical organisational communication scholars (among others) have questioned the need for face-to-face conferences (Broadfoot *et al.*, 2010), fear of flying is not part of the discussion.

It is worth considering where fear of flying fits in relation to rights of persons with disabilities. In the United States, the Americans with Disabilities Act (ADA) prohibits an employer from discriminating against an individual who is a 'qualified individual with a disability'. This means an employer is required to make reasonable accommodation for those who have known physical or mental limitations so long as that accommodation does not interfere with the essential function of the individual's job. To be qualified as having a disability, the impairment must *substantially* [our italics] limit a major life activity (however, under certain US state laws, the life activity may be merely 'limited'). Where an employee has a fear of flying, teleconferencing or telecommuting may be a satisfactory option. Reed (2018) reports the high-profile case of Royce White, a US basketball player with the Houston Rockets who requested that he be permitted to travel by bus, rather than fly to certain away games, because he suffered from obsessive-compulsive disorder and generalised anxiety disorder which included a fear of flying. In this case, The Rockets agreed to White taking alternative transport. However, Reed (2018) makes the point that 'while anxiety disorders and OCD have been recognized as qualified disabilities, several courts have held that fear of flying itself doesn't rise to that level'.

Moving Forward...

Much of the knowledge we have of fear of flying comes from Western, English-speaking passengers and has been framed within the mental health perspective. For a large part, it comes from quantitative data – questionnaires and behavioural scales, for example, the Fear Survey Schedule. It largely reflects contemporary, Western neoliberal society's focus on the individual and responsibility for the self. The passenger narrative above illustrates absorption of this discourse: individual ownership of the anxiety and responsibility for managing it – the onus is on her to control her emotions. We have argued here that it is helpful to turn to the sociocultural environment to understand how emotions have been constructed. The first step would be to rethink how we view and evaluate emotion and reason, how we label and classify fear of flying. Despite modern labelling which considers such a fear 'irrational', this fear is not beyond our comprehension. While statistics might confirm the safety of travel, being aloft is not a 'natural' way of being and being confined to a small space, often for an extended period of time, with strangers, can be confronting especially when their behaviours are at odds with our own.

A critical approach to fear of flying sees the flying experience as social activity that is inherently political. Power relations are reflected and reinforced through the airline industry (its products, service etc.), media (representation of air travel) and businesses (requirement to travel by air). To understand the experience of flying requires an appreciation of the interconnection of the representation and discourse of flying, the practice of flying (embodied and emotional) and the materialities of air travel (the features of airport and aircraft). The degree of anxiety that emerges at the intersection differentiates passengers. While the airline industry can work to make changes to the physical and sociocultural environments of air travel, the media can consider how they frame air incidents. Businesses can work to avoid disadvantaging their workers who fear air travel. Today's technology, permitting online participation, can offer an alternative to the necessity for air travel. Providing a means for all workers to participate, facilitates 'a rich diversity of voices and ideas to flourish' (Broadfoot *et al.*, 2008: 347) and, at the same time, benefits the environment by reducing the carbon cost of flying. Examining flying from this wider social discourse and critical perspective allows us to identify possibilities for change in the service that may help reduce fear of flying and lower the chance of damaged career prospects. The consequences of fear of flying are far reaching and thus require us to expand how we view this fear. We suggest looking beyond the individual to the social construction of fear of flying in the hope that we can go some way to move the individual from that of an excluded group of anxious or non-flyers to 'the club' of 'normal' flyers. Mobility justice warrants it.

Flyer's Reflexive Postscript

When agreeing to contribute to this chapter, I thought that the process of reflection and writing might cure my fear of flying. Thinking, reading and planning for this chapter has heightened my emotions, awareness of my body and thinking around flying. However, I would not say that I am 'cured'. Indeed, I now think that my fear of flying may not be fully resolved and eradicated. However, what I would say, more importantly, is that reflection has highlighted the wider societal discourses and how these have been used in the communications about flying. If the airline industry changed various aspects of their language, impersonal communication, physical environment and offerings then my fear would reduce and I would fly more often for work and with family and friends.

References

American Psychiatric Association (2013) *Diagnostic and Statistical Manual of Mental Disorders*. Washington, D.C.: Elsevier.

Bilder, R. (2015) Dimensional and categorical approaches to mental illness: Let biology decide. In L. Kirmayer, R. Lemelson. and C. Cummings (eds) *Revisioning Psychiatry: Cultural Phenomenology, Critical Neuroscience, and Global Mental Health* (pp. 179–205). New York, NY: Cambridge University Press.

Broadfoot, K.J., Cockburn, T., Cockburn-Wootten, C., do Carmo Reis, M., Gautam, D.K., Malshe, A., Munshi, D., Nelson-Marsh, N., Zakari Okwori, J., Simpson, M. and Srinivas, N. (2008) A mosaic of visions, daydreams, and memories: Diverse inlays of organizing and communicating from around the globe. *Management Communication Quarterly* 22 (2), 322–350. https://doi.org/10.1177/0893318908323574.

Broadfoot, K.J., Munshi, D. and Nelson-Marsh, N. (2010) COMMUNEcation: A rhizomatic tale of participatory technology, postcoloniality and professional community. *New Media & Society* 12 (5), 797–812. https://doi.org/10.1177/1461444809348880.

Campos, D., Bretón-López, J., Botella, C., Mira, A., Castilla, D., Baños, R., Tortella-Feliu, M. and Quero, S. (2016) An Internet-based treatment for flying phobia (NO-FEAR Airlines): Study protocol for a randomized controlled trial. *BMC Psychiatry* 16. DOI: 10.1186/s12888-016-0996-1.

Cockburn-Wootten, C., Pritchard, A., Morgan, N. and Jones, E. (2008) 'It's her shopping list!' Exploring gender, leisure, and power in grocery shopping. *Leisure/Loisir* 32 (2), 407–436. https://doi.org/10.1080/14927713.2008.9651416.

Crawford, J., Kippax, S., Onyx, J., Gault, U. and Benton, P. (1992) *Emotion and Gender: Constructing Meaning from Memory*. London: Sage.

Foreman, E. and van Gerwen, L. (2008) *Fly away Fear: Overcoming your Fear of Flying*. London: Karnac Books.

Foreman, E.I., Bor, R. and van Gerwen, L. (2006) The nature, characteristics, impact and personal implications of fear of flying. In R. Bor and T. Hubbard (eds) *Aviation Mental Health: Psychological Implications for Air Transportation* (pp. 53–68). London: Routledge.

Gillovic, B., McIntosh, A., Darcy, S. and Cockburn-Wootten, C. (2018) Enabling the language of accessible tourism. *Journal of Sustainable Tourism* 26 (4), 615–630. https://doi.org/10.1080/09669582.2017.1377209.

International Air Transport Association (IATA) (2018) *Safety Report 2017* (54th edn). See https://cdn.aviation-safety.net/airlinesafety/industry/reports/IATA-safety-report-2017.pdf (accessed March 2019).

International Air Transport Association (IATA) (2019) *Safety Fact Sheet*. See https://www.iata.org/pressroom/facts_figures/fact_sheets/Documents/fact-sheet-safety.pdf (accessed March 2019).

International Air Transport Association (IATA) (2020a) *IATA Releases 2019 Airline Safety Report*, 6 April. Press Release No: 27. See https://www.iata.org/en/pressroom/pr/2020-04-06-01/ (accessed March 2022).

International Air Transport Association (IATA) (2020b) *Safety Report 2019*, 1 April. Edition 56. See https://libraryonline.erau.edu/online-full-text/iata-safety-reports/IATA-Safety-Report-2019.pdf (accessed March 2022).

Kinderman, P. (2014) How to think slow and fight the fear of flying. *The Conversation*, 29 July. See https://theconversation.com/how-to-think-slow-and-fight-the-fear-of-flying-29793 (accessed March 2019).

Lakritz, T. (2019) 22 horrible things passengers have done while flying. *Insider*, 24 July. See https://www.insider.com/flying-airport-horror-stories-tourists-2018-4 (accessed November 2019).

Martinussen, M., Gundersen, E. and Pedersen, R. (2011) Predicting fear of flying and positive emotions towards air travel. *Aviation Psychology and Applied Human Factors*, 1(2) 70–74. https://doi.org/10.1027/2192-0923/a000011.

Maul, T. (2016) On the photography of An-My Lê. *DIVISION/Rev.* 14.3.

Medialdea, J. and Tejada, F. (2005) Phobic fear of flying in aircrews: Epidemiological aspects and comorbidity. *Aviation, Space, and Environmental Medicine* 76 (6), 566–568.

Mills, A.J. (1996) Strategy, sexuality and the stratosphere: Airlines and the gendering of organisations. In L. Morris and E. Stina Lyon (eds) *Gender Relations in Public and Private* (pp. 77–94). London: Palgrave Macmillan.

Oakes, M. and Bor, R. (2010a) The psychology of fear of flying (part I): A critical evaluation of current perspectives on the nature, prevalence and etiology of fear of flying. *Travel Medicine and Infectious Disease* 8 (6), 327–338. https://doi.org/10.1016/j.tmaid.2010.10.001.

Oakes, M. and Bor, R. (2010b) The psychology of fear of flying (part II): A critical evaluation of current perspectives on approaches to treatment. *Travel Medicine and Infectious Disease* 8 (6), 339–363. https://doi.org/10.1016/j.tmaid.2010.10.002.

Open Access Government (2018) Brits more scared of flying than ever before. *Transport News*, 21 February. See https://www.openaccessgovernment.org/brits-scared-of-flying/42966/ (accessed November 2019).

Pickersgill, M. (2014) Debating DSM-5: Diagnosis and the sociology of critique. *Journal of Medical Ethics* 40, 521–525. http://dx.doi.org/10.1136/medethics-2013-101762.

Popp, R.K. (2016) Commercial pacification: Airline advertising, fear of flight, and the shaping of popular emotion. *Journal of Consumer Culture* 16 (1), 61–79. https://doi.org/10.1177/1469540513509640.

Preston, A. (2014) Fear of flying: The spectre that haunts modern life, *The Guardian*, 28 December. See https://www.theguardian.com/world/2014/dec/28/fear-of-flying-phobia-we-cant-overcome (accessed November 2019).

Reed, T. (October 24, 2018) *NBA prospect's fear of flying reflects potential limits of employers' obligation to accommodate disabilities*, ENERTAINHR:A Ford Harrison Blog, 24 October. See https://hrdailyadvisor.blr.com/2018/10/24/nba-prospects-fear-of-flying-reflects-potential-limits-of-employers-obligation-to-accommodate-disabilities/ (accessed March 2019).

Simpson, R. (1996) Neither clear nor present: The social construction of safety and danger. *Sociological Forum* 11, 549–562. https://doi.org/10.1007/BF02408392.

Smith, L. (2015) The vast beast-whistle of space. *The Paris Review*, 23 January. See https://www.theparisreview.org/blog/2015/01/23/the-vast-beast-whistle-of-space/ (accessed March 2019).

Stuff (2016) Passengers share their worst ever travel experiences. *Stuff*, 26 April. See https://www.stuff.co.nz/travel/travel-troubles/79314988/passengers-share-their-worst-ever-travel-experiences (accessed November 2019).

Tsang, S., Masiero, L. and Schuckert, M. (2018) Investigating air passengers' acceptance level of unruly in-flight behavior. *Tourism Analysis* 23 (1), 31–43. https://doi.org/10.3727/108354218X15143857349477.

Tversky, A. and Kahneman, D. (1973) Availability: A heuristic for judging frequency and probability. *Cognitive Psychology* 5, 207–232. https://doi.org/10.1016/0010-0285(73)90033-9.

Van Gerwen, L. and Koopmans, T. (2018) Self-help treatment for fear of flying. *Aeronautics and Aerospace Open Access Journal* 2 (3), 184–189. DOI: 10.15406/aaoaj.2018.02.00049.

Van Gerwen, L., Spinhoven, P., Diekstra, R. and Van Dyck (1997) People who seek help for fear of flying: Typology of flying phobics. *Behavior Therapy* 28, 237–251. https://doi.org/10.1016/S0005-7894(97)80045-7.

Webber, D. (2009) Who stopped flying around September 11? *Applied Economics Letters* 16 (13), 1375–1381. https://doi.org/10.1080/13504850701452031.

8 The Flyers' Dilemma: Confronting the Negative Psychological Effects of Air Passenger Travel

James Higham and Martin Young

Introduction

The latter part of the 20th century witnessed tremendous growth of tourism, paralleled with increasingly widespread concerns arising from social and environmental impacts (Stovall *et al.*, 2019). Timothy (2019) critically explores global tourism in relation to the 'exhausted Earth', insisting that new forms of 21st century tourism need to be imagined and enacted. Despite the individual benefits of air travel, passenger air travel is perhaps *the* key driver of exhaustive tourism in two respects. First, jet aircraft and their associated transport infrastructures enable the transport of millions of tourists per day. Indeed 4.3 billion passenger trips were made by scheduled air services in 2019 (International Civil Aviation Organization, 2018). These 11.7 million daily trips create social and environmental impacts at destinations on an unprecedented global scale. Second, the air transport system itself has become a globally significant emitter of greenhouse gases. Air travel has been described as the most efficient means by which consumers can cheaply and effortlessly add significant volumes of carbon dioxide (among other greenhouse gases) to the global atmospheric sink (Peeters *et al.*, 2016). The growing demand for air travel has been matched by public pressure to resolve the aviation-climate challenge (Sgouridis *et al.*, 2011).

The association between leisure air travel and climate change is now firmly established in the consciousness of consumers in highly aeromobile societies (Higham *et al.*, 2016a). As set out in Air New Zealand's (2017: 4) Sustainability Report,

> ...the dilemma for anyone who cares passionately about addressing the multiple threats of climate change: either stop flying altogether (the

logical but somewhat unworldly idealist's position), or fly as little and as discriminatingly and responsibly as possible (the often uncomfortable pragmatist's position).

This places environmentally aware consumers in a difficult position whereby the attractiveness of international tourism has increased and become more accessible across social classes, while scope to simply ignore the inherently damaging nature of air passenger travel has narrowed. It is this evolving tension that is expressed in the concept of the *'flyers' dilemma'*. This concept arises from the increasingly inescapable interplay of air travel desire and environment concern, driven in part by social movements such as *flygskam* (flight shame) (Mkono, 2020). In this chapter we first contextualise the debate surrounding the sustainability of air travel in the light of air transport trends over the past 50 years. We go on to explain the conditions responsible for the emergence of the flyers' dilemma and review the body of empirical research that has teased out its negative psychological effects. We conclude with a critical consideration of an alternative conceptual approach to resolution of the flyers' dilemma, one that elaborates its structural causes and preconditions as a necessary project of collective social action.

Tourist Air Travel and Climate Change

Largely unquestioned tourism growth strategies have driven steep growth in global tourism emissions, while the systemic challenges facing the sector have been generally ignored (Scott *et al.*, 2012). To overcome this, the global tourism system faces the daunting challenge of rapid decarbonisation if it is to become environmentally sustainable (IPCC 2018). This will require system-wide transitions to a low carbon economy (Stern, 2007). Within this, it is also recognised that the difficulty in reducing emissions will vary by tourism subsector (Gössling & Higham, 2021). High energy intensity combined with limited efficiency gains under the current technical regime and high costs of technology change present a deeply problematic set of circumstances (Larsson *et al.*, 2019; Peeters *et al.*, 2016).

The transportation sector presents, undoubtedly, the greatest challenge to a sustainable and climate safe tourism system. Not only does transport account for almost a quarter (23%) of total global energy-related CO_2 emissions, but these emissions are also projected to double by 2050 (Creutzig *et al.*, 2015). A feature of tourism development has been rapid growth in demand for aviation, which has become critical to the competitiveness of international destinations (Cornelissen, 2017). Prior to the paralysis brought about by the global

COVID-19 pandemic (January 2020), global passenger demand for air travel had sustained 5–6% annual growth over a period of decades (Bows-Larkin et al., 2016). The growth of the global civil aviation fleet is remarkable, increasing more than sixfold over the past 50 years. In 1970, the global tourism system was served by 3700 civil aircraft, growing to 9100 in 1990, 21,000 in 2010 and 23,100 in 2018 (Airbus, 2014; Boeing, 2019). Across this 50-year period, revenue passenger kilometres (RPK) increased sixteenfold from 500 billion (1970) to 8157 billion in 2018 (Boeing, 2019).

This growth rate, prior to COVID-19, was forecast to continue, with Boeing predicting a global fleet of 50,660 civil aircraft producing almost 20,000 billion RPK per annum by 2038 (Boeing, 2019). This projection was based on a global air passenger growth rate of 4.6% per annum which far outstrips the annual efficiency improvement target (2.0% per annum 2020–2050) set by the International Civil Aviation Organization (ICAO) (EFTE, 2016). Due to this rapid growth, aviation emissions between 2015 and 2050 were forecast to account for over one quarter (27%) of the total carbon budget required to stabilise global temperatures between +1.5–2.0°C. Indeed, following the Paris Climate Accord (2015), ICAO accepted that '… aviation emissions are expected to grow by up to 300% by 2050 unless action is taken' (EFTE, 2016: 2). Clearly, climate stabilisation will not be achieved without confronting the energy and carbon intensive nature of the tourism industry (Becken, 2011), most notably air passenger transport emissions (Scott et al., 2012).

Tourist air travel, as a form of consumption, presents its own set of unique management challenges. Air travel has become an increasingly affordable and routine consumer product (Young et al., 2014), offering the possibility of personal air travel to a widening range of social classes (Randles & Mander, 2009). The increase in the social accessibility of air travel across social groups has been facilitated by the advent of budget airlines or 'low-cost carriers' (LCCs). These new airlines dramatically reduced their operating costs by increasing labour productivity, reducing levels of add-on service and increasing the use of technology to compete solely on the basis of ticket price. This trend commenced with US airline deregulation in 1978 and has accelerated heavily over the past two decades (Gössling & Peeters, 2015). For example, the 5% market share for LCCs in Europe in 2001 increased to over a quarter (26%) in 2011 (UNWTO, 2012). The innovation of the LCC model has steadily cheapened airfares. This has, in turn, driven an acceleration in the frequency of travel and in the level of international tourists arriving by air, which increased from 43.7% in 1998 to 57% in 2018 (UNWTO, 2018). Decreasing air fares have also changed the spatio-temporal patterns of leisure travel, with tourists travelling greater distances for shorter periods. These trends have been responsible for inevitable year-on-year increases in aviation emissions (Gössling & Higham, 2021). This has produced the situation where demand for leisure-based passenger air transport has been steadily increasing, while the environmental consequences of that travel are becoming impossible to ignore. It is to this tension that we now turn.

The Flyers' Dilemma

Given that leisure-based air transport is a 'discretionary' activity (Higham *et al.*, 2019), it stands to reason that voluntary behavioural change may have a role to play in the reduction of air transport consumption. Therefore, close attention needs to be paid to the relationships between tourist air travel behaviour on the one hand, and climate change discourses on the other, if we are to understand the potential role of voluntary behavioural change in reducing aviation emissions (Lassen, 2010). It is clear that, over the last two decades, awareness of climate change and public concern for the climate consequences of personal leisure air travel have become increasingly evident in western societies (e.g. Cohen & Higham, 2011; Higham & Cohen, 2011; Mkono & Hughes, 2020). Equally evident is the dissonance that exists between increasing climate concern among consumers and behaviours that remain almost entirely unchanged. This cognitive dissonance arises in relation to a wide range of domestic (day to day) sustainability issues (Miller *et al.*, 2010). It appears particularly entrenched in the case of discretionary air travel (e.g. Hares *et al.*, 2010; Hibbert *et al.*, 2013; Kroesen, 2013).

Some two decades ago, Kollmuss and Agyeman (2002) described this dissonance between mental conceptions and behaviour as the 'value-action gap'. In tourism studies, the 'value-action gap' has been found to vary between behaviours that take place in 'home' (ordinary) and 'away' (extraordinary) settings. Pro-environmental behaviours that have been adopted and are conducted routinely in the home setting may be temporarily suspended by tourists. This raises a particularly acute challenge confronting sustainability behaviour change in the context of tourism. Tourists may seek to escape the stress of their lives while on holiday and this may extend to the temporary suspension of climate concerns (Cohen *et al.*, 2013; see also Barr *et al.*, 2010).

Of course, the 'value-action gap' plays out in relation to air travel in various ways. Rosenthal (2010) used the term 'the flyers' dilemma' to highlight the internalised psychological burden that emerges from the conflict between an individual's self-identity as an environmentally responsible consumer, and knowledge of the environmental impacts produced by their travel (Young *et al.*, 2014). The flyers' dilemma thus expresses a cognitive dissonance between the air travel behaviours of those who consider themselves environmentally responsible, and growing awareness these flyers have of the contribution of air travel to the climate crisis, which threatens the very existence of the places that tourists seek to experience (Gössling & Higham, 2021). It arises from the inescapable reality of high and damaging aviation emissions combined with the absence of a technical solution to the high climate cost of unrestrained air travel (Peeters *et al.*, 2016). The flyers' dilemma is perhaps felt most acutely by 'new puritans' (Burns & Bibbings, 2009), ethical consumers and environmental activists who are vocal on the need to reduce levels of personal aeromobility (Cohen *et al.*, 2011).

Not only does the flyers' dilemma draw into question the travel behaviour of those who engage in high personal aeromobility (Cohen *et al.*, 2011; Urry, 2010), it also highlights the processes by which environmental consequences can become sublimated through the internal psychological processes of individual travellers to allow continued travel (Clark & Calleja, 2008; Elliott, 1994). This cognitive dissonance may be a cause of guilt and anxiety, leading to negative emotions of denial, blame and suppression (Cohen *et al.*, 2011). The irony of the flyers' dilemma is that the most frequent flyers are from the middle classes who tend to be the most environmentally aware (Leviston *et al.*, 2011; Princen *et al.*, 2002). This draws the discourse of air travel as a socially desirable form of leisure consumption into deep question (Young *et al.*, 2014).

Not all flyers experience a dilemma, including those who are ignorant (willingly or otherwise) of the environmental impacts of flying and those who are aware of the environmental impacts of flying but don't care. The latter have been shown to deploy strategies such as denial and blame to overcome an inescapable but inconvenient flyers' dilemma (Higham *et al.*, 2014). However, the suspension of climate concerns by tourists is increasingly difficult to maintain. The freedom of unconstrained consumption is increasingly interrupted by discursive evidence about the environmental costs of air travel (Peeters *et al.*, 2016); costs that are largely unaccounted for, challenging to resolve, and increasingly difficult to ignore (Gössling, 2009; Higham *et al.*, 2016a).

Empirical Insights into the Flyers' Dilemma

The flyers' dilemma construct has been the subject of a number of empirical studies prompted by the growing public demand for climate action (Garnaut, 2011; Gössling, 2009; Hares *et al.*, 2010). In 2009, researchers at the University of Otago (New Zealand) initiated a series of studies that examined consumer responses to the flyers' dilemma in various highly aeromobile long-haul markets in Norway, the United Kingdom and Germany (Higham *et al.*, 2016a). A subsequent study led by Reis (University of Western Sydney) developed further insights into the flyers' dilemma in the Australian context (Higham *et al.*, 2016b; Reis

& Higham, 2016). These studies revealed growing climate concerns and increasing conscious awareness of the climate impacts of air travel in all four societies. Evidence of a range of negative psychological emotions associated with air travel was found in all four studies. However, it was also evident that consumer responses to the flyer's dilemma contrasted sharply between different societies (Higham *et al.*, 2016a, 2016b). These contrasts can be highlighted within the framing of three important findings that emerged from the research.

(1) Logic favours the unsustainable option

Within the established socio-technical transport regime, air travel has become a 'default setting' despite increasing environmental concerns, because it usually out-competes more sustainable transport modes in terms of both cost and convenience (Cohen & Higham, 2011; Higham *et al.*, 2016a, 2016b). Studies of the flyer's dilemma conducted in Norway and Germany revealed the view that policy interventions such as cross-subsidisation are required to support more sustainable transport modes (Higham *et al.*, 2016a). Cross-subsidisation may take the form of removing tax exemptions on aviation fuel (Gössling *et al.*, 2017), allowing for investment in alternative low-carbon transport infrastructures to support modal shifts and accelerate revolutionary transport technology uptake (Hopkins & Higham, 2016). As reported by Higham *et al.* (2016a), these structural issues, expressed by a 63-year-old British citizen (male), illustrate the factors that may lead people to choose to fly rather than travel by train:

> *if the roads were less crowded, if the train service was better, then people wouldn't use airplanes. It's just that the country is so crowded, often there's no point in travelling by car, well there is, but it could take you ages. So fly or go by train? The train service is not particularly reliable, so you go by plane. So you've got lots of things interacting and it* [the decision to fly] *is not simply a question of – 'I won't do it because of greenhouse gases or pollution or environmental effects'. You've got to take into account the other things as well.*

The German study conducted by Higham *et al.* (2016a) revealed the reality that logical and pragmatic consumer decision-making inevitably promotes cost and convenience over environmental concerns. In this case, cost was clearly the critical factor that determined tourists' transport modal choice, even for those who claimed to be the most climate-aware and climate-conscious. Those who, all other things being equal, would prefer to travel by train rather than aeroplane (including those who declared a fear of flying) expressed sentiments arising from a sense of 'locked-in' decision-making.

(2) Air travel consumers as agents of social change

Social marketing and 'nudge' campaigns engage consumers as active agents of social change (Ampt & Gleave, 2004). These approaches are predicated upon the need for persuasive strategies to foster pro-climate decision making. Information and advice, as well as nudging consumer decision making through social marketing approaches, are avenues that may help to address excessive air travel consumption. The importance of marketing and media communications to encourage less travel is evident in the body of empirical research (Higham et al., 2016a). Empowerment through awareness was considered an important persuasive strategy to counter the convenience of pleading ignorance which is clearly evident in this line of research (Higham et al., 2014).

> *Perhaps if somebody showed me (relative to) daily living... that's a huge amount, maybe that would make me rethink. I've never seen anything that tells me that.* (British female, 41)

Reporting the environmental impacts of air travel is an important step towards wider public dissemination and discussion. Expert opinion pieces may lead to social marketing campaigns and blog discussions that, when distributed via social media, may influence consumers to fly less (Gössling & Hall, 2008). Some consumers argued that providing clear and accurate information on aviation emissions to inform consumer decision making should be a fundamental responsibility of airlines themselves. Such efforts are advanced in the recent KLM 'Fly Responsibly' online marketing campaign (KLM Royal Dutch Airlines, 2020).

Carbon offsetting, while conceptually contentious and lacking credibility in the eyes of many consumers (Gössling et al., 2007), was also viewed as an important means to engage consumers as agents of social change. Offsetting was viewed as a form of social marketing because it encourages consumers to be informed about their personal carbon emissions, as well as voluntary actions, such as purchasing offsets and reducing air miles. This was considered particularly important in cases, such as air travel, where emissions from 'necessary' air travel are unavoidable under the current technical regime (Peeters et al., 2016). Of course, 'necessary' can be defined in many different ways. While the practice of compensating in some way for the environmental costs of air travel was considered important, the majority of study participants viewed offsetting with uncertainty and distrust (Broderick, 2009). The low uptake of offsetting contributed to it being viewed as nothing more than a cheap way of buying a clear conscience (Higham & Cohen, 2011). Adjusting 'choice architecture' (Hall, 2013) of offset purchases, such that the cost of offsetting is included in the cost of flights by default, or included as an opt-out rather than opt-in decision, was considered necessary if offsetting was to have any prospect of playing a part in reducing emissions (Mair, 2011).

However, a limitation of social marketing and peer group efforts that is widely recognised in the literature is the failure of sustained behaviour change (Avineri & Goodwin, 2010). Insights into the flyers' dilemma, as expressed by regular air travellers living in highly aeromobile societies, makes it abundantly clear that a carbon conscience is insufficient to radically alter entrenched consumer behaviours. Policy interventions to enable structural change are clearly required. It appears that persuasive information and peer influence are more likely to be effective if they nudge consumers to support the strong government policy interventions that are required to meaningfully address the climate crisis, rather than focusing on directly influencing consumer decision-making, relating to such entrenched behaviours.

(3) The need for strong policy interventions

More than anything, the flyers' dilemma makes it clear that unconstrained travel freedom is an aspect of mobile societies that is very difficult to address (Higham et al., 2014). While the dilemma is commonly expressed in terms of resistance to policy interventions, resignation to the inevitable need for government regulation emerged in different societies. In Norway, relying on individual responses to the flyers' dilemma was viewed by consumers as a failed approach. The need for carbon costs to be included in the purchase price for all flights was deemed to be long overdue. Incorporation of the environmental externalities of flying in the cost of travel was considered an initial step towards comprehensive government policy intervention, a view which reflects high trust in the Norwegian government (Higham & Cohen, 2011). The views of German and British nationals reflected lower levels of trust in government. In these cases, resistance to any constraints on travel freedoms was expressed in combination with scepticism that governments would invest revenue from carbon pricing in low-carbon transport transitions. Yet, in these cases, too, the inevitability of government policy intervention was acknowledged (Cohen & Higham, 2011).

Competing views on government regulation of air travel were particularly evident among British consumers (Barr et al., 2010; Hares et al., 2010). The dominant view was one of distrust of government and opposition to taxation measures to reduce air travel demand. This arose from concerns about constraints being imposed upon personal travel freedoms (Hares et al., 2010) and distrust in government to effectively use income from taxes to build future low-carbon transport systems. Central to the debate was where responsibility lies for an environmentally flawed transport sector. The view was expressed among UK consumers that airlines should face the environmental costs of production, rather than pass those costs to air travel consumers. Gössling *et al.* (2007) have observed that assigning the carbon costs of flying to the consumer is a strategy that absolves airlines of responsibility and any sense of urgency to confront and respond to increasing aviation emissions (Young *et al.*, 2014). Interestingly, a subsequent study of public attitudes towards climate policy interventions for aviation in the UK has found some support for policies that place financial and regulatory responsibility with airlines rather than individuals (Kantenbacher *et al.*, 2018).

Extending the Concept of the Flyers' Dilemma

Various studies have subsequently extended the concept of the flyer's dilemma, offering new theoretical and empirical insights. A study of the Australian air travel market conducted by Reis and Higham (2016) found similar consumer resistance to constraints being imposed upon entrenched air travel freedoms. The empirical research conducted by Reis and Higham (2016) highlights the enormity of the challenge inherent in shifting established consumer behaviours. The capacity of consumers to suppress sentiments of guilt when engaging in air travel arose from the widespread conviction that airlines should be responsible for the environmental impacts of air travel production, rather than the consumers of air travel. This line of research builds on the work of McDonald *et al.* (2015) who identified a range of strategies deployed by self-identifying 'green consumers' in response to the flyers' dilemma. McDonald *et al.* (2015) found that many chose to resist compromising their air travel appetites, but offered justifications (e.g. relating to personal identity) to excuse their continued and unrestrained consumption of air travel. Others felt a sense of guilt to the extent that they actively sought to reduce, or otherwise account for, their air travel emissions by compensating through the purchase of offsets or discontinuing flying wherever possible.

Font and Hindley (2017) used resistance theory to critically explore the relationship between climate concerns and travel decisions. In exploring the importance of freedom of choice, they found that air travellers can overcome the flyers' dilemma by denying the threat of climate change, devising ways to reduce tensions and seeking out destinations that are most at risk from climate change while they are still able to. Resistance theory, as used in this case, draws the effectiveness of awareness-raising campaigns into question, because environmentally aware consumers were, prior to the COVID-19 pandemic, still unlikely to compromise or reduce their longstanding flying behaviours. This line of research is usefully extended by Hales and Caton's (2017) use of co-constructed narratives to address the proximity ethics that underpin the flyer's dilemma. They examine their own flying behaviours in relation to the '... ethical proximal relations that compel intimate contact with others, create the need for face-to-face contact and impel obligation in family/work/social domains in a globalised world' (Hales & Caton, 2017: 94). In this sense, Gössling *et al.* (2018: 1586) argue that '... travel is no longer an option, rather a necessity for sociality, identity construction, affirmation or alteration', whereby non-tourism becomes a threat to self-identity. Both studies conclude that, in the minds of most consumers, the flyers' dilemma is secondary to social obligations and personal identity interests.

Failure of the Flyers' Dilemma to Trigger Behaviour Change

A number of approaches are available that attempt to directly engage with public flying behaviours. These avenues include education campaigns, social marketing, constraints on advertising and/or 'nudge' initiatives that seek to foster and encourage behaviour change. The use of these persuasive and economic interventions aimed at reducing the consumption of damaging products is already well established in the field of public health (Avineri & Goodwin, 2010; Marteau *et al.*, 2011). Such interventions have been explored in the field of transport and environmental responsible behaviour more generally (e.g. Barr *et al.*, 2010; Peattie & Peattie, 2009; Steg & Vlek, 2009). However, studies in the context of sustainable tourism have shown that established flying behaviours are extremely resistant to manipulation. For example, despite growing sentiments of eco-anxiety, the *flygskam* (flight shame) movement has failed to become mainstream (Mkono, 2020). Despite the psychological burden felt by air travellers, voluntary consumer-led responses to the problem of aviation emissions have failed (Higham *et al.*, 2019; Mair, 2011; Miller *et al.* 2010).

This point has been long argued by Gössling *et al.* (2010: 9) who report that 'air travellers put their own responsibility last; after aircraft producers, airlines, government and intergovernmental organisations'. Indeed, Cohen *et al.* (2011) have suggested that frequent flying may represent a site of behavioural addiction, characterised by guilt, suppression and denial. They reframe air travel as a pathological form of consumption and argue that such a framing shifts air travel from a socially desirable form of leisure consumption to a form of consumer addiction that is difficult to dislodge. Unlike other forms of addictive consumption, such as alcohol and tobacco, the damaging consequences of air travel (as expressed through a changing climate) are globally dispersed and unevenly distributed (Hill, 2007; Young *et al.*, 2014). They are felt most acutely by those in poor and vulnerable economies who do not fly, rather than frequent flyers in the developed world who are principally responsible for the problem (Cohen *et al.*, 2011). This has led to increasing calls for progressive political action to curtail aviation emissions (cf. Higham *et al.*, 2014).

The Production of Travel Anxiety

Perpetuation of the air passenger transport system is deeply problematic. The aviation industry has become central to the global tourism production system (Cornelissen, 2017). Sustained high growth in air travel has resulted in increases in carbon emissions that dwarf marginal efficiency gains in the current aviation technical system (Peeters et al., 2016). For even the most environmentally aware consumers, who feel the flyers' dilemma particularly acutely, frequent flying continues because, in the case of air travel, a deep disconnect exists between environmental attitudes and behaviour (Barr et al., 2010; Cohen et al., 2013; Hales & Caton, 2017). The environmental costs of air travel production are actively denied by the aviation industry (Wakefield, 2020) in order to divert the environmental burden of aviation to individual consumers (Young et al., 2014). In denying meaningful accountability, the air transport industry requires travellers to accept and internalise the psychological burden of air travel consumption. This formulation allows for continued unrestrained growth in the global aviation system. Thus, new forms of travel emerge that are characterised by anxiety rather than pleasure (Young et al. 2015). For some, the psychological burden of an unsustainable industry is relieved by bearing the economic cost of carbon offsetting (Higham & Cohen, 2011). For most, the economic and psychological burden of the flyer's dilemma is suppressed and denied (Higham et al., 2019). However, as long as the momentum of an inherently unsustainable industry and its high carbon footprint remain unresolved, the guilt and anxiety felt by air travellers will continue to increase, as the Paris Climate targets become more remote with the passage of time (Cohen et al., 2011; Higham et al., 2014).

Reformulation of the Flyers' Dilemma

The need to tackle the problems arising from high and unrestrained aeromobility is well established (Gössling & Higham, 2021; Scott et al., 2012). Studies of tourist attitudes towards aviation emissions have now been conducted in various societies including the United Kingdom, Sweden, Poland, Norway, Germany, Australia and New Zealand (Becken, 2004; Cohen & Higham, 2011; Dickinson et al., 2013; Hares et al., 2010; MacIntosh & Downie, 2008; Reis & Higham, 2016; Shaw & Thomas, 2006). These studies highlight the embedded nature of the unconstrained consumption of air passenger travel (Urry, 2010), such that a reformulation of the flyers' dilemma is necessary (Young et al., 2014). The aviation industry itself has made the case for special consideration on the grounds of its importance to global business (Aviation Benefits, 2016; Wood et al., 2012). Aviation industry interests have been expressed through the lobbying of state governments for favourable trading conditions (Bowen, 2010; Young, 2020). Efforts have also been sustained to convince policymakers, such as the International Civil Aviation Organization (ICAO), that sustainable aviation can be achieved through technology, alternative fuels and operational innovations (Sustainable Aviation, 2011). Such promises have perpetuated a lack of meaningful regulation of international aviation emissions (Peeters *et al.*, 2016).

The critique of the flyers' dilemma offered by Young *et al.* (2014, 2015) draws attention to the inescapable structural issues that lie at the heart of the aviation-environment predicament. They argue that contemporary tourist (aero)mobility is founded upon global and regional transport systems that are carbon intensive and deeply unsustainable (Creutzig *et al.*, 2015). The design and maintenance of high-cost transport systems that are intended for public use lie entirely beyond the reasonable accountability of individual consumers. Thus, notwithstanding the individual psychological effects of the flyers' dilemma, consumers are largely powerless to engage in sustainable transportation in the absence of meaningful structural change geared towards near future low-carbon transportation systems. However, transportation systems are difficult to redirect (Geels, 2012). Radical transitions performed through coordinated action are required to support changes in behavioural practices (Schwanen *et al.*, 2011).

At the global level, coordinated action is the domain of the industry-dominated International Civil Aviation Organization (ICAO) which has been accused of three decades of ineffective climate leadership (Peeters *et al.*, 2016). Following the Paris Climate Agreement in 2015, ICAO was charged with the urgent responsibility of developing and implementing a global regime to address aircraft CO2 emissions (Scott *et al.*, 2016). In October 2016, the ICAO 39th General Assembly passed a resolution to implement a global market-based mechanism (GMBM). The so-called 'Montréal Agreement' is a carbon offsetting and reduction scheme for international aviation (CORSIA). A critical review of the Montréal Agreement reveals that CORSIA lacks ambition, distorts behaviour, is voluntary and riddled with exemptions (see Higham *et al.*, 2019). It is expected that CORSIA, given its focus on offsetting emissions over and above a future benchmark, will not achieve the absolute reductions in emissions required to stabilise levels of carbon and other GHGs in the Earth's atmosphere (Becken & Mackey, 2017). A similar critique has been empirically mounted against other market-based mechanisms for air transport reduction (Markham *et al.*, 2018).

The prevailing lack of conviction and longstanding failure of global governance heighten the need for strong sub-global (national) policy interventions to respond to the structural issues underpinning the flyers' dilemma. The European Union's Emissions Trading Scheme, or similar schemes such as Australia's short-lived carbon tax on domestic aviation (Markham *et al.*, 2018), if adopted more widely, may lead to a tipping point beyond which it becomes part of all national interests to advance rather than resist low carbon transport transitions. Only then will wide-reaching regulation of air travel become the rule. Countries that adopt air transport carbon charges may well become destinations of choice for 21st century carbon-conscious travellers who seek relief from the psychological burden of the flyers' dilemma (among other aspects of tourist climate guilt). They may generate revenue to be invested in the low carbon transportation transitions and wide emissions mitigation projects (Higham et al., 2019).

In doing so, progressive destinations have the opportunity to abandon the focus on high volume based on price, and transition to highly marketable low-carbon tourism under a new regime (Gössling & Higham, 2021). As Higham et al. (2019: 543) note, once some destinations have '… seized the advantages available to early adopters, the constellation of interests constraining the rest of the world shifts'. Only when the tipping point is reached, and serious global measures are finally implemented by the ICAO to advance a low-carbon tourist transportation regime, will it be possible to resolve the flyers' dilemma.

Conclusion

Aviation emissions represent an existential threat to all life on Earth (IPCC, 2018). The urgency of radical aviation emissions mitigation cannot be overstated (Peeters et al., 2016). To date, national and global policy responses have ranged from ineffective to non-existent. Airlines, and the aviation industry more broadly, have resisted implementation in much the same way that gambling and tobacco companies have historically resisted, confused, downplayed or ignored the public health costs of their products (Cohen et al., 2011; Young & Markham 2017). Governments have gone to extraordinary lengths to avoid constraining the economic contribution of the aviation industry or to be seen to impose upon freedoms to travel. Where governments have expressed climate concerns, the response to aviation emissions has been to rely on individuals to forego or offset their personal air travel. The freedom to travel (and therefore the freedom to add carbon to the global atmospheric sink) has remained politically untouchable (Higham et al., 2019).

While the flyers' dilemma has existed in some form for as long as the link between aviation emissions and climate change has been embedded in the public consciousness, it has long been wilfully ignored by consumers. However, neglect and denial have become increasingly untenable in the face of an intensifying climate emergency, the growth of aviation emissions in both absolute and relative terms, and increasingly dramatic evidence of the social, economic and environmental toll of climate change (Timothy, 2019). The responsibility to respond to the threat of aviation emissions has hitherto been allocated by governments to the uncoordinated efforts of individual consumers (Peeters *et al.*, 2016). In this chapter, we have presented a body of empirical evidence that reveals the failure of uncoordinated individual responses to this problem (Hales & Caton, 2017; Higham *et al.*, 2016a; Kollmuss & Agyeman, 2002; Kroesen, 2013; Miller *et al.*, 2010). Thus, the flyers' dilemma will remain unresolved in the absence of state intervention in the form of strong policy to achieve low carbon transitions by way of coordinated action (Higham *et al.*, 2019).

This conclusion leads us to confront two decades of failed global measures on the part of the ICAO and – with very few notable exceptions – the failure of governments to even attempt to regulate aviation emissions through the deployment of state apparatus (Young, 2020). Creutzig *et al.* (2015: 911) note that, to date, there has been '… little appetite among policy-makers for seriously discussing thorny transport issues in public debates and international climate negotiations'. Now, belatedly, the COVID-19 pandemic has crippled the global tourism system and created an opportunity to disrupt aviation's contribution to high-risk emissions (Gössling *et al.*, 2020). The paralysis of the global economy, brought about by the COVID-19 pandemic, reduced global carbon emissions by 9% – a level of reduction that needs to be sustained year in, year out in order to meet the +1.5–2.0 °C target established by Paris Climate signatories (Scott *et al.*, 2016). As tourism re-emerges from the global pandemic, consumers may immediately resume flying and continue to resist environmental concerns. Equally, it may be that many will be ready to accept that the industry must be made accountable for its heavy environmental cost. A unique and fleeting opportunity for disruption is upon us.

References

Air New Zealand Sustainability Advisory Panel (2017) Sustainability Report 2017. See https://p-airnz.com/cms/assets/PDFs/sustainability-report-2017-v2.pdf (accessed August 2018).

Airbus (2014) Global Market Forecast for 2014–2033. See http://www.airbus.com/company/market/forecast/ (accessed March 2017).

Ampt, E. and Gleave, S.D. (2004) Understanding voluntary travel behaviour change. *Transport Engineering in Australia* 9, 53–66.

Aviation Benefits (2016) Climate action takes flight. See http://aviationbenefits.org/environmental-efficiency/our-climate-plan/ (accessed June 2018).

Avineri, E. and Goodwin, P. (2010) Individual behaviour change: Evidence in transport and public health. Centre for Transport and Society. See https://uwe-repository.worktribe.com/output/983014/individual-behaviour-change-evidence-in-transport-and-public-health (accessed August 2011).

Barr, S., Shaw, G., Coles, T. and Prillwitz. J. (2010) A holiday is a holiday: Practicing sustainability, home and away. *Journal of Transport Geography* 18 (3), 474–481. https://doi.org/10.1016/j.jtrangeo.2009.08.007.

Becken, S. (2004) How tourists and tourism experts perceive climate change and carbon-offsetting schemes. *Journal of Sustainable Tourism* 12 (4), 332–345. https://doi.org/10.1080/09669580408667241.

Becken, S. (2011) A critical review of tourism and oil. *Annals of Tourism Research* 38 (2), 359–379. https://doi.org/10.1016/j.annals.2010.10.005.

Becken, S. and Mackey B. (2017) What role for offsetting aviation greenhouse gases in a deep-cut carbon world? *Journal of Air Transport Management* 63 (August), 71–83. https://doi.org/10.1016/j.jairtraman.2017.05.009.

Boeing (2019) Commercial Market Outlook 2019–2038. See https://www.boeing.com/resources/boeingdotcom/commercial/market/commercial-market-outlook/assets/downloads/cmo-sept-2019-report-final.pdf (accessed February 2020).

Bowen, J. (2010) *The Economic Geography of Air Transportation*. London: Routledge.

Bows-Larkin, A., Mander, S.L., Traut, M.B., Anderson, K.L. and Wood, F.R. (2016) *Aviation and Climate Change: The Continuing Challenge*. Tyndall Centre for Climate Change Research, School of Mechanical Aerospace and Civil Engineering, University of Manchester, Manchester, UK. See https://www.researchgate.net/publication/303446744.

Broderick, J. (2009) Voluntary carbon offsetting for air travel. In S. Gössling and P. Upham (eds) *Climate Change and Aviation: Issues, Challenges and Solutions* (pp. 329–346). London: Earthscan.

Burns, P. and Bibbings, L. (2009) The end of tourism? Climate change and societal challenges. *21st Century Society* 4 (1), 31–51. https://doi.org/10.1080/17450140802642424.

Clark, M. and Calleja, K. (2008) Shopping addiction: A preliminary investigation among Maltese university students. *Addiction Research & Theory* 16 (6), 633–649. https://doi.org/10.1080/16066350801890050.

Cohen, S.A. and Higham, J.E.S. (2011) Eyes wide shut? UK consumer perceptions on aviation climate impacts and travel decisions to New Zealand. *Current Issues in Tourism* 14 (4), 323–335. https://doi.org/10.1080/13683501003653387.

Cohen, S.A., Higham, J.E.S. and Cavaliere, C.T. (2011) Binge flying: Behavioural addiction and climate change. *Annals of Tourism Research* 38 (3), 1070–1089. https://doi.org/10.1016/j.annals.2011.01.013.

Cohen, S.A., Higham, J.E.S. and Reis, A. (2013) Sociological barriers to developing sustainable discretionary air travel behaviour. *Journal of Sustainable Tourism* 21 (7), 982–998. https://doi.org/10.1080/09669582.2013.809092.

Cornelissen, S. (2017) *The Global Tourism System: Governance, Development and Lessons from South Africa*. Abingdon, Oxon: Routledge.

Creutzig, F., Jochem, P., Edelenbosch, O.Y., Mattauch, L., van Vuuren, D.P., McCollum, D. and Minx, J. (2015) Transport: A roadblock to climate change mitigation? *Science* 350 (6263), 911–912. DOI: 10.1126/science.aac8033.

Dickinson, J.E., Robbins, D., Filimonau, V., Hares, A. and Mika, M. (2013) Awareness of tourism impacts on climate change and the implications for travel practice: A Polish perspective. *Journal of Travel Research* 52 (4), 506–519. https://doi.org/10.1177/0047287513478691.

EFTE (European Federation for Transport and Environment) (2016) Aviation Emissions and the Paris Agreement: Europe and ICAO Must Ensure Aviation Makes a Fair Contribution to the Paris Agreement's Goals. See http://www.transportenvironment.org (accessed October 2017).

Elliott, R. (1994) Addictive consumption: Function and fragmentation in postmodernity. *Journal of Consumer Policy* 17 (2), 159–179.

Font, X. and Hindley, A. (2017) Understanding tourists' reactance to the threat of a loss of freedom to travel due to climate change: A new alternative approach to encouraging nuanced behavioural change. *Journal of Sustainable Tourism* 25 (1), 26–42. https://doi.org/10.1080/09669582.2016.1165235.

Garnaut, R. (2011) *The Garnaut Review 2011: Australia in the Global Response to Climate Change*. Cambridge: Cambridge University Press.

Geels, F.W. (2012) A socio-technical analysis of low-carbon transitions: Introducing the multi-level perspective into transport studies. *Journal of Transport Geography* 24, 471–482. https://doi.org/10.1016/j.jtrangeo.2012.01.021.

Gössling, S. (2009) Carbon neutral destinations: A conceptual analysis. *Journal of Sustainable Tourism* 17 (1), 17–37. DOI: 10.1080/09669580802276018.

Gössling, S. and Hall, C.M. (2008) Swedish tourism and climate change mitigation: An emerging conflict? *Scandinavian Journal of Hospitality and Tourism* 8 (2), 141–158. https://doi.org/10.1080/15022250802079882.

Gössling, S. and Higham, J.E.S. (2021) The low carbon imperative: Destination management under urgent climate change. *Journal of Travel Research* 60 (6), 1167–1179. https://doi.org/10.1177/0047287520933679.

Gössling, S. and Peeters, P. (2015) Assessing tourism's global environmental impact 1900–2050. *Journal of Sustainable Tourism* 23 (5), 639–659. https://doi.org/10.1080/09669582.2020.1758708.

Gössling, S., Broderick, J., Upham, P., Ceron, J.P., Dubois, G., Peeters, P. and Strasdas, W. (2007) Voluntary carbon offsetting schemes for aviation: Efficiency, credibility and sustainable tourism. *Journal of Sustainable Tourism* 15 (3), 223–248. https://doi.org/10.2167/jost758.0.

Gössling, S., Cohen, S.A. and Hibbert, J.F. (2018) Tourism as connectedness. *Current Issues in Tourism* 21 (14), 1586–1600. https://doi.org/10.1080/13683500.2016.1157142.

Gössling, S., Fichert, F. and Forsyth, P. (2017) Subsidies in aviation. *Sustainability* 9 (8), 1295. https://doi.org/10.3390/su9081295.

Gössling, S., Hall, C.M., Peeters, P. and Scott, D. (2010) The future of tourism: Can tourism growth and climate policy be reconciled? A climate change mitigation perspective. *Tourism Recreation Research* 35 (2), 119–130. https://doi.org/10.1080/02508281.2010.11081628.

Gössling, S., Scott, D. and Hall, C.M. (2020) Pandemics, tourism and global change: A rapid assessment of COVID-19. *Journal of Sustainable Tourism* 29 (1), 1–20. https://doi.org/10.1080/09669582.2020.1758708.

Hales, R. and Caton, K. (2017) Proximity ethics, climate change and the flyer's dilemma: Ethical negotiations of the hypermobile traveller. *Tourist Studies* 17 (1), 94–113. https://doi.org/10.1177/1468797616685650.

Hall, C.M. (2013) Framing behavioural approaches to understanding and governing sustainable tourism consumption: Beyond neoliberalism, 'nudging' and 'green growth'? *Journal of Sustainable Tourism* 21 (7), 1091–1109. https://doi.org/10.1080/09669582.2013.815764.

Hares, A., Dickinson, J. and Wilkes, K. (2010) Climate change and the air travel decisions of UK tourists. *Journal of Transport Geography* 18 (3), 466–473. https://doi.org/10.1016/j.jtrangeo.2009.06.018.

Hibbert, J.F., Gössling, S., Dickinson, J.E. and Curtin, S. (2013) Identity and tourism mobility: An exploration of the attitude-behaviour gap. *Journal of Sustainable Tourism* 21 (7), 999–1016. https://doi.org/10.1080/09669582.2013.826232.

Higham, J.E.S. and Cohen, S.A. (2011) Canary in the coalmine: Norwegian attitudes towards climate change and extreme long-haul air travel to Aotearoa/New Zealand. *Tourism Management* 32 (1), 98–105. https://doi.org/10.1016/j.tourman.2010.04.005.

Higham, J.E.S., Cohen, S.A. and Cavaliere, C.T. (2014) Climate change, discretionary air travel and the 'flyers' dilemma'. *Journal of Travel Research* 53 (4), 462–475. https://doi.org/10.1177/0047287513500393.

Higham, J.E.S., Cohen, S.A., Cavaliere, C.T., Reis, A.C. and Finkler, W. (2016a) Climate change, tourist air travel and radical emissions reduction. *Journal of Cleaner Production* 111, 336–347. https://doi.org/10.1016/j.jclepro.2014.10.100.

Higham, J., Ellis, E. and Maclaurin, J. (2019) Tourist aviation emissions: A problem of collective action. *Journal of Travel Research* 58 (4), 535–548. https://doi.org/10.1177/0047287518769764.

Higham, J., Reis, A. and Cohen, S.A. (2016b) Australian climate concern and the 'attitude–behaviour gap'. *Current Issues in Tourism* 19 (4), 338–354. https://doi.org/10.1080/13683500.2014.1002456.

Hill, A. (2007) Travel: The new tobacco, *The Observer*, 6 May. See http://www.guardian.co.uk/travel/2007/may/06/travelnews.climatechange/ (accessed October 2016).

Hopkins, D. and Higham, J.E. (eds) (2016) *Low Carbon Mobility Transitions*. Wolvercote, UK: Goodfellow Publishers Ltd.

International Civil Aviation Organization (ICAO) (2018) Annual Report. See https://www.icao.int/annual-report-2018/Pages/the-world-of-air-transport-in-2018.aspx (accessed May 2019).

IPCC (Intergovernmental Panel on Climate Change) (2018) Special Report on Global Warming of 1.5°C. See http://www.ipcc.ch/report/sr15/ (accessed April 2019).

Kantenbacher, J., Hanna, P., Cohen, S., Miller, G. and Scarles, C. (2018) Public attitudes about climate policy options for aviation. *Environmental Science & Policy* 81, 46–53. https://doi.org/10.1016/j.envsci.2017.12.012.

KLM Royal Dutch Airlines (2020) Fly responsibly. See https://flyresponsibly.klm.com/gb_en#home (accessed September 2020).

Kollmuss, A. and Agyeman, J. (2002) Mind the gap: Why do people act environmentally and what are the barriers to pro-environmental behavior? *Environmental Education Research* 8 (3), 239–260. https://doi.org/10.1080/13504620220145401.

Kroesen, M. (2013) Exploring people's viewpoints on air travel and climate change: Understanding inconsistencies. *Journal of Sustainable Tourism* 21 (2), 271–290. https://doi.org/10.1080/09669582.2012.692686.

Larsson, J., Elofsson, A., Sterner, T. and Åkerman, J. (2019) International and national climate policies for aviation: A review. *Climate Policy* 19 (6), 787–99. https://doi.org/10.1080/14693062.2018.1562871.

Lassen, C. (2010) Environmentalist in business class: An analysis of air travel and environmental attitude. *Transport Reviews* 30 (6), 733–751. https://doi.org/10.1080/01441641003736556.

Leviston, Z., Leitch, A., Greenhill, M., Leonard, R. and Walker, I. (2011) *Australians' Views on Climate Change*. Canberra: CSIRO.

Macintosh, A. and Downie, C. (2008) Aviation and climate change: Can the airline industry continue to grow in a carbon-constrained economy? *Australasian Journal of Environmental Management* 15 (4), 253–265. https://doi.org/10.1080/14486563.2008.9725209.

Mair, J. (2011) Exploring air travellers' voluntary carbon-offsetting behaviour. *Journal of Sustainable Tourism* 19 (2), 215–230. https://doi.org/10.1080/09669582.2010.517317.

Markham, F., Young, M., Higham, J.E.S. and Reis A. (2018) Does carbon pricing reduce air travel? Evidence from the Australian 'Clean Energy Future' policy, July 2012 to June 2014. *Journal of Transport Geography* 70, 206–214. https://doi.org/10.1016/j.jtrangeo.2018.06.008.

Marteau, T.M., Ogilvie, D., Roland, M., Suhrcke, M. and Kelly, M.P. (2011) Judging nudging: Can nudging improve population health? *British Medical Journal* 342. https://doi.org/10.1136/bmj.d228.

McDonald, S., Oates, C.J., Thyne, M., Timmis, A.J. and Carlile, C. (2015) Flying in the face of environmental concern: Why green consumers continue to fly. *Journal of Marketing Management* 31 (13–14), 1503–1528. https://doi.org/10.1080/0267257X.2015.1059352.

Miller, G., Rathouse, K., Scarles, C., Holmes, K. and Tribe, J. (2010) Public understanding of sustainable tourism. *Annals of Tourism Research* 37 (3), 627–645. https://doi.org/10.1016/j.annals.2009.12.002.

Mkono, M. (2020) Eco-anxiety and the flight shaming movement: Implications for tourism. *Journal of Tourism Futures* 6 (3), 223–226. https://doi.org/10.1108/JTF-10-2019-0093.

Mkono, M. and Hughes, K. (2020) Eco-guilt and eco-shame in tourism consumption contexts: Understanding the triggers and responses. *Journal of Sustainable Tourism* 28 (8), 1223–1244. https://doi.org/10.1080/09669582.2020.1730388.

Peattie, K. and Peattie, S. (2009) Social marketing: A pathway to consumption reduction? *Journal of Business Research* 62 (2), 260–268. https://doi.org/10.1016/j.jbusres.2008.01.033.

Peeters, P., Higham, J.E.S., Kutzner, D., Cohen, S. and Gössling, S. (2016) Are technology myths stalling aviation climate policy? *Transportation Research Part D: Transport and Environment* 44, 30–42. https://doi.org/10.1016/j.trd.2016.02.004.

Princen, T., Maniates, M. and Conca, K. (eds) (2002) *Confronting Consumption.* Cambridge, MA: The MIT Press.

Randles, S. and Mander, S. (2009) Practice(s) and ratchet(s): A sociological examination of frequent flying. In S. Gössling and P. Upham (eds) *Climate Change and Aviation: Issues, Challenges and Solutions* (pp. 245–271). London: Earthscan.

Reis, A. and Higham, J.E.S. (2016) Climate change perceptions among Australian non-frequent flyers. *Tourism Recreation Research* 42 (1), 59–71. https://doi.org/10.1080/02508281.2016.1215889.

Rosenthal, E. (2010) Can we kick our addiction to flying? *The Guardian.* See http://www.guardian.co.uk/environment/2010/may/24/kick-addiction-flying/ (accessed January 2011).

Schwanen, T., Banister, D. and Anable, J. (2011) Scientific research about climate change mitigation in transport: A critical review. *Transportation Research Part A: Policy and Practice,* 45 (10), 993–1006. https://doi.org/10.1016/j.tra.2011.09.005.

Scott, D., Hall, C.M. and Gössling, S. (2012) *Tourism and Climate Change: Impacts, Adaptation and Mitigation.* New York: Routledge.

Scott, D., Hall, C.M. and Gössling, S. (2016) A report on the Paris Climate Change Agreement and its implications for tourism: Why we will always have Paris. *Journal of Sustainable Tourism* 24 (6), 1–16. https://doi.org/10.1080/09669582.2016.1187623.

Sgouridis, S., Bonnefoy, P.A. and Hansman, R.J. (2011) Air transportation in a carbon constrained world: Long-term dynamics of policies and strategies for mitigating the carbon footprint of commercial aviation. *Transportation Research Part A: Policy and Practice* 45 (10), 1077–1091. https://doi.org/10.1016/j.tra.2010.03.019.

Shaw, S. and Thomas, C. (2006) Discussion note: Social and cultural dimensions of air travel demand: Hyper-mobility in the UK? *Journal of Sustainable Tourism* 14 (2), 209–215. https://doi.org/10.1080/09669580608669053.

Steg, L. and Vlek, C. (2009) Encouraging pro-environmental behaviour: An integrative review and research agenda. *Journal of Environmental Psychology* 29 (3), 309–317. https://doi.org/10.1016/j.jenvp.2008.10.004.

Stern, N. (2007) *The Economics of Climate Change: The Stern Review.* Cambridge: Cambridge University Press.

Stovall, W., Higham, J.E.S. and Stephenson J. (2019) Prepared for take-off? Anthropogenic climate change, 21st-century tourism, and the global challenge of 21st century tourism. In D. Timothy (ed.) *Handbook on Globalization and Tourism* (pp. 174–187). Cheltenham: Edward Elgar Publishing.

Sustainable Aviation (2011) Progress Report 2011. See http://www.sustainableaviation.co.uk/progress-report/ (accessed May 2012).

Timothy, D. (ed.) (2019) *Handbook on Globalization and Tourism.* Cheltenham: Edward Elgar.

UNWTO (United Nations World Tourism Organization) (2012) Global Report on Aviation. See http://cf.cdn.unwto.org/sites/all/files/pdf/unwto_globalreportonaviation_lw_eng_0.pdf (accessed May 2013).

UNWTO (United Nations World Tourism Organization) (2018) Tourism Highlights 2018. Madrid: UNWTO. See https://www.e-unwto.org/doi/book/10.18111/9789284419876 (accessed March 2019).

Urry, J. (2010) Sociology and climate change. *The Sociological Review* 57 (2), 84–100. https://doi.org/10.1111/j.1467-954X.2010.01887.x.

Wakefield, A. (2020) Airlines want you to think they're serious about the climate crisis. They're not. *The Guardian.* See https://www.theguardian.com/commentisfree/2020/feb/04/airlines-climate-crisis-plant-trees-carbon-emissions (accessed April 2020).

Wood, F.R., Bows, A. and Anderson, K.L. (2012) Policy update: A one-way ticket to high carbon lock-in: The UK debate on aviation policy. *Carbon Management* 3 (6), 537–540. https://doi.org/10.4155/cmt.12.61.

Young, M. (2020) Capital, class and the social necessity of passenger air transport. *Progress in Human Geography* 44 (5), 938–958. https://doi.org/10.1177/0309132519888680.

Young, M. and Markham, F. (2017) Coercive commodities and the political economy of involuntary consumption: The case of the gambling industries. *Environment and Planning A* 49, 2762–2779. https://doi.org/10.1177/0308518X17734546.

Young, M., Higham, J.E. and Reis, A.C. (2014) 'Up in the air': A conceptual critique of flying addiction. *Annals of Tourism Research* 49, 51–64. https://doi.org/10.1016/j.annals.2014.08.003.

Young, M., Markham, F., Reis A.C. and Higham, J.E.S. (2015) Flights of fantasy: A reformulation of the flyers' dilemma. *Annals of Tourism Research* 54, 1–15. https://doi.org/10.1016/j.annals.2015.05.015.

9 Epilogue

Jennie Small

March 2020

There is a strange and befuddling moment in Dubai airport. All the world seems to be there. We are Australians and New Zealanders, Nigerians and Ghanaians, Pakistani and Bangladeshi, North American and Latin American, many of us scrolling on phones and laptops and iPads, seeking information on which borders have been closed, whether we can indeed go home. Some of us are sitting still and staring out into space, shifting in those uncomfortable vinyl chairs, trying to not touch and not to breathe on one another.

I am two seats away from a young woman, poised and elegantly dressed, her hair hidden under a rainbow-coloured turban. She is speaking on her phone in rapid French. My own French is weak but I gather she has managed to get on a flight to Lagos and from Lagos she will do her best to head home. Wherever home may be. 'Paris was strange,' she says into her phone. 'Everything was closed, everything was shut. I've never seen it like that.'

And it's at that precise moment, overhearing her conversation, looking around me at the people staring at their screens, that it strikes me how bizarre and ridiculous it is that we all have only so recently been zig-zagging around the world, taking this freedom and this movement and this privilege for granted. It isn't a moral aversion that I am experiencing. It isn't righteousness; it is more a recognition of absurdity. I turn to Wayne when he comes back from the long wait for the toilets.

'All of this, it's unnecessary.'

'No, we need to get home, this is serious.'

'No, not that. All this travel, all this movement, that is what is unnecessary.'

(Tsiolkas, 2020: 12)[1]

The Passenger Experience Disrupted

In the Introduction to *The Routledge Handbook of Mobilities*, the editors (Adey *et al.*, 2014: 2) ask: 'How have we become so reliant upon mobilities that, should they fail, our lives may be thrown into chaos?'. Six years later, the unthinkable happened and the mobility of much of the world's population was brought to a standstill by coronavirus disease (COVID-19), declared a global pandemic by the World Health Organization (WHO) on 11 March 2020 (an upgrade from the January 30th declaration of the virus as a 'Public Health Emergency of International Concern'). The world became aware that human mobility, usually associated with modernity, freedom and social and economic opportunities, has a downside in the part it can play in the transmission of disease: as we humans move, so does the *non-human* thing, the virus (SARS-CoV-2), moving from place to place, mutating as it moves. With its global reach, air transport has both contributed to the rapid spread of the virus and been heavily affected by the disease. For the aviation industry, it has been a 'financial crisis' with aircraft grounded (see Figure 9.1) and terminals near empty as governments, in an attempt to control the virus, closed state and international borders and imposed quarantine periods for incoming passengers.

From a total number of 4.5 billion passengers carried on scheduled services in 2019 (International Civil Aviation Organization [ICAO], 2019), 90% of business had disappeared at the peak of the crisis in April 2020 (International Air Transport Association [IATA], 2020a).

Figure 9.1 Parked aircraft (Brisbane Airport, 2020 © Andrew Dawson with permission)

The worldwide chaos that has ensued highlights our taken-for-granted reliance on air transportation. While previously we have seen changes to air travel due to environmental incidents (volcanic eruption), terrorism (9/11), infections (SARS, MERS) and industrial action which have affected services and surveillance, none has affected air transportation on such a global scale. IATA (2020a) reports that since World War II 'COVID-19 is the largest shock to commercial air travel and aviation' (2020a: 11); 'the most profound de-connecting of modern society' (2020a: 8). As Schaberg (2020: 47) says, aviation is 'an index of certain common aspirations, such as professional mobility, vacation travel, and social connection'. When aviation ceases, the impact on society is profound.

In the early months of 2020, as governments advised against any but non-essential travel and recalled their citizens, the passenger experience was changing. With the original rush of citizens to return, overcrowded airports with long queues and wait times were reported. Media images of returning passengers (for example, in the United States) prompted concern about passenger behaviour when breaking the newly-introduced 1.5 metre social distancing rule. In these early months, passengers returning to their home countries were frequently shocked that airports (often those of their home country) were not doing more in terms of safety and surveillance, as evidenced in media headlines:

- 'Coronavirus: Kiwi traveller stunned at lack of health checks at New Zealand airports or displaying any information'.
- 'Logan Airport arrivals say screening was too easy'.
- 'London coronavirus: Heathrow Airport passengers alarmed by lack of health checks at the terminals'.
- 'Coronavirus: US airports in disarray over screening'.
- 'Coronavirus confusion: Lisbon airport "not controlling arrivals from China"'.

Safety and surveillance regulations, which might have been considered tedious, inconvenient and frustrating prior to COVID-19, were now demanded. Passengers were critical of authorities which failed to enquire about the passenger's prior movements, state of health and/or neglected to provide information about the virus and self-isolation requirements. Lack of hand sanitisers and masks were also cited as cause for alarm. Airports were compared in their screening procedures, especially in their use of thermal scanners and hand-held thermometers.

What surprised me was the fact that from arriving at the airport [Sydney] to embarkation there were no other checks other than the normal emigration ones. In other words, no temperature test nor any travel or health questionnaire... On arrival in London I passed straight through immigration using the automated passport check and baggage collection. What surprised me most was not once since leaving my place in Sydney to arriving in London (where I understood I would be told to be self-isolated for seven days) had I been asked any questions. In fact, in London, there was nothing stopping me taking public transport to my home, even though I might have been running a high temperature and been infectious and carrying the COVID 19 virus [Sydney to London – March 19]. (Bernard, personal communication, 13 April 2020)

They didn't swab us, they didn't take our temperatures, they didn't do anything but ask us how we felt. (Linda Cole, from Williamsburg, Virginia, who was returning from a vacation in Portugal via Heathrow – as cited in Fausset et al., 2020)

In Thailand and Singapore at airports and shopping centres and hotels, they (temperature scanners) were everywhere…Then we fly back into Brissy [Brisbane] and nothing … we were mortified. (as cited in Bedo, 2020)

While temperature screening has been used in the past (SARS in 2003 and bird flu in 2009), its effectiveness remains controversial (Quilty et al., 2020; St John et al., 2005). Even with the correct equipment and use, there are many reported reasons for not testing: a fever could be a symptom of illness other than COVID-19; many of those with the virus are asymptomatic; and passengers may have taken a fever-reducing medication (Rauhala, 2020).

Advice from the World Health Organization on 10 January 2020, in the early days of the virus, was as follows: 'WHO does not recommend any specific health measures for travellers. It is generally considered that entry screening offers little benefit, while requiring considerable resources' (World Health Organization, 2020a). Later advice recommended that temperature screening could be part of a broader strategy including health messages (World Health Organization, 2020b). As Rauhala, (2020) reported for *The Washington Post*, it is important that authorities are seen to be doing something. According to the infectious disease specialist, Bogoch (as cited in Rauhala, 2020), 'If the community thinks you're doing nothing, they are not going to buy into your other public health policies like the social distancing measures that everyone should be employing on a mass scale right now…' With time, health messages increased at airports; see Figures 9.2 and 9.3.

The variability amongst countries in the onset, spread, preparedness and approach to the virus meant different regulations and policies in respect to air transportation. For those permitted to fly, flights were often difficult to obtain and costly. In Australia, for example, 'travel caps' on international arrivals drove up flight cost and decreased availability (Bourke, 2021a) such that 18 months into the pandemic, 45,000 Australians remained 'stranded' overseas waiting to return

Epilogue 201

Figure 9.2 COVID-safe message (Sydney Domestic Airport, 2020 © Brian Dawson with permission)

Figure 9.3 COVID-safe message (Sydney Domestic Airport, 2020 © Brian Dawson with permission)

Figure 9.4 Masks – the new look – flying during COVID-19

home (Visontay, 2021). On many international flights, the demographic makeup of the passenger body changed with flights restricted to returning citizens or those who met specific criteria. Social distancing, the wearing of masks and hand sanitising became the mantra for all; see Figure 9.4.

However, airlines differed in their enforcement of COVID-19-safe policies.[2] On some airlines, mask wearing was mandatory, on others, merely 'encouraged'. Onboard, passengers might be socially distanced from each other with empty seats either side, or not distanced at all; see Figure 9.5. Passengers might encounter a reduced meal service, suspension of in-flight entertainment removal of magazines, pillows, blankets and duty-free service. At the airport, lounges, meeting rooms and shops could be closed, and valet parking suspended. Perhaps the strangest experience for the air traveller was finding a terminal near empty and silent, a contrast from the usual crowded, noisy space particularly so at the start of the pandemic as citizens rushed home; see Figures 9.6 and 9.7.

Schaberg (2020: 4) observes that empty terminals can be read in two ways:

> Such a space can represent the wish image of air travel: a personalized adventure, the individuated feeling of being spirited up and across a continent or ocean with no apparent obstacles. But a deserted security checkpoint can also signify something quite different. It underscores the

Figure 9.5 No social distancing on a QantasLink flight (Queensland, 2020 © Andrew Dawson with permission)

Figure 9.6 An empty Brisbane Domestic Terminal (2020 © Andrew Dawson with permission)

Figure 9.7 An empty Sydney Domestic Terminal (2021 © Brian Dawson with permission)

baseline fragility and collectivity of our interconnected and networked world, where something as small and site-specific as a novel virus can travel fast and thereby ensnarl—and threaten to terminate—the whole system.

In addition to measures enforced by governments, airlines and airports, passengers also reported taking their own safeguards for extra protection from infection.

> *[At the airport] I usually buy something to eat or drink while waiting for departure but didn't this time while trying to keep at distance from staff and fellow passengers. I avoided using handrails, or anything in restrooms or any areas that others may have touched* [Sydney to Hobart – 1 March, 2020]. (Mary, personal communication, 17 April 2020)

I tried to drink as few fluids as necessary as I wanted to use the WC facilities as little as possible. Doha airport was heaving with people. I tried to make my way to the Business class as quickly as possible ... and isolating myself until my flight was called [Sydney to London- 19 March 2020]. (Bernard, personal communication, 13 April 2020)

As discussed in Chapters 3 and 4, the behaviour of other air passengers can be both irritating and frustrating, negatively affecting the travel experience. During a pandemic, contact with other passengers (those in close proximity) can be a lot more sinister and threatening. As demonstrated in the earlier chapters, underlying passenger–passenger conflict are issues of individual rights and responsibilities, power and resistance.

The plane was surprisingly full. I usually exchange some words with the person seated beside me but avoided doing so this time. I was somewhat alarmed when, just before landing, the gentleman seated next to me leaned over to tell me he was on his way home from a two-week trip to Singapore. Authorities there had taken his temperature numerous times, etc etc. and he said he was fine but, as we were only about 40cm apart, I was very relieved that, 2 weeks later, I was symptom free.... [Sydney to Hobart – 1 March, 2020]. (Mary, personal communication, 17 April 2020)

While seated on the plane, I also felt some revulsion towards the persons sitting next to me ... I was wearing a face mask and wished for them to be doing so too, as I felt their breath might get on me ... [Lumbini to Melbourne – 20 March 2020]. (Sally, personal communication, 21 April 2020)

Sat in window seat 10A. Young man, mid to late 20s, then sat next to me. Not wearing mask. I asked did he have a mask. Answer was NO so I offered him my Qantas pack with mask enclosed (as I had brought my own). He sat there for 5 or so minutes, didn't put it on so I asked whether he was going to wear a mask. Answer – didn't like them. I asked whether there was a reason he wouldn't wear one – health/breathing issue (?) – and he became abusive. Told me it wasn't compulsory, didn't have to, to shut the fu—up and, with clenched fist raised towards me, said 'You'd better be careful or I'll ...'. He had rows of large brown beads around his hand and wrist – which sat on his clenched fist like knuckle duster [Sydney to Adelaide – 16 October 2020]. (Kerry, personal communication, 1 November 2020)

Shawn Kathleen, the creator of the popular Instagram account, Passenger Shaming, (see Chapter 3), confirmed that, while the normal complaints regarding fellow travellers have not abated during the pandemic, there has been a new genre of conflict in relation to mask wearing and social distancing protocols. The content on the site was also considered to be more physically and verbally violent than previously (Compton, 2021). On a more positive note, the joint experience of travelling during a crisis can create a bond between passengers. As countries went into lockdown and citizens were recalled home, their shared experiences – disrupted lives and anxieties to make it home safely – were grounds for connection. One passenger reported how the crisis provided an opportunity for passenger interaction at the airport, (a subject Gottdiener [2001] and Anderson [2006] have discussed – see Chapter 2).

> [Kathmandu Airport] *there were a lot of foreigners. The big difference that I noticed now was talking to other passengers much more than I normally would. It was as though, all of a sudden, there was a change in permission to talk to total strangers. I heard lots of stories of the change of plans to come home early... I made friends with a woman from Tasmania travelling on the same flights as me to Melbourne before she flew onwards after customs checks. We met up before check-in, after check-in, before security check, after security check, and also in Singapore we shopped and coffee-ed together. We have subsequently emailed each other and I will meet her again if I go to Hobart, as she me if she comes to Melbourne* [Lumbini to Melbourne – 20 March 2020]. (Sally, personal communication, 21 April 2020)

After so many uncertainties of return travel, to arrive safely home has been an emotional experience for many passengers.

> *There was a great feeling of relief on landing in Melbourne, much stronger than usual. I would not have been surprised if a cheer or clap had resounded through the cabin* [Lumbini to Melbourne – 20 March 2020]. (Sally, personal communication, 21 April 2020)

Throughout the pandemic, the toll of border restrictions on separated families and friends has been evident in the poignant reunions. Barlass (2020: 6) describes the reunion of passengers with family when an Air New Zealand flight from Auckland landed in Sydney after seven months of border closure: 'The emotions of birth, death and marriage were all laid bare...'

While the pandemic restricted the capacity to travel by air from A to B, especially internationally, the cessation of destination flights led to opportunities for other kinds of flying experience – sightseeing flights. When the Qantas 'Great Southern Land' sightseeing flight went on sale, it sold out in 10 minutes. According to a Qantas spokesperson 'It's probably the fastest selling flight in Qantas history' (Reddy, 2020). As Joyce, the CEO of Qantas says, 'many frequent flyers missed the experience of flying as much as the destination themselves' (as cited in

Reddy, 2020). In other parts of the Asia Pacific Region, scenic flights/ destination-free flights/'Flights to nowhere' became a trend. Elsewhere, Sampson (2021) reports a destination-free flight over the site of the Chernobyl nuclear disaster. Non-flight experiences were also developed. In Taiwan, 'passengers' could go through the boarding procedures without actual take-off before having a meal in the airport. In Bangkok, would-be passengers could have an in-flight meal sitting in an airline seat at Thai Airways headquarters, while, in Sydney and Brisbane, in-flight meals could be bought to eat at home. In Tokyo, virtual air travel experiences, while not new, were reported to be experiencing a resurgence of interest. Meanwhile, on social media, TikTok users were posting videos pretending to be air travellers (ABC News, 2020).

It has been difficult to ignore the politics of mobility with governments limiting and regulating citizens' access to air travel. On the one hand, the pandemic has been referred to as a social equaliser; hierarchies of privilege flattened considerably with many of the previously mobile joining the ranks of the immobile. Indeed, we might hope that the curtailment in air travel has led to an awareness amongst the hypermobile of the privileges of mobility and understanding and empathy for those who are usually denied this opportunity (Tremblay-Huet, 2020). Yet, the inequalities associated with air travel did not completely dissolve. Access to flights depended on government approval, flight availability (often limited) and cost (often escalated).

In Australia, border restrictions (affecting both inbound and outbound travel) have been controversial. Many Australians were incensed that foreign celebrities (actors, sports stars etc.) could easily enter the country (Mao, 2021) when government travel caps limited the number of Australian citizens who could secure an airline seat and return home. In April 2021, the government was accused of racism, when it banned its own citizens from returning from India (as the pandemic surged there) with threats of fines or jail if they attempted to do so (Visentin, 2021). No such restrictions were applied to Australian citizens from the United Kingdom or the United States even during their worst days of the pandemic. As Australia's primary response to the pandemic, border restrictions were not limited to inbound travel. Legislation was introduced (an amendment to the Biosecurity Act) preventing Australian citizens leaving the country unless with government exemption (for reasons such as business, medical, compassionate or in the national interest). 'Compelling' reasons often required the individual to be out of the country for at least three months. Many applications were refused. The stated reasons were often not clear – 'murky' – and the threshold for decision-making 'arbitrary' (Jefferies & McAdam, 2021). In prohibiting Australian citizens from leaving the country (unless meeting specific criteria) and prohibiting some citizens entry, the government has been accused of violating human rights under international law (Hicks et al.,

2021). The freedom of mobility principle, as recognised in Article 13 of the Universal Declaration of Human Rights (United Nations, 1948), was superseded by the desire to contain the virus through controlling mobility. Within Australia, state border closures further disrupted air travel.

However, as mobility scholars have reflected, mobility is not always associated with freedom and privilege. Some, such as Fly-in Fly-out workers, business travellers and air crew, might have been mobile but reluctantly so, especially in the face of a pandemic.

The Future of Air Travel

As Adey (2010a: 208) says, 'Air travel has always been about the future', yet any 'certainty' for the future of air travel, tourism and global relations has been disrupted by COVID-19. It is now over two years since COVID-19 was declared a global pandemic by the World Health Organization. In that time the development of a vaccine and other health measures have enabled many countries to bring the pandemic under ('enough') control to open their borders and skies to air travel. Yet, we are still in a pandemic and being told we have to 'learn to live' with the virus. For the present, this means that passengers may continue to experience the materialities of COVID air travel. Depending on the airline, airport, governments and type of travel (domestic or international), these can include social distancing, masks, hand sanitisation, proof of vaccination/s, COVID test pre-departure and maybe even quarantine. Those who have returned to air travel are having to familiarise themselves with the evolving protocols of air travel. Whereas pre-pandemic, the practice of air travel could be performed unreflexively by the experienced 'frequent flyer', today, new 'skill-kits' (Mertena *et al.*, 2022) are required (new skills learned or existing ones adapted), especially when travelling internationally.

For some passengers the development of a new skill-kit might be all too much – a disincentive to travel. Pandemic travel fear (Zheng *et al.*, 2021) is real, especially with international travel: the fear of not having the correct documents (or concern about accessing them digitally), of being uninsured, of sudden border closures (and possibly locked out of one's home country – it happened before!) and, of course, the fear of contracting the virus (and the financial, social and health care implications of illness when away from home). Chapter 7 focused on the passenger experience of fear of flying. With the emergence of the pandemic, our understanding of fear of flying may need revision. Beyond those fears typically associated with flying – plane crashing, closed space, height of plane etc. – are pandemic-related fears. We may need to relook at passenger social anxiety as individuals may now be more fearful of their co-passengers – their airborne transmissions and touched surfaces. As Schaberg (2020: 53) suggests, 'We'll be sensitized, perhaps, to the inconvenient facts of interconnectedness. Whereas once it was about my miles, my status, my legroom—social distancing practices have rejiggered our collective senses of space'.

It is too early to say how COVID-19 has affected different groups of passengers but it would not be surprising if the more vulnerable groups (those with underlying health conditions and/or of older age) were more cautious about the prospect of flying than they had been previously (especially if the virus remains active). Studying older UK residents, early in the pandemic, Graham *et al.* (2020) found that many planned to travel but to take fewer trips, more domestic trips and/or means of transport other than air. Other groups may be precluded from travel – those who have experienced financial hardship as a consequence of the virus, those who have chosen not to be vaccinated and those who cannot access the vaccine. Questions have been raised by the World Health Organization of the ethics of a vaccine passport/certificate, warning that it would isolate those poorer countries which do not have the vaccine (Bourke, 2021b). In all likelihood, COVID-19 has further contributed to the immobilities/uneven mobilities of air travel as discussed in earlier chapters. There may also be a decline in the number of business travellers (and the associated cultural capital associated with flying). The pandemic has taught us that travel is not always required to enact business as meetings can occur virtually.

The long-term future of air travel is a critical issue on many fronts. The unexpected collapse of the travel and tourism sector exposed the crises and issues historically inherent in the industry (Benjamin *et al.*, 2020). Where previously, critical scholars were grappling with concerns of excessive (over) tourism and the unsustainability of the exponential growth in travel and tourism, the pause in activity not only gave the planet a reprieve (time to breathe) but also provided an opportunity to consider the future of air travel and tourism. We are, as Ioannides and Gyimothy (2020) say, at a 'fork in the road'. Which direction will we take?

Amongst critical scholars has been the fear that, once safe to do so, it would be 'business as usual' with governments, industry (including those represented by ICAO) and the majority of tourists keen to revert to pre-2020 travel with even more aggressive growth to compensate for the lost opportunities created by the pandemic (Gössling *et al.*, 2021; Lew *et al.*, 2020). As Hall (as cited in Brouder *et al.*, 2020: 743) says, 'The race to the bottom of special offers and discounts has begun', an example being the half price airfares to priority tourist destinations in Australia by the Australian Government in 2021 (Crowe, 2021). To describe this potential surge in tourist travel some are even using the term 'revenge travel' – in part 'retribution' against COVID-19 (Bologna, 2021).

A more hopeful view is that there will be a paradigm shift away from the growth trajectory in post-pandemic travel and tourism. Critical scholars argue that the temporary process of de-globalisation and undermining of the neoliberal agenda resulting from COVID-19 provides an 'unrepeatable opportunity' (Niewiadomski, 2020: 654) to transform travel and tourism, 'to recalibrate, regenerate, remake and rethink tourism' (Cheer, 2020: 515), to 'socialise' tourism (Higgins-Desbiolles, 2020), to move the planet in a new direction (Lew as cited in Lew *et al.*, 2020: 3) by making structural changes, making tourism more just (Rastegar *et al.*, 2021). For many, it is more than an opportunity; it is an obligation.

A reset travel and tourism would include addressing the previous question of immobilities in air travel. As argued in the preceding chapters, individuals are not equal in the air travel experience; certain bodies are favoured over others in their access to air travel and the quality of their experience whether in the air or traversing the airport. A critical approach to the air travel experience argues for inclusion and social equity, for researchers to expose uneven mobilities and the hierarchies of power which contribute to the unevenness. If mobility is capital, then this should be more equitably shared. It recognises that aeromobility contributes to differential mobility associated with class, age, sexuality, gender, dis/ability, body size, appearance, culture, race etc. and the intersections of these subjectivities. We now see new forms of unevenness as a consequence of the pandemic, particularly related to health – a person's vulnerability to the disease. As Adey (2010b: 93) says 'The ultimate issue… is much more than a recognition of difference; it is rather how those differences are reflected and come to reinforce societal inequalities and differences'. Urry (2002: 270) argues for all to have access to the benefits of corporeal travel and co-presence that air travel allows:

> if all other things were equal, then we could imagine that a 'good society' would not limit, prohibit or re-direct the desire for such copresence. The good society would seek to extend the possibilities of co-presence to every social group and regard infringements of this as involving undesirable social exclusion.

However, as Chapter 8 demonstrates, and Urry (2002, 2011) underlines, there is a tension between consumption in the neoliberal society – the right for all to travel – and the sustainability of the planet. We cannot consider inequities of air travel without focusing on air travel's impact on the environment, what Adey *et al.* (2007: 787) refer to as the true inequity of air travel. A 'good society' must also preserve the planet. A reset travel and tourism must address the externalities of air transport – carbon (GHG) emissions, nitrogen oxides (NOx) emissions and noise. It must address air transport's contribution to 'overtourism' and the unsustainability of many destinations as a consequence of transporting so many people from one place to another. COVID-19 has made the future of air travel less certain but critical scholars know we cannot afford the pre-pandemic forecasts – around 10.0 billion scheduled passengers with departures around 90 million by 2040 (ICAO, 2019). Such growth in demand, coupled with the current lack of technological solution to the problem of aircraft emissions, is incompatible with the targets set to reduce global emissions.

A further issue relates to the distribution of benefits and costs of air travel. Whereas the benefits accrue to the individual passenger, the environmental costs are felt globally and unevenly (Young et al., 2014). It is the highly mobile, located in a few countries, who are responsible for a large share of environmental damage. Constituting, at most, 1% of the global population, they are likely to be responsible for more than 50% of the emissions from passenger air travel (Gössling & Humpe, 2020). Indeed, in many ways, those least likely to enjoy the benefits of air travel (those from lower income regions) are the ones who disproportionately bear the cost of the environmental damage of air travel. The uneven distribution of emissions from air travel has led some to propose a levy aimed at excessive frequent flying (Carmichael, 2019). At the same time, appeals are made to the business and academic communities to avoid excessive flying by changing their way of doing business (Caset et al., 2018; Higham & Font, 2020).

Now is the time to reconsider the growth models from which air travel and tourism businesses and organisations have profited. Capitalism's manipulation of the desire to fly is clearly at odds with a healthy planet – an alternative narrative is required to the one that forever sees flying as a socially desirable activity. While the largely European movement, *flygskam* (flight shaming), has had some effect in persuading travellers to curtail their flying behaviour, Higham and Martin (Chapter 8) and others maintain that, for the most part, environmental arguments do not have the desired effect when it comes to flying. Responsibility for change must go beyond the micro-level (the individual) to industry and government. Much of the research on hypermobility has focused on Western perspectives, yet we need a better understanding of the values of those from the Asia Pacific region when considering mobility and the environment since this region constitutes the largest share of the air passenger market (Cocolas et al., 2020) – 34.7% of the global market in 2019 (IATA, 2020b). While many have decried government bail-out of airlines during the pandemic at the expense of clean industries (Monbiot, 2020), a positive outcome of COVID-19 has been the early retirement of older, inefficient aircraft due to the significant decline in demand (Pallini, 2020).

Central to a critical approach to the passenger experience of air travel is concern for *mobility justice*. Sheller (2018a: 130) claims that the hierarchies of mobility observed in air travel make it 'an issue of mobility justice par excellence'. She sees a comprehensive theory of mobility justice as going beyond transport justice approaches related to accessibility and infrastructure planning (individual injustices) to include environmental justice (transnational injustices) (Sheller, 2019). However, when there are competing injustices, the question of mobility justice can become tricky as Freire-Medeiros and Name (2013) identify in their study of first-time air travellers from a Brazilian favela where environmental awareness competes with a right to travel. The authors explain:

> These people have waited their whole lives to have access to possessions and to a mobile world embedded into an imaginary of prosperous life and full citizenship (as opposed to a restricted and fragmented one). It should not come as a surprise that they resist the idea of having to give up their recently acquired consumption and mobility possibilities. (2013: 180)

While environmental justice demands we limit our air travel, questions arise as to how we, in practice, ensure equitable access to air travel within these limitations. Should air transport be rationed? Farrelly (2019), in arguing that plane travel is not endless, suggests to her Australian readers that they limit their air travel to two or three trips in a lifetime, not two or three a year. However, the question arises: do some individuals have more right to air travel than others? Is entitlement dependent on the absence of alternative modes of transport? Are certain purposes of travel (visiting friends and relatives, education, business, health, leisure or migration) more legitimate than others, or do the newly mobile, as in the Brazilian favela example above, have more right to air transport than the hypermobile, the kinetic elite? These are just a few of many questions that highlight the complexity of mobility justice.

Drawing on Iris Young's theorisation of social justice and domination, Cook and Butz (2016) argue that mobility justice is more than the equitable distribution of motility. Sheller (2019) explains that mobility justice requires distributive justice (deliberation of which activities should be protected and which reduced), procedural justice (the participation of disempowered groups in decision making), restorative justice (whereby the kinetic elites make reparations to those harmed by their mobility such as in climate change) and epistemic justice (inclusion of alternative modes of knowing and creation of new facts). She concludes:

> Deliberation over mobility justice... pertains not simply to expanding transport infrastructures or even accessibility, but also to the cultural meanings and hierarchies surrounding various means of mobility, infrastructures for mobility, their valuation and who determines value, relevant facts and meaning. Even more radically, it would take into account how kinopolitics shape space, subjects and difference in the first place. (2019: 33)

As many would argue, mobility justice must involve 'caring justice' – recognition of others and their needs (caring about) as well as supporting the fulfilment of such needs (caring for) (Sevenhuijsen as cited in Verlinghieri & Schwanen, 2020). A justice of care would recognise and support individuals' needs in their access to air travel and their onboard and airport experiences. At the same time, it would mean limiting aviation to 'save the planet' and 'help to fulfil everybody's needs' (Verlinghieri & Schwanen, 2020: 6). The COVID-19 pandemic has brought to the fore debate about mobility justice as the aviation industry, media, individuals, governments (and opposition) argue over travel restrictions and air travel rights – the right to travel, the right to travel safely and the right of citizens at home to be protected from infected travellers. Mobility justice is a complex matter. To 'reset' air travel necessitates a careful consideration of the many requirements for mobility justice as outlined above.

And to Conclude……

We have seen how the passenger experience of air travel has evolved from the early days of the jet engine through to the 21st century, halting abruptly in 2020 with the emergence of COVID-19. During this time, we have seen how the passenger experience both reflects and shapes Western culture. With air travel central to social connections, business, leisure and migration, its absence has meant profound societal change. Border closures and halted air travel have led to questions regarding government control, individual freedom and human rights. The pandemic has brought with it a 'demise of certainty' (Tsiolkas, 2020: 12), shaking confidence in predictions over the future of air travel and the passenger experience. At the same time, the pandemic has provided us with *some* certainties. It has confirmed that the passenger experience of air travel is not a trivial subject, but rather a complex social phenomenon warranting scholars' attention.

From a critical perspective, it is a phenomenon which needs to be situated within the politics of mobility. Meaning and experience of air travel need to be understood within capitalism's consumption practices, neoliberalism's focus on individual autonomy, human rights ideological concerns for equality and the environmental movement whose discourse demands us to confront the future of our planet and its inhabitants. Now, the global pandemic, with its discourse on health and disease, coupled with significant state power to control flyers' access and experience, is added to the sociocultural context through which to understand meaning and experience of air travel. The issues at hand are what Sheller (2018b) refers to as: the macro-mobilities at the planetary scale, the micro-mobilities at the bodily scale and, at the nanoscale, the viral mobilities.

To be a passenger is, clearly, not a non-event but an embodied and emotional experience where discourse, practice and materialities are enmeshed. Air travel can never be considered 'dead time', nor air transport a mere conduit of space (Vannini 2009). Aeroplanes and airports will never be 'non-places' but places with meaning where passengers interact with others, behaviours are contested, and identities are enacted. Despite the many changes to air travel resulting from the pandemic, the words of Adey et al. (2007: 776) remain relevant: 'aeromobility demands to be theorized as a complex set of social representations, imaginations and practices as much as the outcome of technological advances'.

While the chapter authors have highlighted the many dimensions to the passenger experience, there remain gaps in our understanding of aeromobility, its discourse and practice, both in the air and at the airport. Much of our knowledge is biased towards those from Western societies, travellers whose purpose is business, and those who move through airports that are large global hubs. We know little about other passenger types and those who use small domestic airports. We need to identify those who are not mobile and to study the inherent power relations and injustices at different scales as outlined by Sheller (2020). We need a greater understanding of how sexism, ableism, racism and other 'isms' have privileged some mobilities at the expense of others. There is still much to be known regarding passenger interactions with other passengers, air crew and the family and friends who farewell and greet the passenger. There are many challenges in the study of mobility. Aeromobility research requires methodologies which allow us to understand the fleetingness of mobility, movement and stillness, semiotics and practice, the embodied and affective dimensions of mobility, human–human interaction and human–nonhuman interaction. Finally, a critical approach which is concerned with mobility justice requires us to consider the ethical implications of our methodological decisions (Cook & Butz, 2019).

Confronted with the immobilities of air travel and two global crises – COVID-19 pandemic and climate change – there is an urgency to rewrite the traditional narrative that associates mobility with freedom, independence, progress and modernity. The industry view that aviation is the 'business of freedom' (IATA, 2020a: 5) is difficult to sustain. We have seen the tension between the 'access to air travel' discourse and the environmental discourse. At the core is the issue of mobility justice. Yet, greater discussion is required as to how we implement the ideals of justice. We need a 'roadmap' (Everuss, 2019). Time will tell if practitioners, policy makers and the travelling public take advantage of the opportunity created by the pandemic to 'reset' air travel in the pursuit of mobility justice. That other crises will come our way is undeniable but, for the time being, we need to address the certainties we have. Whichever fork in the road (or sky) is taken, the passenger experience will remain a subject worthy of study, not least because the health and wellbeing of our citizens and planet depend upon it.

Notes

(1) Licensed by Copyright Agency.
(2) At the time of writing, we are two and a half years into the pandemic and while some regulations have relaxed, others are still in place.

References

ABC News (2020) 'Flights to nowhere' and other ways travel junkies are getting their fix during coronavirus lockdowns. *ABC News*, 20 September. See https://www.abc.net.au/news/2020-09-20/qantas-sightseeing-flights-sydney-uluru-coronavirus-airlines/12675086 (accessed December 2020).

Adey, P. (2010a) *Aerial Life: Spaces, Mobilities, Affects*. Chichester: Wiley-Blackwell.

Adey, P. (2010b) *Mobility*. London: Routledge.

Adey, P., Bissell, D., Hannam, K., Merriman, P. and Sheller, M. (2014) Introduction. In P. Adey, D. Bissell, K. Hannam, P. Merriman and M. Sheller (eds) *The Routledge Handbook of Mobilities* (pp. 1–20). London: Routledge.

Adey, P., Budd, L. and Hubbard, P. (2007) Flying lessons: Exploring the social and cultural geographies of global air travel. *Progress in Human Geography* 31, 773–791. https://doi.org/10.1177%2F0309132507083508.

Anderson, B. (2006) *Imagined Communities*. London: Verso.

Barlass, T. (2020). NZ103: Love, death and new beginnings. *The Sydney Morning Herald*, 20 October, p. 6.

Bedo, S. (2020) Coronavirus: Travellers 'freaking out' as they arrive in Sydney amid self-isolation restrictions. *News.com.au*, 16 March. See https://www.news.com.au/travel/travel-advice/coronavirus-travellers-freaking-out-as-they-arrive-in-sydney-amid-selfisolation-restrictions/news-story/49fae0bed2ac5b2f53b51ff6f50a3b9b (accessed November 2020).

Benjamin, S., Dillette, A. and Alderman, D. (2020) 'We can't return to normal': Committing to tourism equity in the post-pandemic age. *Tourism Geographies* 22 (3), 476–483. https://doi.org/10.1080/14616688.2020.1759130.

Bologna, C. (2021) 'Revenge Travel' will be all the rage over the next few years. *Huffington Post*, 6 April. See https://www.huffpost.com/entry/revenge-travel-future_l_6052b724c5b638881d29a416 (accessed April 2021).

Bourke, L. (2021a) International borders closed until June with 40,000 stranded. *The Sydney Morning Herald*, 3 March, p. 9.

Bourke, L. (2021b) WHO urges against vaccine passports, even for international travel. *The Sydney Morning Herald*, 7 April. See https://www.smh.com.au/world/europe/who-urges-against-vaccine-passports-even-for-international-travel-20210407-p57h0d.html (accessed May 2021).

Brouder, P. Teoh, S., Salazar, N., Mostafanezhad, M., Mei Pung, J., Lapointe, D., Higgins Desbiolles, F., Haywood, M., Hall, C.M. and Balslev Clausen, H. (2020) Reflections and discussions: Tourism matters in the new normal post COVID-19. *Tourism Geographies* 22 (3), 735–746. https://doi.org/10.1080/14616688.2020.1770325.

Carmichael, R. (2019) *Behaviour Change, Public Engagement and Net Zero*. A Report for the Committee on Climate Change. See https://www.theccc.org.uk/publication/behaviour-change-public-engagement-and-net-zero-imperial-college-london/ (accessed March 2021).

Caset, F., Boussauw, K. and Storme, T. (2018) Meet & fly: Sustainable transport academics and the elephant in the room. *Journal of Transport Geography* 70, 64–67. DOI: 10.1016/j.jtrangeo.2018.05.020.

Cheer, J. (2020) Human flourishing, tourism transformation and COVID-19: A conceptual touchstone. *Tourism Geographies* 22 (3), 514–524. https://doi.org/10.1080/14616688.2020.1765016.

Cocolas, N., Walters, G., Ruhanen, L. and Higham, J. (2020) Air travel attitude functions. *Journal of Sustainable Tourism* 28 (2), 319–336. https://doi.org/10.1080/09669582.2019.1671851.

Compton, N. (2021) Inside Passenger Shaming, the notorious Instagram of bad travel behavior. *The Washington Post*, 14 April. See https://www.washingtonpost.com/travel/tips/passenger-shaming-instagram-shawn-kathleen/ (accessed April 2021).

Cook, N. and Butz, D. (2016) Mobility justice in the context of disaster. *Mobilities* 11 (3), 400–419. http://dx.doi.org/10.1080/17450101.2015.1047613.

Cook, N. and Butz, D. (2019) Moving toward mobility justice. In N. Cook and D. Butz (eds) *Mobilities, Mobility Justice and Social Justice* (pp. 3–21). London: Routledge.

Crowe, D. (2021) Cut-price flights to help lift tourism. *The Sydney Morning Herald*, 11 March, pp. 1, 4. https://www.smh.com.au/national/nsw/air-fair-cut-price-flights-will-land-in-marginal-seats-20210310-p579i8.html.

Everuss, L. (2019) 'Mobility Justice': A new means to examine and influence the politics of mobility. *Applied Mobilities* 4 (1), 132–137. https://doi.org/10.1080/23800127.2019.1576489.

Farrelly, E. (2019) Cheap, easy and endless: The big lie about plane travel. *The Sydney Morning Herald*, 20 August. See https://www.smh.com.au/national/nsw/cheap-easy-and-endless-the-big-lie-about-plane-travel-20190829-p52m3i.html (accessed March 2021).

Fausset, R., Stockman, F. and Kanno-Youngs, Z. (2020) Airports reel as new coronavirus screening goes into effect. *The New York Times*, 15 March. See https://www.nytimes.com/2020/03/15/us/airports-coronavirus.html (accessed April 2021).

Freire-Medeiros, B. and Name, L. (2013) Flying for the very first time: Mobilities, social class and environmental concerns in a Rio de Janeiro favela. *Mobilities* 8 (2), 167–184. https://doi.org/10.1080/17450101.2012.655974.

Gössling, S. and Humpe, A. (2020) The global scale, distribution and growth of aviation: Implications for climate change. *Global Environmental Change* 65 (November), 102194. https://doi.org/10.1016/j.gloenvcha.2020.102194.

Gössling, S., Scott, D. and Hall, C.M. (2021) Pandemics, tourism and global change: A rapid assessment of COVID-19. *Journal of Sustainable Tourism* 29 (1), 1–20. https://doi.org/10.1080/09669582.2020.1758708.

Gottdiener, M. (2001) *Life in the Air: Surviving the New Culture of Air Travel*. Lanham, MD: Rowman & Littlefield.

Graham, A., Kremarik, F. and Kruse, W. (2020) Attitudes of ageing passengers to air travel since the coronavirus pandemic. *Journal of Air Transport Management* 87 (August), 101865. https://doi.org/10.1016/j.jairtraman.2020.101865.

Hicks, L., McAdam, J. and Jefferies, R. (2021) The government just made it even harder for Australians to come home. Is this legal? *UNSW NewsRoom*, 10 August. See https://newsroom.unsw.edu.au/news/general/government-just-made-it-even-harder-australians-come-home-legal (accessed March 2022).

Higgins-Desbiolles, F. (2020) Socialising tourism for social and ecological justice after COVID-19. *Tourism Geographies* 22 (3), 610–623. DOI: 10.1080/14616688.2020.1757748.

Higham, J. and Font, X. (2020) Decarbonising academia: Confronting our climate hypocrisy. *Journal of Sustainable Tourism* 28 (1), 1–9. https://doi.org/10.1080/09669582.2019.1695132.

International Air Transport Association (IATA) (2020a) *Annual review 2020*. See https://www.iata.org/en/publications/annual-review/ (accessed April 2021).

International Air Transport Association (IATA) (2020b) *Slower but steady growth in 2019*. Press Release No: 5, 6 February. See https://www.iata.org/en/pressroom/pr/2020-02-06-01/ (accessed April 2020).

International Civil Aviation Organization (ICAO) (2019) *Annual report 2019: The world of air transport in 2019.* See https://www.icao.int/annual-report-2019/Pages/the-world-of-air-transport-in-2019.aspx (accessed March 2021).

Ioannides, D. and Gyimothy, S. (2020) The COVID-19 crisis as an opportunity for escaping the unsustainable global tourism path. *Tourism Geographies* 22 (3), 624–632. https://doi.org/10.1080/14616688.2020.1763445.

Jefferies, R. and McAdam, J. (2021) Who's being allowed to leave Australia during COVID? FOI data show it is murky and arbitrary. *UNSW Law*, 5 July. See https://www.kaldorcentre.unsw.edu.au/publication/who%E2%80%99s-being-allowed-leave-australia-during-covid-foi-data-show-it-murky-and-arbitrary (accessed March 2022).

Lew, A., Cheer, J., Haywood, M., Brouder, P. and Salazar, N. (2020) Visions of travel and tourism after the global COVID-19 transformation of 2020. *Tourism Geographies* 22 (3), 455–466. https://doi.org/10.1080/14616688.2020.1770326.

Mao, F. (2021) Celebrities in Australia anger stranded citizens over 'double standard'. *BBC News*, Sydney, 1 April. See https://www.bbc.com/news/world-australia-55851074 (accessed May 2021).

Mertena, I., Kaaristo, M. and Edensor, T. (2022) Tourist skills. *Annals of Tourism Research* 94, 103387. https://doi.org/10.1016/j.annals.2022.103387.

Monbiot, G. (2020) Airlines and oil giants are on the brink. No government should offer them a lifeline. *The Guardian*, 29 April. See https://www.theguardian.com/commentisfree/2020/apr/29/airlines-oil-giants-government-economy (accessed March 2021).

Niewiadomski, P. (2020) COVID-19: From temporary de-globalisation to a re-discovery of tourism? *Tourism Geographies* 22 (3), 651–656. https://doi.org/10.1080/14616688.2020.1757749.

Pallini, T. (2020) Even more iconic planes are disappearing from the sky earlier than planned as the coronavirus continues to wreak airline havoc. *Business Insider Australia*, 14 March. See https://www.businessinsider.com.au/coronavirus-havoc-forces-airlines-to-retire-iconic-planes-sooner-2020-3?r=US&IR=T (accessed March 2021).

Quilty, B., Clifford, S., CMMID nCoV working group2, Flasche S. and Eggo, R. (2020) Effectiveness of airport screening at detecting travellers infected with novel coronavirus (2019-nCoV). *Eurosurveillance* 25 (5), 4–9. https://doi.org/10.2807/1560-7917.ES.2020.25.5.2000080.

Rastegar, R., Higgins-Desbiolles, F. and Ruhanen, L. (2021) COVID-19 and a justice framework to guide tourism recovery. *Annals of Tourism Research* 91 (November), 103161, 1–5. https://doi.org/10.1016/j.annals.2021.103161.

Rauhala, E. (2020) Some countries use temperature checks for coronavirus. Others don't bother. Here's why. *The Washington Post*, 15 March. See https://www.washingtonpost.com/world/coronavirus-temperature-screening/2020/03/14/24185be0-6563-11ea-912d-d98032ec8e25_story.html (accessed April 2021).

Reddy, J. (2020) Qantas sightseeing flight: 'Great Southern Land' scenic trip over Australia. *Traveller*, 17 September. See https://www.traveller.com.au/qantas-sightseeing-flight-great-southern-land-scenic-trip-over-australia-h1qrtk (accessed February 2021).

Sampson, H. (2021) An airline is taking a flight to nowhere over the Chernobyl nuclear disaster. *The Washington Post*, 22 April. See https://www.washingtonpost.com/travel/2021/04/22/chernobyl-flight-pandemic-ukraine-airline/ (accessed April 2021).

Schaberg, C. (2020) *Grounded: Perpetual Flight… and then the Pandemic.* Minneapolis, MN: University of Minnesota Press.

Sheller, M. (2018a) *Mobility Justice: The Politics of Movement in an Age of Extremes.* London: Verso.

Sheller, M. (2018b) Theorising mobility justice. *Tempo Social* 30 (2), 17–34. https://doi.org/10.11606/0103-2070.ts.2018.142763.

Sheller, M. (2019) Theorizing mobility justice. In N. Cook and D. Butz (eds) *Mobilities, Mobility Justice and Social Justice* (pp. 22–36). London: Routledge.

Sheller, M. (2020) Mobility justice. In M. Büscher, M. Freudendal-Pedersen, S. Kesselring and N. Grauslund Kristensen (eds) *Handbook on Research Methods and Applications for Mobilities* (pp. 11–20). Cheltenham: Edward Elgar Publishing.

St John, R., King, A., de Jong, D., Bodie-Collins, M., Squires, S. and Tam, T. (2005) Border screening for SARS. *Emerging Infectious Diseases* 11 (1), 6–10. https://doi.org/10.3201/eid1101.040835.

Tremblay-Huet, S. (2020) COVID-19 leads to a new context for the 'right to tourism': A reset of tourists' perspectives on space appropriation is needed. *Tourism Geographies* 22 (3), 720–723. https://doi.org/10.1080/14616688.2020.1759136.

Tsiolkas, C. (2020) The demise of certainty. *The Sydney Morning Herald*, 4–5 April, pp. 12–13, 19.

United Nations (1948) *Universal Declaration of Human Rights*. See https://www.un.org/en/universal-declaration-human-rights/index.html (accessed February 2021).

Urry, J. (2002) Mobility and proximity. *Sociology* 36 (2), 255–274. https://doi.org/10.1177/0038038502036002002.

Urry, J. (2011) *Climate Change and Society*. Cambridge: Polity Press.

Vannini, P. (2009) The cultures of alternative mobilities. In P. Vannini (ed.) *The Cultures of Alternative Mobilities: Routes Less Travelled* (pp. 1–18). Farnham: Ashgate.

Verlinghieri, E. and Schwanen, T. (2020) Transport and mobility justice: Evolving discussions. *Journal of Transport Geography* 87, 102798. https://doi.org/10.1016/j.jtrangeo.2020.102798.

Visentin, L. (2021) 'Extraordinary action': Labor says government must justify India ban. *The Sydney Morning Herald*, 2 May. See https://www.smh.com.au/politics/federal/extraordinary-action-labor-says-government-must-justify-india-ban-20210502-p57o71.html (accessed May 2021).

Visontay, E. (2021) More than 45,000 Australians stranded overseas registered for government help. *The Guardian*, 21 September. See https://www.theguardian.com/business/2021/sep/21/more-than-45000-australians-stranded-overseas-registered-for-government-help (accessed March 2021).

World Health Organization (2020a, January 10) WHO advice for international travel and trade in relation to the outbreak of pneumonia caused by a new coronavirus in China. See https://www.who.int/news-room/articles-detail/who-advice-for-international-travel-and-trade-in-relation-to-the-outbreak-of-pneumonia-caused-by-a-new-coronavirus-in-china (accessed April 2021).

World Health Organization (2020b, January 24) Updated WHO advice for international traffic in relation to the outbreak of the novel coronavirus 2019-nCoV. See https://www.who.int/news-room/articles-detail/updated-who-advice-for-international-traffic-in-relation-to-the-outbreak-of-the-novel-coronavirus-2019-ncov-24-jan/ (accessed April 2021).

Young, M., Higham, J. and Reis, A. (2014) 'Up in the air': A conceptual critique of flying addiction. *Annals of Tourism Research* 49, 51–64. http://dx.doi.org/10.1016/j.annals.2014.08.003.

Zheng, D., Luo, Q. and Ritchie, B. (2021) Afraid to travel after COVID-19? Self protection, coping and resilience against pandemic 'travel fear'. *Tourism Management* 83, 104261, 1–13. https://doi.org/10.1016/j.tourman.2020.104261.

Index

Note: References in *italics* are to figures, those in **bold** to tables; 'b' refers to boxes; 'n' refers to chapter notes.

Abranches, M. 54, 68
accessible tourism 120–1
Adam, H. 98
Adams, D. 47
Adey, P. *et al.* 2, 10, 14, 17, 31, 36–7n1, 44, 45, 46, 54–5, 62, 66, 69, 118, 197–8, 208, 210, 214
Advertising Standards Authority 109, *109*
aeromobility 2, 31–2, 214
aeronautical expertise 32
aerophobia *see* fear of flying
aerotropolis 3
affective experiences 21
age
    of airline staff 105–7, 113
    of passengers 120, 122–3
age ordering 98
Agyeman, J. 181
Air Asia 12, 29, 48, 82
air crew 89–90, 112, 164
Air New Zealand 18, 178–9, 206
air passenger–passenger interaction 76–8
    air rage 87–90
    companion animals 86–7, 155–6
    contested behaviours 78–80
    crying babies 80–2
    passenger size – obesity 82–6
air rage
    causes of 88–9
    defined 87
    impact on air crew 89–90
    and passenger safety 88
    public reaction to 89
    reporting of 87–8
    unacceptable passenger behaviour 87
air safety 173
air traffic rights 32

air travel 2
    desirability of 20
    to fly or not to fly? 32–3
    impact on environment 20, 33, 35, 174, 179–81, 210–11
    representation of 17–20
air travel experience: a critical approach 14–17
aircraft evacuation 91
Airfarewatchdog 83
airline advertising 7, 8, 17, 18, 25, 109
airline booking 142
airline 'greed' 89
airline safety performance **165**, 165–6
airline staff
    'aesthetic labour' 107–8
    age 105–7
    appearance of 97, 102, 104, 105–6, 107
    'emotional labour' 107
airlines
    deregulation of 8
    and disability 121–4
    as national symbols 18–20
    responsibility of 90–1, 92
airport experience 34, 44–6
    the changing airport 46–8
    places or non-places 49–51
    signage 44, *45*
    spaces of consumption 64, 64–6, *65*
    spaces of liminality and transition 51–4, *52*, 62
    spaces of mobility and immobility 54–8
    spaces of surveillance and control 47, 58, 61–4, 92
    spaces shared with others 58–61
    and vision impairment 142–5, *143*
    conclusion 66–9

airport farewells 9, 10, 11
airport information
    and hearing 146–8
    and vision impairment 144–5
airport lounges 61, 142, 152
airport websites 142
airportness 3–4, 18
airports 2–3
airspace 3
alcohol use 88, 89
Alzheimers 152
Ambrose, I. 125
Ampt, E. 184
Ancell, D. 131–2
Anderson, B. 59
Anderson, J. 23
animal rights 87
animals: companion animals 86–7, 155–6
anxiety 5, 164, 166–8, 173, 174, 188
appearance *see* flying and appearance
architecture 47
ASDs (Autism Spectrum Disorders) 152–3
Asia Pacific region 207, 211
Aspers, P. 98–9
Association of Flight Attendants-CWA 86, 110–11
Auckland International Airport 52–3, 68
Augé, M. 49–50, 51
Australia 19
    air travel market 186
    Biosecurity Act 207
    carbon tax 189–90
    and COVID-19 pandemic 200–2, *201, 202, 203, 204,* 207
    Disability Discrimination Commissioner 124, 144
    passengers with disability 124
    post-COVID-19 209
    sexual harassment at work 110
    unruly passenger incidents 88
    see also Brisbane Airport; Perth Airport; Qantas; Sydney Domestic Airport; Sydney International Airport; Tullamarine Airport, Melbourne
Autism Spectrum Disorders (ASDs) 152–3
aviation emissions 33, 180, 181, 182, 184, 211
aviation–climate challenge 178, 179–81
aviophobia *see* fear of flying
Ayuttacorn, A. 108, 111

babies, crying 80–2
background to the book 1–6
Bailey, B. 130, 131

Ballard, T.J. *et al.* 110
Banham, Reyner 47
Barlass, T. 206
Baron, S. 76–7
Barry, K. 105
Baum, T. 107, 108
BBC News 105
Beal, J. 83, 84, 85
Becken, S. 33
Bedo, S. 200
Beijing Airport 48
Bergman, A. 107
Berry, S. 139–40
Betjeman, J. 14
Bibbings, L. 182
Bilder, R. 169
'binge flying' 32, 33
bird flu 200
Bissau Airport, Guinea-Bissau 68
Bissell, D. 2, 16, 20, 36, 57, 75, 76, 78, 91, 92
Blackburn, H. 47
blind travellers *see* vision impairment
BOAC flight attendants 108
boarding order of passengers 28, 84
'body project' 98
Boeing 7, 8, 180
Boorstin, D. 25
Bor, R. 28, 166–7, 168, 169
Bosch, S. 122
Bovone, L. 98
Braniff 109
Brazil
    older passengers 122–3
    passengers with vision impairment 144–5
Brisbane Airport 151, *198,* 200, *203,* 207
Broadfoot, K.J. *et al.* 174
Brouder, P. *et al.* 209
Brown, Bob 25–6
Brownell, K. 100
Brussels Airport 65
Budd, L. 7, 25
budget airlines 11, 180
    see also low-cost carriers
Buhalis, D. 120
Bullock, C. 111
Burns, P. 182
Burrell, K. 28–9, 77
Busch, S. 78–9
Business Class travel 18, 29–30, 37n2, 60, 61, 81
business travellers 13, 29–31, 173, 174, 209
Butler, J. 98
Butz, D. 119, 212

CAA *see* UK Civil Avation Authority
cabin crew 82, 89–90
    see also female flight attendants; flight attendants
Calder, C. 86
Cambridge English Dictionary 87
Campos, D. *et al.* 169
capital 16
carbon offsetting 32, 174, 184–5, 188, 189–90
Carr, N. 87
Caton, K. 186–7
Cerdan Chiscano, M. 153
Champion Autism Network 152
Chang, Y. 122
changing passenger experience 6–14
Cheer, J. 210
Chen, C. 122
children with a disability 131–2
Christie, N. 124, 128, 131–2
Chua, B.-L. *et al.* 61
Churchill, Sir Winston 47
'civil inattention' 58
class of travel 28
    see also Business Class travel; Economy Class; First Class travel
climate change 178–82, 189, 214
cloud formation 26
club lounges 103
cockpit visits 9, *11*
cognitive behavioural techniques 168–9
cognitive impairment 148–9
    autism 152–3
    dementia 149–51, 150–1b
    epilepsy 153–5
    hypoxia 172
    spatial disorientation 172
    vestibular dysfunction 172
cognitive vulnerability 166–7, 168
Cohen, S. *et al.* 13, 18, 30, 31, 32
Cohen, S.A. *et al.* 187
Cole, Linda 200
Cole, S. 132
comfort 12, 99, 101
companion animals 86–7, 155–6
Conde Nast Traveler Editors 105
connected time 23
Connell, J. 139, 149, 151
Convention on the Rights of People with Disabilities (CRPWD) 119
Cook, N. 119, 212
CORSIA (carbon offsetting and reduction scheme for international aviation) 189
cost of air travel 11–12
COVID-19 pandemic 35–6, 180, 186, 191, 198, 204–5
    effects on family and friends 206
    and fear of flying 208–9
    and the future of air travel 208, 209–10
    and mobility justice 119, 211–13, 214–15
    non-flight experiences 207
    passenger numbers 11, 198, *198*, 199, 200, *203*, *204*
    passenger–passenger interaction 205–6
    politics of mobility 207–8
    safety and surveillance 199–202, *201*, *202*, *203*, 204–6
Cox, C. 87
Crang, M. 15, 59
Crawford, J. *et al.* 170
Crede, M. *et al.* 88
Cresswell, T. 1, 2, 4, 15, 16, 36, 60, 63–4, 67, 90, 119
Creutzig, F. *et al.* 191
critical approach to air travel 14–17
critical disability studies 16, 119–21
Critical Discourse Analysis 99, 106
critical tourism studies 6, 14, 16, 120–1
Crossley-Holland, K. 1, 24
Crouch, D. *et al.* 15
CRPWD (*Convention on the Rights of People with Disabilities*) 119
crying babies 80–2
Cui, M. *et al.* 81
customer service 123
customer-to-customer interaction 74–5
cyber security 173

da Silva, T. *et al.* 122, 144, 157
Dahlberg, A. 89
Dann, E. and G. 147
DAPB (Disruptive Airline Passenger Behaviour) 87–8
Darcy, S. 120, 123, *125*, 126, 127, *127*, 128, 129, *129*, 131, 132, 133–4, *134*, 141, 147, 155
Darda, J. 4
Davies, A. 124, 128, 131–2
Day-Lewis, Cecil: *The Tourists* 1
de Botton, A. 44, 46, 62
de Certeau, M. 49
deaf travellers *see* hearing impairment
deafblind travellers 147
    see also hearing impairment; vision impairment
DeCelles, K.A. 88–9
delayed flights 59, 76
DeLillo, D. 55

Delta Airlines 83, 152, 156
dementia 149–51, 150–1b
Dementia Australia 149
'democratisation' of air travel 12, 32, 102, 103
Denver, J. and J. 11
Devkota, A.R. 154
Dewsbury, J. *et al.* 15
Diagnostic and Statistical Manual of Mental Disorders-5 (DSM-5) 166
Dickson, T.J. 120
direct flights 83
disability
 and airlines 121–4
 children 131–2
 critical disability studies 16, 119–21
 flying with disability 31–2, 34
 social model of disability 119–20
 see also flying with mobility disability; flying with non-mobility disabilities
discipline 91, 92
discrimination 97
disembarking and vision impairment 144
disrupted passenger experience 197–208
Disruptive Airline Passenger Behaviour (DAPB) 87–8
distributive justice 212
diversity of practice 28–32
dogs 86, 87, 142, 145, 156
Doha Airport 48, *143*
Dombroff, M. 156
dress codes 99, 100, 102–5, *103*, 111
Drew, C. 19
drug use 88
DSM-5 (*Diagnostic and Statistical Manual of Mental Disorders-5*) 166
Dubai International Airport 48, *64*, *143*
Duffy, K. *et al.* 110, 113
Dye, J. 19

e-gates and passengers with disability 123
Eastern 114n
EasyJet 8
Economy Class 8, 9, 12, 13, 18, 30, 82, 88, 92, 105
Edelheim, J. 20
Edensor, T. 21, 34
EFTE (European Federation for Transport and Environment) 180
Eghtesadi, C. *et al.* 148
Eiselin, S. *et al.* 48
Elliott, A. 16
embodied experience of air travel 20–8, 91
embodied ontology 120

embodied semiotics 15
Emirates Business Class 18
emotional support animals 86–7, 155–6
emotions 28, 44, 53, 55, 61, 66–7, 89
 see also fear of flying
empty seats 84
'enclavic space' 21
enclothed cognition 98
environment, impact of air travel on 20, 33, 35, 174, 179–81, 210–11
environmental justice 212
epilepsy 153–5
epilogue 35–6, 197
 future of air travel 208–15
 passenger experience disrupted 197–208
epistemic justice 212
Escolme-Schmidt, L. 107, 108–9
European Federation for Transport and Environment (EFTE) 180
European Network for Accessible Tourism 125
European Union 123
 Emissions Trading Scheme 189–90
executive departure lounges 30, 61, 67
Expedia.com 79, 80, 82
experienced (business) travellers 29–30
Ezeh, C. 47

Facebook 18, 20, 79
Fairclough, N. 80, 99, 101, 106
fairness 119
'familiar stranger' 77
Farrelly, E. 212
fashion 98
Faulconbridge, J. 30
Fausset, R. *et al.* 200
fear of aeroplanes 166
fear of flying 5, 35, 164–5, 174
 and COVID-19 208–9
 a critical approach 169–73, 174
 A Fearful Flyer's Narrative 162–3
 gendering of 170–1
 media responsibilities 172, 174
 mental health perspective 165–9
 moving forward 174
 programmes 168–9
 role of transport industry 171–2
 sociology of psychiatric critique 170
 solutions 172
 Flyer's Reflexive Postscript 175
 see also travel anxiety
fear of heights 166
Fear Survey Schedule 174

female flight attendants 113
   appearance 104, 105–11
   dress code 104, 111
   sexual harassment of 110–11
First Class travel 8, 18, 81
Fisk, R. 90
fitness to fly 150
flight attendants 34
   ageism 113
   behaviour of 89, 92
   and larger passengers 83
   male flight attendants 113–14n
   and passenger behaviour 78, 79
   and passengers with reduced mobility 132–4, **134**
   sexism 113
   sexualisation of 113–14n
   see also female flight attendants
flight duration 12
flight shame *see flygskam*
'floundering hypermobile' 31
'flourishing hypermobile' 31
flyers' dilemma 178–9, 181–2
   extending the concept 186–7
   failure to trigger behaviour change 187
   to fly or not to fly? 32–3
   production of travel anxiety 188
   reformulation of 35, 188–90
   tourist air travel and climate change 179–81
   'value-action gap' 181–2
   conclusion 190–1
flyers' dilemma: empirical insights 182–3
   air travel consumers as agents of social change 184–5
   logic favours unsustainable option 183
   need for strong policy interventions 185–6
flygskam (flight shame) 179, 187, 211
flying and appearance 97–8
   airline staff 97, 102, 104, 105–6, 107
   passenger appearance 34, 98–105
   passenger experience of female flight attendants' appearance 105–11
   conclusion 111–14
flying into uncertainty *see* flying with mobility disability; flying with non-mobility disabilities
Flying Nannies 83
flying with disability 34
   see also passengers with reduced mobility
flying with mobility disability 31–2, 118–21
   and ageing 122–3
   airlines and disability 121–4

airport security 126, 140, 142, 144
defining mobility 119
differential mobility 118
mobility disability 124–34, *127*, *129*
   phases of air travel procedure 124–5, **127, 128, 129, 134**
   terminology 135n1
   toilets 124, 126–7, 130–1
   unevenness of mobility 118
   conclusion 134–5
   see also passengers with reduced mobility
flying with non-mobility disabilities 34–5, 139–40
   cognitive impairment 148–55, 172
   guidelines for airlines 140
   hearing impairment 146–8
   hidden disabilities 34–5, 139–40, 147, 151, 152, 157
   mental health conditions 155–6, 157
   toilets 124
   vision impairment 141–6
   conclusion 156–7
flying with reduced mobility *see* passengers with reduced mobility
Flying Without Fear 162
Fodness, D. 65
Font, X. 186
Foreman, E. 164, 166, 168, 169
Foster, Sir Norman 48
Franklin, A. 15
Freire-Medeiros, B. 29, 212
frequent flyers 13, 30, 187
Frith, J. 118
Fuller, G. 2, 13, 44, 45, 47, 48, 65
future of air travel
   benefits and costs 211
   and COVID-19 208, 209–10
   inclusion and social equity 210
   and mobility justice 119, 211–13, 214–15
   and sustainability 210

Gale, S. *et al.* 110
Galinsky, A. 98
Gatwick Airport, London 81, 151
gay stewards 114n
Gebicki, M. 25–6
gender of passengers 31, 77
   and appearance 98
   and fear of flying 170–1
Germany 185
Geuens, M. *et al.* 64, 65
Gharaveis, A. 122

Gilboa, S. 101
Gillberg, G. 107
Gillovic, B. et al. 171
Giner-Sorolla, R. 88
glamorization of hypermobility 13
Glancey, J. (2014) 7
Gleave, S.D. 184, 191
global civil aviation fleet 180
global market-based mechanism (GMBM) 189
Godart, F. 98–9
Goffman, E. 58, 98
Goggin, G. 135
Goldsmid, S. et al. 88
Gordon, A. 46, 47, 48, 61, 62, 63, 68
Gössling, S. et al. 12, 13, 18, 30, 31, 33, 186, 187
Gottdiener, M. 22, 51, 54, 55, 57, 58, 59
Graham, A. et al. 46, 47, 48, 121–2, 131–2, 209
greenhouse gases 178
Grove, S. 90
guide dogs 142, 145
Gustafson, P. 30
Gyimothy, S. 209

Hagood, M. 30
Haldrup, M. 15
Hales, R. 186–7
Hall, C.M. 118, 134
Hancock, P. 111
Hannam, K. et al. 54, 118
Hares, A. et al. 33
Harley, R. 2, 44, 45, 65
Harpaz, B. 152
Harris, C. 6, 18, 20, 59, 78, 79–80, 81, 82, 83, 84–6, 89, 99, 101, 106
Harris, K. 76–7
Harris, L. 47
Harris, S. 78, 102
Hart, M. 3
Hartsfield-Jackson Atlanta International Airport 152
Harvard Flight Attendant Health Study 110
Harvey, D. 22
headphones 30
health costs 30–1
health sciences approach 5
hearing impairment
    airport information 146–8
    deafblind travellers 147
    in-flight entertainment 148
    speech-to-text translation 147–8
    visual communication strategies 147

Heathrow Airport, London 48, 55, 55, 56, 151, 199–200
Heidegger, M. 48
Hemmings, C. 76
Hersh, M.A. 147
Higgins-Desbiolles, F. 210
Higham, J.E.S. et al. 181, 182–3, 184, 190
hijackings 47
Hindley, A. 186
Hirsh, M. 29, 45, 47
Hochschild, A. 107
Hokanson, B. 98
Hong Kong International Airport 48
Hope, Francis 23
Hu, H. et al. 90
Huang, W. et al. 51, 52
hub airports 46
Hubbard, S.M. 123, 126, 129, 130, 131
human rights 156, 207–8
Humpe, A. 12
Hunter, J.A. 88
hypoxia 172

IATA see International Air Transport Association
ICAO see International Civil Aviation Organization
identity
    personal identity 100
    and prejudice 100–1
    and status 51
immobilities 31, 54–5
Incheon Airport, Korea 68
IndiGo 83
infants 61
infected time 23
in-flight controls and vision impairment 144
in-flight entertainment 12, 148
in-flight experience 6
Innes, G. 124, 130–1, 144
Instagram (passengershaming) 79, 205–6
intellectual disability see cognitive impairment
International Air Transport Association (IATA) 11, 87, 88, 153, 166, 199, 214
International Civil Aviation Organization (ICAO) 11, 180, 189, 191, 198
    global market-based mechanism (GMBM) 189
Ioannides, D. 209
Ireland, K.: 'Airport Blues' 48

Jain, D. et al. 147–8
Jaworski, C. 15, 18
Jefferies, R. 207

Jensen, O. 15, 20–1, 22, 23
jet aircraft 7
jet lag 21, 23, 27, 30, 154
Jet Set 7, 8
Jetstar 12
Johnson, K. 98
Johnston, Sir Charles: *Air Travel in Arabia* 24
journey 2, 5–6
Joyce, Alan 19
Judge, A. 82
justice 85–6, 119, 173, 212–13

Kandola, Binna 111
Karki, A.R. 154
Kasarda, J. 3
Kathmandu Airport 206
Kaufman, V. *et al.* 16
Kellerman, A. 58, 61, 63, 91
Kelly, Mark 19
Khoshneviss, H. 53–4, 60
Kim, S. 130
Kinderman, P. 167
KLM Royal Dutch Airlines 184
Kokonis, Robert 78, 102
Kollmuss, A. 181
Koopmans, T. 166
Kroesen, M. 33
Kuala Lumpur International Airport 29, 48
Kubrick, Stanley 164

Lagrave, K. 105
Lakritz, T. 173
Larsen, J. 15
Las Vegas Airport 68
Lassen, C. 13, 29–30
Lather, P. 17
Latif, Amar 145–6
Lawton, L. 102
LCCs *see* 'low-cost carriers'
Lee, S. *et al.* 61
Lehto, X. 130
Lehtonen, P. 120, 123–4
Lew, A. *et al.* 210
Lewis, L. *et al.* 79
life-threatening behaviour 87
lighting 91
liminality 51–4, 52, 62
Lin, W. 2, 14, 32, 108
Lindsay, G. 3
Lisbon Airport 199
literature review 17
    diversity of practice 28–32
    embodied practice of air travel 20–8, 91
    to fly or not to fly? 32–3
    passenger experience of movement and speed 22
    passenger experience of space and time- 22–3
    representation of air travel 17–20
    visual gaze from above 23–8, 26, 27b
Logan Airport 199
'lookism' 97
Los Angeles International Airport 63
Losekoot, E. 44
'low-cost carriers' (LCCs) 101–2, 180
    see also budget airlines
luggage, weight of 29, 84, 85, 100, 101
Lunday, J. 49
Lyons, G. 22–3

McAdam, J. 207
MacArthur, M. 18, 24
McCabe, T. 150
MacCannell, D. 1
McCarthy, M.J. 126
McDonald, S. *et al.* 186
McIntosh, A. 154, 155
McLinton, S. *et al.* 87, 88, 110–11
McNeill, D. 67
Majima, S. 99
Major, W.L. 123, 126, 129, 130, 131
Malaysia Airlines 83
male flight attendants 113–14n
Mander, S. 12, 13
Martin, C. 73, 74, 75, 77
Massey, D. 16
Matousek, M. 82
Maul, T. 164
meal service 9, 144, 147, 172, 202, 207
media: framing of air incidents 172, 174
mementoes of flying 7–8, *9*, *10*
memories of air travel 12
mental health conditions 155–6, 157
mental health perspective 165–9
    airline safety performance **165**, 165–6
    behavioural responses 167
    cognitive responses 167–9
    computer-assisted treatments 169
    intervention programmes 168–9
    physiological responses 5, 167, 168
    see also fear of flying
Merriman, P. 15, 36, 45, 50, 51
Mertena, I. *et al.* 29, 208
Metz, D. 121–2
Millward, L. 7, 12–13, 24
mobile semiotics 15
mobility 18, 34, 53, 54, 118, 119

mobility disability *see* flying with mobility disability
mobility justice 119, 211–13, 214–15
mobility, politics of 53, 67, 119, 207–8, 213
mobility rights 14, 16
mobility studies 2, 3, 16, 118
'Montréal Agreement' 189
moral judgements 91
Morgan, N. 16, 51, 53, 63, 69, 97, 98, 104
mothers and infants 61
motility 16
movement 2, 22
multi-sensory rooms 152
Munoz, Oscar 86
Murray, B. 65
Muther, C. 102
Myrtle Beach Airport, South Carolina 152

Name, L. 15, 212
Napolitano, F. 151
Nasseri, Mehran Karimi 57
National Academies of Sciences Engineering and Medicine 127, 135
National Airlines 109
national borders 3
National Geographic 173
negative psychological effects of air passenger travel 35, 178–9
  flyers' dilemma 179, 181–2
  tourist air travel and climate change 179–81
Nelson, Sara 86, 111
network capital 16
Neulinger, J. 103–4
'new mobilities' paradigm 1–2, 5, 54, 118
'new puritans' 182
New Zealand 52–3, 68, 172, 182, 199
  see also Air New Zealand
Nicholls, R. 77, 91
Niewiadomski, P. 210
non-flight experiences 207
non-places 49–50, 51
Norton, M.I. 88–9
Norway 185
nostalgia 36–7n1
nouveaux globalisés 45
novice passengers 29

Oakes, M. 166–7, 168, 169
obesity 82–6
  and financial exploitation 85
  health and safety 83, 84, 85, 91
  'personal space violators' 82–6, 88
  and power 92
  reactions to 85
  and social justice 85–6
  vs. tall/broad-shouldered people 85
  vs. weight of luggage 84
obsessive-compulsive disorder (OCD) 173
older passengers 122–3
O'Leary, Michael *109*
Oliver, M. 119
Oostveen, A. 120, 123–4
O'Reilly, M. *et al.* 148, 150, b150–1
Orwell, G. 23
overhead bins 78, 82, 89, 91
overweight passengers *see* obesity
Oxford English Dictionary 87

Page, S. 139, 149, 151
Pan Am
  Clipper Service 7, *8*
  gay stewards 114n
panic attacks 164
Parent, L. 119
Paris Charles de Gaulle Airport 57
Paris Climate Agreement (2015) 180, 189
Pascoe, D. 3, 17, 23, 51
'pass riders' 104
passenger appearance 34, 98–105
  'appropriate' passenger dress 99–100
  comfort 99, 101
  control 103
  'democratisation' of air travel 102, *103*
  dress codes 99, 100, 102–5, *103*, 111
  'offensive' dress 99, 100, 103, 104
  personal identity 100
  political slogans 100
  rights and responsibilities 102
  'travel clothing' 101
passenger behaviour
  responses to flying 167, 168
  unacceptable behaviour 78–80, 87–90
passenger experience
  disrupted 197–208
  of female flight attendants' appearance 105–11
  of movement and speed 22
  of space and time 22–3
passenger lanyards/bracelets 140, 151, 152
passenger numbers 11, 198, *198*, 199, 200, *203*, *204*
Passenger Shaming sites 79, 80
passenger size *see* obesity
passenger space 91, 101
passenger–passenger interaction 34, 73, 76–80
  air rage 87–90
  critical approach 75–6

customer-to-customer interaction 74–5
during pandemic 205–6
discussion and conclusion 90–3
passengers
  age of 120, 122–3
  diversity of practice 28–32
  enjoyment of 13
  gender of 31, 77, 98, 170–1
  lived experience of 4
  safety of 88
  weight of 84
passengers with reduced mobility (PRMs) 132
  airline costs of 132, **133**
  and flight attendants 132–4, **134**
  see also flying with mobility disability
passports 12, 32, 51, 67
'pay by the pound' 84
Pearce, P. 59, 77
Peeters, P. 33
people watching 55, 56
performance 21
performativity 98
Perng, S.-W. *et al.* 65
personal identity 100
'personal space violators' 82–6, 88
personality traits 167
Perth Airport, Western Australia 152–3
phobias 164, 165, 166, 169, 170
physical abuse 87, 88
physiological effects of air travel 5, 167, 168
Pickersgill, M. 170
poetry 18
Poling, M. 152
political slogans 100
Popp, R.K. 170, 171
Poria, Y. *et al.* 83, 84, 85, 122, 124, 126, 130, 131, 145
power relations 16, 92, 174
Pranter, C. 73
prejudice 100–1
Preston, A. 172
Pritchard, A. *et al.* 5, 16, 51, 53, 63, 69, 97, 98, 104
PRMs *see* passengers with reduced mobility
procedural justice 212
psychological effects of air travel 5, 30–1, 83
psychosocial conditions 157
public access 9
Puhl, R. 100
purpose of travel 28
Pütz, O. 58

Qantas 18–20, 155
  747 36–7n1
  club dress code 103
  'Great Southern Land' sightseeing flight 206–7
Qantas Spirit of Australia commercials 19
QantasLink *203*
Qatar Airways 105
Qatar International Airport *60*
quiet rooms 152

Randles, S. 12, 13
Rastegar, R. *et al.* 210
Rauhala, E. 200
Reddit 172
Reddy, J. 206–7
Reed, T. 173
Reid, Charles 108–9
Reis, A. 182–3, 186
relativist ontological worldview 14–15
Relph, E. 49
resistance theory 186
responsibility, individual *vs.* corporate 33, 38
restorative justice 212
retail 55, 64–6, *65*, *66*
'revenue customers' 104
rhythms of air travel 21
rights and responsibilities
  of airlines 90–1, 92
  of passengers 34, 80, 93, 102, 205
Rink, B. 3, 7, 23, 24
Rosenkvist, J. *et al.* 148–9
Rosenthal, E. 181
Routledge Handbook of Mobilities, The 197–8
Rowley, J. 59, 61, 64
Royal Society for the Blind, The 146
Rushdie, Salman 62
Ryanair 8, 28, 109, *109*

safety 12, 86, 88
  COVID-19 199–202, *201*, *202*, *203*, 204–6
Saltes, N. 134
Sampson, H. 104, 207
SARS virus 198, 199, 200
Sawchuck, K. 118
Scandinavian Airlines (SAS) cabin attendants 107
Schaberg, C. 3–4, 10, 11, 13–14, 17, 18, 22, 25, 28, 31, 59, 62, 67, 79, 101, 199, 202, 204, 209
Schiphol Airport, Amsterdam 46, *50*, 60, 63–4, 68

Schivelbusch, W. 25
Schwanen, T. 213
Scoot Airlines 83
seat belt extenders 83
seat selection 28
seat size 83–4, 89, 91
Sebald, G.: *The Rings of Saturn* 24
second seat purchase 84
security measures 9, *11*, 21, 47, 51, 58, 61–4, 67
   cyber security 173
   and disability 31–2, 126, 140, 142, 144
   frequent flyers 30
   inequalities 31–2
Sedgley, D. *et al.* 82, 152
Seeman, M.V. 155
self-respect 91
service animals 86
sexism 105, 113, 214
sexual harassment 110–11
Shakespeare, T. 120
Shannon Airport, Ireland 152
Sharma, S. 63, 69
Shaw, S. 32
Sheller, M. 1, 14, 15, 17, 34, 118–19, 210–11, 212, 213, 214
Shepherd, N. 148, 150, b150–1
Shilling, C. 98
shorter-haul flights 83
sightseeing flights 206–7
Simmel, G. 59, 77
Simpson, R. 170
Singapore Airlines 108
Sky Nannies 83
Slack, F. 59, 61, 64
Small, J. *et al.* 6, 18, 20, 59, 78, 79–80, 81, 82, 83, 84–6, 89, 99, 101, 106, 119–20, 121, 141, 142
Smith, G.E.K. 48
Smith, L. 166
smoking 12, 73, 78, 88
social change 184–5
social class 28, 100–1
social enquiry 14–15
social equity 210
Social Identity Theory 100
social justice 85–6, 173, 212
social model of disability 119–20
sociality of the airport 9
South-East Asia 47–8
space, lack of 82–3, 84–5, 89
spatial cognition 22–3, 122
spatial disorientation 172
speech-to-text translation 147–8
speed 22, 49

Spiess, L. 107–8, 110
Stadiem, W. 7, 107
Stansted Airport 48
status
   and identification 51
   inequality 88–9
Straker, K. 64
stress 5, 44, 89
structure of the book 34–6
summary of the book 36
surveillance 47, 58, 61–4, 92
Sydney Domestic Airport *201*, 204, *204*
Sydney International Airport 9, 10, 36–7n1, 56, 57, 58, 65, 66, 69, 199–200, 207
Sydney Morning Herald, The 102, 103
   Letters to the Editor of Traveller 27, 27b

tactile information 147
Taiwan 207
   Kaohsiung airport 65
   Taoyuan International Airport 122
Tajfel, H. 100
technological change 10, 12, 146
temperature 91
Terminal, The 57
Thai Airways 9, 108, 111, 207
Thomas, C. 32
Thompson, B. 64, 65
Thrift, N. 75, 92
Thurlow, C. 15, 18
Tiemeyer, P. 113–14n
TikTok 207
time out 23
Timmis, A. *et al.* 87–8
Timothy, D. 178
toilets 29
   and dementia 150
   and obese passengers 83, 84
   and passengers with disability 124, 126–7, 130–1
   and vision impairment 144
Tokyo: virtual air travel experiences 207
tourism studies 1, 2, 6, 14, 83, 97, 181
tourist air travel and climate change 179–81
tourist attractions 64, *64*
The Tourist: A New Theory of the Leisure Class 1
Trailblazers Young Campaigners' Network, The 131, 133
transient communities 59
transition time 23
transport industry 171–2
Transport Workers Union 19, 110

travel anxiety 188
   see also fear of flying
'travel clothing' 101
travel disorientation 23
travel insurance 156
travel time 22–3
Traveleyes 145
Traveller.com.au 81
Tripadvisor 19
Tsang, S. *et al.* 88
Tsiolkas, C. 197, 213
Tullamarine Airport, Melbourne 68
Tulloch, L. 62, 102, 103
turbulence 162–3
Turner, J. 100
Turner, V. 51, 62
Twigg, J. 98, 99
Tyler, M. 111

UK
   Civil Aviation Authority (CAA) 122, 139–40, 149, 152, 157
   Dementia Challenge Group for Air Transport 151
   government regulation of air travel 33, 185–6
Unger, O. *et al.* 30, 61
United Airlines 86
United States
   Access Board 135
   Air Carrier Access Act (ACAA) 125, 126, 127, 148
   airline deregulation 180
   Americans with Disabilities Act (ADA) 125, 126, 173
   and COVID-19 pandemic 199
   Department of Transportation (DOT) 86, 126, 148
   emotional support animals 86, 155
   people with disability 123
   Rehabilitiation Act of 1973 125
   Transportation Security Administration (TSA) 126
   travel processes for people with disabilities 125, *125*
University of Otago, New Zealand 182
Unruly Passenger Behaviour (UPB) 87, 88
Urry, J. 1, 14, 16, 54, 61, 145, 210

Valtonen, A. 20, 31, 110
Van Gerwen, L. *et al.* 164, 166, 168, 169, 174
Vancouver International Airport, Canada 152
Vannini, P. 20–1, 22, 23, 214

Varley, P. *et al.* 51
Vartanian, L. 85
Veijola, S. 20, 31, 110
verbal abuse 87, 88
Verlinghieri, E. 213
vestibular dysfunction 172
Victorian Equal Opportunity and Human Rights Commission (VEOHRC) 156
Vilnai-Yavetz, I. 101
Virgin Atlantic
   flight attendants 111
   Still Red Hot 109, 110
virtual reality 169
vision impairment 122, 141
   airline booking 142
   at airport 142–5, *143*
   and airport information 144–5
   airport websites 142
   and communication with staff 145–6
   deafblind travellers 147
   and disembarking 144
   guide dogs 142, 145
   and in-flight controls 144
   in-flight entertainment 148
   lounge facilities 142
   and meals 144
   and technology 146
   and toilets 144
visits to the cockpit 9, *11*
visual gaze from above 23–8, *26*, 27b

waiting 44, 46, 54, 55, 57
Wang, W. 132
Waring, P. 107–8, 110
Warren, A. *et al.* 150, 151
Washington Post, The 89, 200
Watson, N. 120
Wattanacharoensil, W. *et al.* 68
Weaver, D. 102
weight of luggage *vs.* weight of passenger 84
Westwood S. *et al.* 31
Wetherell, M. *et al.* 79
wheelchairs 122, 124, 126–8, *127*, *128*, 129, 130–1, 135
White, Royce 173
'Wings for All' 152–3
World Digest 108–9
World Health Organization (WHO) 82–3, 121, 198, 200, 208, 209
Wrigley, C. 64

Young, I. 212
Young, M. *et al.* 32, 33, 189